Enforcement Jurisdiction in International Law and Arbitration

International Arbitration Law Library

VOLUME 75

Editors

Professor Julian D.M. Lew QC has been involved with international arbitration for more than forty years as counsel, as arbitrator and as an academic. He is the founder and has been the Head of the School of International Arbitration, Centre for Commercial Law Studies, Queen Mary University of London since its creation in 1985. He is now an independent international arbitrator at 20 Essex Street, London.

Stavros Brekoulakis is the Michael & Laura Hwang Professor in International Arbitration at the National University of Singapore and a member of 3 Verulam Buildings (Gray's Inn). He is a leading academic in international arbitration and has led, or been involved in, several projects with ICCA, ICC Commission and ILA. He also acts as an independent arbitrator and has been appointed as a chairman, sole arbitrator, co-arbitrator and emergency arbitrator under all the major arbitration rules.

Introduction

Since its first volume published in 1993, this authoritative practitioner-oriented series has published in-depth and analytical works on niche aspects of international arbitration, authored by specialists in the field.

Objective

This authoritative and established series covering in-depth analyses of niche areas appeals to both practitioners and academics. The series includes specific monographs and PhD dissertations of high quality, which are practical and cover issues not fully explored in general texts.

Frequency

A volume is published whenever an interesting topic presents itself.

The titles published in this series are listed at the end of this volume.

Enforcement Jurisdiction in International Law and Arbitration

Satya Talwar Mouland

Wolters Kluwer

Published by:
Kluwer Law International B.V.
PO Box 316
2400 AH Alphen aan den Rijn
The Netherlands
E-mail: lrs-sales@wolterskluwer.com
Website: www.wolterskluwer.com/en/solutions/kluwerlawinternational

Sold and distributed by:
Wolters Kluwer Legal & Regulatory U.S.
920 Links Avenue
Landisville, PA 17538
United States of America
E-mail: customer.service@wolterskluwer.com

ISBN 978-94-035-4158-7

e-Book: ISBN 978-94-035-4168-6
web-PDF: ISBN 978-94-035-4178-5

Table of Contents

Foreword

International law is expected to be a coherent body of laws applying to the many and various issues which it regulates. The rules and principles of international law should be the same and given the same meaning and application in all the courts, national and international, and by all international organisations and sovereign states.

Although international law is often considered to apply principally to the relationship between sovereign states, it is also relevant and may regulate the obligations and actions of many other entities. This includes international institutions and agencies, governments and their organs and subdivisions, multinational and national corporations and to private entities and individuals in some circumstances. These rules and principles relate to rights, obligations and protections.

Article 38 of the Statute of the International Court of Justice (ICJ) states there are four sources of international law. This is where the ICJ finds the rules and principles to apply to any given system situation when it '*is to decide in accordance with international law*'. These are stated as follows:

(a) international conventions, whether general or particular, establishing rules expressly recognized by the contesting states;
(b) international custom, as evidence of a general practice accepted as law;
(c) the general principles of law recognized by civilized nations;
(d) subject to the provisions of Article 59, judicial decisions and the teachings of the most highly qualified publicists of the various nations, as subsidiary means for the determination of rules of law.

There are essential and constant questions as to what specific rules are applied in given situations, and whether those rules are applied in the same way, assuming the same basic rule, by different national courts and institutions. It is important to understand where and how the rules are determined and applied is particularly important because the rules determined by courts of law may differ in content, understanding and application among national courts and international national institutions.

This is not surprising or negative. On the contrary, it is necessary to enable intentional law rules to be analysed and applied as relevant, to be developed and varied as considered to be appropriate in the particular case. A complicating factor is that many rules will be reviewed and changes or applications adopted will be subjective, influenced by the circumstances of the case, the national court and sometimes external factors including political, economic and commercial opinions. For legal practitioners to understand how and why the courts and other institutions have determined issues in particular ways is crucial to enable parties affected to receive up-to-date advice and know how best to deal with commercial, business and other issues, e.g., interpretation of treaties, environmental law, human rights.

This book provides an analysis of national court practice as a source of international law, i.e., the third source of international law in Article 38 ICJ statute. In particular, the book concerns the extent to which states review and enforce the international arbitral practices and international arbitration agreements and awards, through their courts. In so doing, this book contributes to a number of distinct areas, including public and private international law, legal theory and international arbitration and practice. Its core contributions are:

- The identification of a 'common practice' or 'common approach' relating to a court's enforcement jurisdiction in respect of arbitral tribunals, identifying the international legal principle of state immunity as an exception, or *lex specialis*.
- The identification of that practice as a source of a 'general principle of international law'.
- Analysis of supervisory, recognition and review, and execution jurisdiction as the core principles emerging from practice.
- The development of a 'public authority' approach to jurisdiction.
- Viewing public and private international law approaches to jurisdiction together in order to identify that 'common approach'.

Adopting a comparative approach, the book also contributes methodologically to the identification of the international law on enforcement jurisdiction. The work has chosen four 'representative' states (UK, US, France and Germany) as a source of state practice and analysed those approaches against the backdrop of harmonising instruments, including the New York Convention, national arbitration and state immunity laws and procedural rules. This approach takes a novel view on the contribution of public and private international law to issues of jurisdiction, advocating for an 'international' approach to harmonisation, moving away from traditional approaches to considering adjudicative jurisdiction as a mere facet of the State's prescriptive jurisdiction.

The analyses and explanations provided by Dr Satya Mouland will be of great assistance to legal practitioners concerned with how the English and other national courts apply and interpret conventions relevant to agreements providing for international arbitration, obligations on tribunals' relating to due process requirements and excess of jurisdiction for enforcement provisions. This in turn, particularly for jurisdictions which have adopted the Model Law on international commercial arbitration, will feed the development of acceptable international rules and procedures, and will forge international arbitration practices.

Julian D M Lew KC
May 2025

Preface

In 2014, the Permanent Court of Arbitration, in the well-known *Yukos* dispute, issued a USD 50 billion award against the Russian Federation - still largely unenforced after years of worldwide litigation. In *Abaclat*, an ICSID tribunal ruled on a claim arising from Argentina's 2001 sovereign bond default - despite issues that national courts would ordinarily treat as barred by state immunity. Why are private tribunals adjudicating public law disputes, and on what legal basis?

State immunity is commonly invoked to frustrate enforcement. Yet national courts increasingly proceed with supervision, review and recognition, and execution in arbitration-related matters. I would argue that this practice, visible across jurisdictions, is crystallising into a general principle of international law. Drawing on representative case law and applying Von Bogdandy and Venzke's 'public authority' theory, this book examines how national courts generate, shape, and legitimise this enforcement jurisdiction.

This study urges arbitral tribunals and national courts to recognise this general principle and to treat state immunity as a limited exception (*lex specialis*), not a blanket bar. It proposes a coherent set of criteria to guide courts - illustrated by cases such as *Yukos* - in narrowing reliance on immunity at the enforcement stage. Furthermore, it recommends extending the methodology beyond arbitration to other areas of international law, using national court practice as a source for enforcement principles.

Acknowledgements

For Mum and Dad,
For Marianne,
For Rita,

In writing this book, I have a large, extended Indian-English family to thank. I have spent my childhood in Gloucester, surrounded by my brother, Rishi, my aunties, uncles, cousins, baby cousins and, as a small child, my grandmother. Most of all, my parents have provided me with the courage, confidence and day-to-day support to pursue my career ambitions, which started with my PhD, and culminated in this book.

My sincere thanks go to Queen Mary University of London for providing me with the Queen Mary University of London Research Studentship and to the Sidney Perry Foundation for enabling me to fund my PhD.

The kernel of this book idea emanated from my Erasmus year in Berlin in 2013-14, where I participated in the Willem C. Vis International Commercial Arbitration moot. Analysing the power of courts in support of arbitration proceedings from common and civil law perspectives provided me with the tools and academic foundation to imagine a wider, public and private international law thesis, which was ambitious in its scope. My principal supervisor, Dr Stephen Allen, supported me in those ambitions and did not allow me to resile from the promise of a wider piece of work. I am furthermore grateful to my supervisor, Professor Julian Lew KC, for supporting my aspiration to turn this piece into a book, and to my supervisor, Professor Paul Gragl, for his support and advice throughout the PhD process. Further thanks go to my PhD examiners, Professor Elaine Fahey and Dr Matthieu Burnay, for their insightful comments, which informed the development of this book. I am additionally indebted to a number of academic mentors, supervisors and friends, of whom I would in particular like to thank Professor Gerry Maher, Professor Veronica Ruiz Abou-Nigm, Dr Katharina Möser and Dr Cameron Miles, who have supported me and my career ambitions over the years.

Finally, to my partner, Carl Altaner, I thank you for your unwavering support throughout the process of making this book a reality.

PART I Enforcement Jurisdiction in International Arbitration

Chapter 1
Introduction

For many, jurisdiction has the reputation of being a technical matter and thus of having a rather dry appeal, and not without cause. At the same time, the study of the rules assigning jurisdiction, limiting it and seeking to handle overlaps and tensions arising in this process of allocation is a fascinating lens through which to view the macro-structure of international law, since these very rules, in manifold ways, mirror the interplay, and conflict, of the governing principles of the international legal order.[1]

'Jurisdiction' stems from the Latin ius dicere, which means 'speaking the law'. Conceived at its widest, jurisdiction therefore denotes the ability of an entity to authoritatively say what the law is. This introductory chapter concerns the importance of national court practice in international arbitration as a source of public international law 'enforcement jurisdiction'. Parties to an arbitration dispute may seek supervisory relief, review and recognition of arbitral awards, and measures of execution before national courts. Across the globe, states and investors encounter barriers to the enforcement of arbitral awards, with the international legal principle of state immunity restricting enforcement in its various forms. Identifying national court practice as the source of an international law on enforcement jurisdiction, this chapter introduces the core tenets of such an approach – reconsidering adjudicative jurisdiction as a manifestation of enforcement authority. This identifies national court practice on enforcement as a general principle of international law within the meaning of Article 38(1)(c) ICJ Statute, with state immunity operating as a lex specialis (or exception).

1. Bruno Simma and Andreas Müller, 'Exercises and Limits of Jurisdiction' in James Crawford and Martti Koskenniemi (eds), *The Cambridge Companion to International Law* (Cambridge University Press 2012).

[A] BACKGROUND TO QUESTION AND CENTRAL CLAIM

In 2014, the largest ever arbitration award, amounting to around USD 50 billion, was rendered by the Permanent Court of Arbitration (PCA) in favour of the Yukos oil company (once Russia's largest oil company) against the Russian Federation for expropriation of its assets.[2] Since then, there has been protracted litigation across the globe concerning the enforcement of that award against Russia.[3] With a Hague District Court overturning the award on the basis that Russia had never consented to arbitrate[4] and that decision only being reversed by the Hague Court of Appeal in 2020, a drawn-out process for recognition and enforcement had already taken five years.[5] Since then, there have been further enforcement proceedings, including in the UK, the US and the Netherlands, with little success in terms of Yukos actually getting its hands on Russian assets.

Similarly, in the *Stati* litigation, Moldovan creditors sought to enforce an award worth USD 500 million obtained in Sweden against Kazakhstan under the Energy Charter Treaty (ECT).[6] The international legal principle of state immunity precludes the exercise of enforcement jurisdiction against a foreign state where it would breach the foreign state's sovereignty.[7] Orthodox approaches to state immunity consider that this form of immunity is maintained in so far as execution against state assets is concerned.[8] Upon seeking to enforce the award against assets held by the National Bank of Kazakhstan in Sweden, the Swedish Court of Appeal found that immunity precluded the jurisdiction where assets were held by the judgment creditor (here Kazakhstan) within its territory, here, being assets held by its central bank.[9] Swedish law in the area of state immunity relies on customary international law. The Swedish Court of Appeal has stated that since assets held by the National Bank of Kazakhstan are assets held by the central bank, such assets are generally, according to a 'categorical' approach under international law, immune from attachment.[10] In separate and further decisions, however, the *Stati* claimants were permitted to enforce against a savings portfolio of the National Fund of Kazakhstan, a sovereign wealth fund managed by the Central

2. *Yukos Universal Limited v. Russian Federation*, Final Award, PCA Case No AA 227, ICGJ 481 (PCA 2014) ('*Yukos*').
3. For context, the second largest award is USD 2.47 billion rendered in favour of Dow Chemical Company against Kuwaiti Petrochemical Industries Company.
4. Within the meaning of Article 26 of the Energy Charter Treaty (adopted 17 December 1991, entered into force April 1994) 2080 UNTS 100.
5. Decision C/09/477160/HA ZA 15-1 para. 5.95 (Hague District Court, Judgment of 20 April 2016), paras 4.5.12-4.5.26.
6. SCC Arbitration V (116/2010), *Anatolie Stati, Gabriel Stati, Ascom Group S.A., Terra Raf Trans Traiding Ltd v. The Republic of Kazakhstan* ('*Stati*').
7. Peter-Tobias Stoll, 'State Immunity' in *Max Planck Encyclopaedia of Public International Law* (April 2011) [4] (the international legal principle of state immunity is based on *par in parem non habet imperium*).
8. Hazel Fox and Philippa Webb, *The Law of State Immunity* (4th edn, OUP 2015) 1 and Chapter 16.
9. Svea Court of Appeal, Decision of 17 June 2020, Matter No. ÖÄ 7709-19.
10. *Ibid.*, [32]-[34] considered in light of the definition of 'central bank' in Article 21 United Nations Convention on Jurisdictional Immunities of States and Their Property ('UN Convention on Jurisdiction Immunities'), which consequently allows for post-judgment measures of constraint in respect of property held by the central bank of the state.

Bank of Kazakhstan, under a trust management agreement between the bank and Kazakhstan, located in Sweden. This was on the basis that such assets were *not* specifically in use or intended for use for government non-commercial purposes.[11] This latter approach promoted a 'functional' approach to immunity. Although immunity was available in principle in respect of a central bank's assets, the removal of an immunity was possible where assets are used exclusively for wealth management on commercial terms and would not constitute an exercise of the National Bank's monetary policy functions.

Approaches by other courts have not been so expansive in relation to enabling execution by reference to the principle of state immunity under international law, relying instead on interpretations under national law as to whether an otherwise available immunity under national law may be removed to justify an exercise of the court's enforcement jurisdiction.[12] Only to the extent that an immunity is removed or waived is the court considered to have jurisdiction based on an exception to the rule of immunity. For example, the general approach in UK courts is that property held by the central bank is excluded by immunity because it is not regarded as 'in use or intended use for commercial purposes' (section 14(4) State Immunity Act 1978 (SIA)).[13] Such an approach is based on the consent of states to the norm – here, the relevant exception in the state immunity legislation.

'Enforcement jurisdiction' lies at the heart of the international legal order, embodying the very power which ensures states comply with the obligations to which they have subjected themselves.[14] Considering this, it is surprising that enforcement jurisdiction is one of the less studied forms of jurisdiction, with a large focus of the literature being on prescriptive jurisdiction.[15] Enforcement jurisdiction is concerned not merely with the power to compel states to act[16] but also to induce their compliance with laws.[17] This notion of 'compliance' is a principle which underpins inter-state

11. *See*, Case No. Ö 3828-20, 'Ascom', Decision of 18 November 2021 (giving leave to appeal and remitting back to the Court of Appeal; *see* especially, paras 41-43, 47-48, on the basis of Article 19(c) Convention on Jurisdictional Immunities of States and Their Property (UNCSI) (adopted on 2 December 2004, not yet in force) that assets were not held for government non-commercial purposes); Svea Court of Appeal, Decision of 16 January 2023, Matter No. ÖÄ 13682-21. Conclusions in relation to state immunity: [58] (denying an appeal brought by Kazakhstan).
12. This is the traditional approach taken in key state immunity textbooks; *see* especially, Fox and Webb (n 8) 392-394.
13. *AIG Capital Partners, Inc. and CJSC Tema Real Estate Company Ltd. v. The Republic of Kazakhstan* [2005] EWHC 2239 (Comm) (UK) (assets held for a sovereign purpose, such as by the central bank, are generally excluded); State Immunity Act 1978, c. 33 (SIA).
14. *See, e.g.*, Harold Koh, 'Why Do Nations Obey International Law?' (1997) *Yale Law Journal* 2599 https://doi.org/10.2307/797228 (accessed 26 September 2025).
15. *See, e.g.*, Cedric Ryngaert, *Jurisdiction in International Law* (OUP 2015), as well as major sections of the main textbooks focused on prescription: *See, e.g.*, Christopher Staker, in Malcolm Evans (ed.), *International Law* (6th edn, OUP 2024) 306 ff.; Malcolm Shaw, *International Law* (9th edn, CUP 2021) 555 ff.; *Oppenheim's International Law* (Longman 1992) 45.
16. The traditional conception of 'enforcement' in public international law might be considered restricted to compelling action: Koh (n 14), Michael Akehurst, 'Jurisdiction in International Law' (1972-1973) 46 *British Yearbook of International Law* 145 (only considering 'enforcement' as the exercise of 'executive' power which, in the way it is considered, is compulsion).
17. *See*, for example, the definition given to enforcement jurisdiction in Restatement (Third) of Foreign Relations Law of the United States (1987) (hereinafter 'Third Restatement') (§431, 'A

relations, ensuring a state's compliance with its laws, which may include international law to the extent that it forms part of those laws.[18] This is also reflected in the private international law context, for example, the Brussels I (Recast) Regulation, which provides a harmonised set of grounds upon which adjudicative jurisdiction for civil and commercial matters may be based in the intra-EU context.[19] Enforcement jurisdiction can thus be described as encompassing any act of a national court where, in its eagerness to ensure compliance with an interest protected by a law or regulation, it adopts a procedure to induce compliance or provide for a sanction for violation of a law or regulation of the enforcing state.

In the arbitration context, a growing number of national courts have been exercising forms of enforcement jurisdiction in respect of the international arbitral process and in respect of awards against states and/or where the tribunal is outside the territorial jurisdiction of the exercising court.[20] Considering 'adjudicative jurisdiction' – being the power of courts and tribunals to render decisions – as a possible manifestation of enforcement jurisdiction, this study examines and determines whether, in the area of international arbitration, there is now a general principle of international law[21] relating to enforcing international arbitral authority under, and as a source of, international law. It will be argued that state immunity arises as a *lex specialis* or exception to this general principle of enforcement being exercised by national courts, such that immunity ought not to apply to limit or exclude enforcement in the described situations pursuant to this general principle. The central practical consequence is that the identification of a common approach would help ease the enforcement of arbitral awards against states, through a clear delineation of when state immunity applies and when it does not. State immunity would operate under its own set of principles, as a *lex specialis* to the general approach to enforcement of arbitration awards.

[B] ARBITRAL TRIBUNALS AND *ABACLAT*

In the arbitration and international law literature, international arbitral tribunals are understood to operate outside state structures based on the notion of private party

state may employ judicial or nonjudicial measures to induce or compel compliance or punish noncompliance with its laws or regulations').

18. Koh (n 14).
19. Regulation (EU) No. 1215/2012 of the European Parliament and of the Council of 12 December 2012 on jurisdiction and the recognition and enforcement of judgments in civil and commercial matters ('Brussels I (Recast)').
20. *See, e.g.*, *Svenska Petroleum Exploration AB v. Lithuania (No. 2)* [2006] EWCA Civ 1529 (UK); *Gold Reserve Inc v. Bolivarian Republic of Venezuela*, Civil Action No. 14-2014 (D.D.C. 2015) (US); Cass. 1e civ., 6 July 2000, *Creighton v. Ministère des Finances de l'Etat du Qatar*, 127 J.D.I. 1054 (2000) (France); BGH, Decision of 30 January 2013 – III ZB 40/12 – juris (Germany) ('Walter Bau 1').
21. Within the meaning of Article 38(1)(c) Statute of the International Court of Justice ('ICJ Statute').

consent to the discrete arbitration dispute.[22] However, selected awards in the arena of investor-state arbitration call into question whether the tribunal's determination on jurisdiction ought to be governed by general principles of international law, including state immunity.

In the *Abaclat* award, a group of Italian bondholders brought claims against Argentina to an ICSID Tribunal, asserting a breach of provisions of the Argentina-Italy bilateral investment treaty (BIT).[23] An ICSID Tribunal is a special type of arbitral tribunal constituted under the International Convention for the Settlement of Investment Disputes, with the provision on jurisdiction being Article 25.[24] The claim arose out of Argentina's 2001 default on its sovereign bonds. However, Article 25 ICSID Convention only extends to 'any legal dispute arising directly out of an investment'. On the one hand, as a matter of interpretation, it was questionable whether a 'sovereign bond' falls within the scope of an 'investment' on a *textual* reading of the Convention.[25] On the other hand, and of greater relevance to this work, was the remark by Abi-Saab in his dissenting opinion, being that the Tribunal *ought* not to have exercised its jurisdiction in respect of the sovereign debt because the government bonds did not have 'any anchorage' or territorial link with the host state.[26]

Ordinarily, if a sovereign matter were to come before a national court, the international legal principle of state immunity may be engaged to limit or exclude that jurisdiction where its exercise would constitute a breach of the foreign state's sovereignty. This is the principle underpinning the concept of state immunity under international law, being *par in parem non habet imperium*.[27] According to current approaches to arbitral tribunal jurisdiction, these bodies – even though they might

22. *See, e.g.*, Nigel Blackaby et al., *Redfern and Hunter on International Arbitration* (7th edn, OUP 2022) para. 7.02 ('a party who agrees to refer disputes to arbitration chooses a *private* system of justice') Chapter 7 (considering the role of national courts as inherently circumscribed by the arbitration agreement); similarly, Margaret Moses, *The Principles and Practice of International Commercial Arbitration* (4th edn, CUP 2024) 1 ('arbitration is a private system of adjudication. Parties who arbitrate have decided to resolve their disputes outside any judicial system'); Julian DM Lew, *Comparative International Commercial Arbitration* (Kluwer Law International, 2003) paras 1-10 ('just as national courts are public, arbitration is generally private ... having selected arbitration, the intention is for the arbitrators to determine the dispute and the entitlements and obligations of the parties in respect of the issues raised'); Jean-François Poudret and Sébastien Besson, *Comparative Law of International Arbitration* (2nd edn, Sweet & Maxwell 2007) 403, 456.
23. *Abaclat and Others v. Argentine Republic*, ICSID Case No. ARC/07/5, Decision on Jurisdiction and Admissibility (4 August 2011).
24. Convention on the Settlement of Investment Disputes between states and Nationals of Other States (opened for signature 18 March 1965, entered into force 14 October 1966) 575 UNTS 159 ('ICSID Convention').
25. *See*, especially, *Abaclat* (n 23) (Dissenting Opinion, Abi-Saab) especially [258]-[262] (finding the Tribunal's jurisdiction 'ultra vires').
26. *Abaclat* (n 23) (Dissenting Opinion, Abi-Saab) [42].
27. Stoll (n 7) [4]; similarly Fox and Webb (n 8) 1 and 84-85 (described as a 'bar' from one state exercising its adjudicative or enforcement power over or in respect of another state); also, this question is of more general application at the international legal level: *Arrest Warrant of 11 April 2000 (Democratic Republic of the Congo v. Belgium)* (Merits) [2002] ICJ Rep 3 [2]; e.g., *Arrest Warrant of 11 April 2000* (Sep. Op. President Guillaume) [1] (treating the court's jurisdiction as a question which arises prior to jurisdiction); but the extent to which state immunity might bar an enforcement power is unresolved: Fox and Webb (n 8) Ch. 16 (recognising that while state

exercise their decision-making authority 'in the public sphere', i.e., over sovereign and/or public matters – they are conceived as being constituted based on private party consent, being consent to the jurisdictional provision within their constituent instrument.[28] Thus, they may escape scrutiny under public international law because the international legal principle of state immunity is not directly applicable to them. In this context, an inconsistency arises: should arbitral tribunals, though formally *private* bodies, be able to escape the otherwise applicable *public international law* norms which apply to limit and restrict the jurisdiction of national courts? What justifies an exercise of decision-making authority by a privately constituted body over a potentially *public* matter which would ordinarily be excluded before a national court under, for example, the principle of state immunity? Would governance by international law lead to better awards? This book seeks to identify whether there are any such enforcement principles relating to the international arbitral process in public international law and if so, what they are.

[C] SOLUTIONS: ENFORCEMENT JURISDICTION

Arbitration scholars might argue for the exclusion of arbitral tribunals from the purview of general principles of public international law based on the notion of private party consent: jurisdiction is ordinarily constituted based on an interpretation of the constituent provision alone. From a private international law perspective, national courts exercising enforcement powers in respect of arbitral tribunals have jurisdiction based on the laws which the given state, deciding on its jurisdiction, has chosen to adopt, i.e., applicable arbitration laws, and where relevant, state immunity laws.[29] Despite this, it is increasingly acknowledged in the arbitration literature that the role of national courts – being the only *public bodies* that may grant certain types of relief or intervene when the arbitration is floundering (e.g., the tribunal is not yet constituted or is otherwise unable to grant relief) – is central to the enforcement or support of the process.[30]

Public international law scholars, such as Von Bogdandy and Venzke, have pointed out that the notion of international court and tribunal jurisdiction as being based on consent alone is artificial in a world where those bodies contribute to the

immunity continues to bar enforcement of judgments in a number of states, a 'change is taking place' for example in relation to assets held for commercial purposes).

28. *See, e.g.*, Blackaby et al. (n 22) para. 7.02; Moses (n 22) 1; Lew (n 22) paras 1-10; Poudret and Besson (n 22) 403-456.
29. Blackaby et al. (n 22) para. 7.02; Moses (n 22) 1; Lew (n 22) paras 1-10; Poudret and Besson (n 22) 403-456. In the principal arbitration textbooks, jurisdiction is considered from a *private international law* perspective, i.e., what is the basis for the court's enforcing jurisdiction *under a state's national laws.*
30. Blackaby et al. (n 22) para. 7.02 (despite the choice of parties, courts are still in 'partnership' with arbitral tribunals); Julian Lew, 'Does National Court Involvement Undermine the International Arbitration Processes?' (2009) 24(3) *American University International Law Review* 489 (acknowledging the central role that the courts play, at least during the arbitral proceeding).

development of a body of public international law.[31] They draw on the example of 'regime-oriented' international courts, such as the International Tribunal for the Law of the Sea (ITLOS), which contributes to a body of law applying the UN Convention for the Law of the Sea (UNCLOS) and the International Court of Justice (ICJ) which expressly, according to its own statute, 'decides' 'in the name of the international community' as a whole. Despite the contribution of those bodies to their 'regimes' and/or to public international law more generally, traditional public international law approaches still conceive of adjudicative jurisdiction as being a question of consent under the relevant court or tribunal's statute, i.e., as being based on formal consent under treaties.

The issue of an arbitral tribunal's jurisdiction under public international law – i.e., its authority to decide – gives rise to the question of whether that jurisdiction ought to be governed by public international law and, if so, what the rules would be. This book considers the first question by developing the normative justification for the governance of international arbitral authority by public international law. Second, assuming that arbitral tribunals ought to be governed by international law in terms of the scope of their authority, what are the rules?

National courts exercise different forms of enforcement in respect of the international arbitral process. For instance, they may render interim relief, enforce arbitration awards, and execute against assets subject to the award. The New York Convention obliges states to 'recognise and enforce' foreign arbitration awards (Article I). 'Recognise' and 'enforce' in the sense of the New York Convention concern both the 'review' and 'recognition' of awards – that is, the court's capacity to review whether the award should be recognised, and the power to declare the award enforceable. 'Execution' instead concerns the power to execute against assets pursuant to the award – for example, by way of third-party debt (TPDOs) or attachment orders. Interim relief is concerned with measures pursued during the arbitral proceeding itself – for example, to prevent dissipation of assets subject to any future award. 'Supervision' will encompass the power to render measures in support of an ongoing arbitral process, such as interim relief and enforcement of peremptory orders and may also include setting aside the arbitration award.

[D] CASE STUDY: NATIONAL COURT DECISIONS

This book focuses on national court decisions in respect of the international arbitral process exclusively as a source for enforcement jurisdiction in public international law. The work encompasses both commercial and investor-state arbitrations, i.e., arbitrations to which both states and private parties may consent – whether by Treaty (typically, a 'bilateral investment treaty' or 'BIT') or via an 'arbitration agreement' in the parties' contract.

31. Armin Von Bogdandy and Ingo Venzke, *In Whose Name? A Public Law Theory of International Adjudication* (OUP 2014).

An example of the practice under consideration is the *ArcelorMittal* decision.[32] The UK Commercial Court granted a worldwide freezing injunction in respect of assets pursuant to a foreign arbitration award. There was no territorial connection between the Court's jurisdiction and the arbitration dispute, the award being one rendered under the International Chamber of Commerce Rules (ICC Rules) in Minnesota.[33] A worldwide freezing injunction is a particular type of enforcement measure which a court may render to freeze the losing party's assets in pursuit of enforcement of any judgment or arbitration award against them.

Ordinarily, private international law requires a 'link' with a court's territorial jurisdiction for that jurisdiction to be exercisable in respect of the subject matter or the parties.[34] Similarly, public international law jurisdictional rules normally require the identification of some link between the dispute and the parties or forum; jurisdiction is usually justified according to this framework, for example, on the basis of 'territoriality', 'nationality', etc.[35]

The Court decided in *ArcelorMittal* that it could permit 'service out' of the jurisdiction pursuant to r. 62.18(8) UK Civil Procedure Rules (CPR).[36] This provision also allows for the enforcing party to apply for enforcement of the arbitral award, in the same manner as a court judgment.[37] Here, one legal basis for the exercise of jurisdiction may be the national civil procedure rules, according to which the court may view itself as being justified to exercise jurisdiction in the particular circumstances of the case. However, the *effect* of the decision was that it *ensured compliance* with a foreign arbitration award, even though the Court had no connection to the arbitration dispute.

Such an exercise of jurisdiction as that described in *ArcelorMittal* – *outside* the court's territory – might be regarded as engaging the public international law norm of 'enforcement jurisdiction'. This principle states that a state's power to compel a foreign state to do something is excluded unless there is consent to the jurisdiction.[38] In this case, there was no consent based on any link to the territory. Is there any legal basis upon which such an exercise of jurisdiction would be justified, and if so, what is it? This study argues that there is a source, drawing on national court decisions as a source of state practice[39] and a general principle of international law.[40]

32. *ArcelorMittal USA LLC v. Essar Steel Limited and others* [2019] EWHC 724 (Comm).
33. International Chamber of Commerce (ICC) Rules (in force since January 2021).
34. Dicey, Morris and Collins, *The Conflict of Laws* (16th edn, Sweet & Maxwell 2023), e.g., Volume 2, para. 32-034 concerning contractual links based on Rome II within the EU; Volume 1, para. 6-120 on habitual residence as an element of 'domicile' as a link.
35. *See, e.g.*, Ryngaert (n 15).
36. RSC 1965 Ord. 73, r. 8 made foreign arbitral awards enforceable in the same way as court judgments.
37. *General Dynamics United Kingdom Limited v. The State of Libya* [2021] UKSC 22, [11], [12], [36].
38. Shaw (n 15) 555; Akehurst (n 16) 145.
39. The first element in the definition of customary international law within the meaning of Article 38(1)(b) ICJ Statute.
40. Within the meaning of Article 38(1)(c) ICJ Statute.

[E] BACKGROUND TO CENTRAL THEORETICAL APPROACH

Central to the development of any approach to reconceiving adjudicative jurisdiction as a manifestation of enforcement jurisdiction is that 'jurisdiction' is used interchangeably with the concept of 'authority' or 'decision-making authority'. This connotes the authority of international arbitral tribunals and national courts to act in accordance with principles applicable to them and the scope of their authority, which it will be argued, are found in public international law.

The concept of decision-making authority is a focus of the work of Von Bogdandy and Venzke.[41] They include international arbitral tribunals within the definition of 'international courts' in order to explore international 'decision-making authority'.[42] Though the work can be criticised, including for its application of a 'public law' theory - based in German legal tradition - on a conceptually distinct legal order (international law), the authors make a number of good observations which are essential for this work. 'Public authority' is defined in the work as 'the ability, grounded in law, to restrict the freedom of other actors, or to shape their use of freedom in a similar way'.[43] It is a norm drawn from Kantian legal philosophy. It has been developed by Von Bogdandy and Venzke to suggest that the legitimacy of a body cannot be explained merely by the concrete legal rule or principle in a body's statute, e.g., Article 25 ICSID Convention in the *Abaclat* decision. Instead, it is determined by the interactions between bodies within the normative legal framework within which they act: in this regard, the argument is that the applicable normative framework is public international law.

Despite the contribution of international legal bodies, such as the ICJ and ITLOS, to their individual 'regimes' and/or to public international law more generally, traditional public international law approaches still conceive of adjudicative jurisdiction as being a question of consent under the relevant court's or tribunal's statute. However, taking a broader approach to jurisdiction as decision-making authority, the body's jurisdiction ought to also be defined by the normative framework within which it acts - i.e., public international law. This study seeks to argue that international arbitral tribunals are no different from those international courts in that, to the extent that they adjudicate on matters arising between parties with no connection to their territorial jurisdiction or in respect of states, the arbitral tribunal's jurisdiction engages the *public* authority of the state. One of the key aspects of Von Bogdandy and Venzke's approach is how decisions may have *effects* beyond the discrete parties to the dispute and thus cannot logically derive their full meaning or contribution to public international law from the parties' consent alone. This is in-keeping with the broader definition of jurisdiction, based on its root '*ius dicere*', meaning 'to speak the law', or the idea that when rendering decisions, courts and tribunals contribute to the law. Applying this approach to national court decision-making authority, national court

41. Von Bogdandy and Venzke (n 31).
42. *Ibid.*, 1.
43. *Ibid.*, 17.

decisions may be interpreted as a direct source of public international law on enforcement jurisdiction.
Another useful descriptive term for 'decision-making authority' in this work is the German definition of jurisdiction, being '*Zuständigkeit*', which translates as 'competence'. This provides a better descriptive word than 'jurisdiction' for the authority of a court to decide in accordance with the scope of its authority under international law. This describes the central theoretical approach adopted in respect of jurisdiction: does the court have authority to decide the question of its jurisdiction, and if so, on what legal basis?

[1] Application of 'Public Authority' to National Courts

The concept of the 'public sphere' will be applied to national court decisions to determine whether they might, first, be conceived as a manifestation of enforcement jurisdiction and, second, whether such practice is sufficiently consistent, widespread and representative to constitute 'state practice'. It will be argued that these two aspects are sufficient to render the practice a 'general principle of international law'. Focusing on the first aspect in this section and the second aspect in the methodology section below, the following types of decisions have been identified. These are potential sources of any practice relating to the scope of a national court's enforcement jurisdiction under public international law:

(1) Where the court exercises jurisdiction, even though there is no territorial connection between the court's jurisdiction and the arbitration dispute.
(2) Where one party to the arbitration proceeding is a foreign state.
(3) Where the national court decision in the public sphere based on a private international legal rule is a manifestation of the public international law rule.

In these three scenarios, the central proposition is that by virtue of the exercise of jurisdiction 'in the public sphere', the court may be contributing to the development of public international law. In the case of (1), the court exercises jurisdiction/renders a decision in respect of an arbitral tribunal *outside* the jurisdiction. In the case of (2), the court renders a decision in respect of a foreign state. The contention is that since the exercise of decision-making authority engages the *state* at the *source* of its authority, these decisions ought to be regarded as arising in the 'public sphere'.

This concept of the public sphere is pivotal to the analysis of whether any national practice ought to be regarded as a general principle of international law because it concerns the *normative legitimacy* of the general principle under examination. General principles are unwritten norms, derived from national legal systems, transposable to the international legal level.[44] They derive their authority from both:

44. Alain Pellet, 'Article 38' in Andreas Zimmermann et al. (eds), *The Statute of the International Court of Justice: A Commentary* (2nd edn, OUP 2012) 768.

(a) their applicability in domestic legal orders; and (b) their relevance in the international legal order, and thus, the need to apply them beyond domestic legal orders in a distinct though similar framework.[45]

In her work on general principles of international law, Saunders found that the function and type of any 'general principle' are determined by the author's choice (or determination) of the 'jurisprudential legitimacy' (or legal basis) for the rule (or principle).[46] That approach derives from the idea that general principles can only be identified by knowing their function, type, methodology *and* jurisprudential legitimacy. The fourth aspect mentioned touches on the other three aspects, forming what Saunders calls a 'tetrahedral framework'. This means that whenever determining a general principle, it is important that the underlying jurisprudential basis for that norm is identified. That, in turn, determines the function, type and methodology. This work identifies the jurisprudential legitimacy as being the question of whether courts exercise powers in the 'public sphere' in the three above-mentioned aspects.

[F] METHODOLOGY

This section is focused on how widespread, representative, and consistent practice is determined which is central to determining why the decisions ought to be regarded as contributing to a general principle of international law.

[1] Harmonisation

Harmonisation is the lens through which any state practice is being determined, with national court decisions in the public sphere as the principal source. Though the term 'harmonisation' is not often used in public international law, it is intended to connote the meaning it has in private international law – that is 'the process of ascertaining the admitted limits of international unification but does not necessarily amount to a vision of total uniformity'.[47] This is distinct from how harmonisation might otherwise be understood as creating 'uniform laws'.[48] Instead, the use of 'harmonisation' here is as a methodological *tool* for understanding the extent to which national courts act in accordance with each other and the applicable principles of international law.

It is not necessary that any norms identified are 'perfectly' harmonised in a doctrinal sense, seeing as different concepts may apply across different jurisdictions. Instead, enforcement norms will be deduced by analysing the consistency of national court 'acts' – being national court decisions and their effects, in so far as they engage

45. Mathias Forteau, 'General Principles of International Procedural Law' (2018) *Max Planck Encyclopaedia of International Law* 16.
46. Imogen Saunders, *General Principles as a Source of International Law* (Hart 2021) 6.
47. Werner Menski, *Comparative Law in a Global Context* (2nd edn, CUP 2006) 39.
48. In any case, it is generally doubted that the adoption of the functional comparative approach could achieve 'unity' of laws since it rests on *functional* (and thus not exact) comparators, i.e., their equivalence *may* be determined through the effects of similar approaches for what they achieve: Ralf Michaels, 'The Functional Method of Comparative Law' (2006) *The Oxford Handbook of Comparative Law* 339, 342.

public international law – with the relevant applicable harmonising instruments. The 'harmonising instruments' used in this book are found in the New York Convention and, to the extent that they are otherwise consistent with any applicable public international legal principles (principally the international legal principle of state immunity), the application by national courts in the public sphere of their national state immunity laws[49] and national arbitration laws.

Viewed from the perspective of 'global law' – that is 'the endorsement … or commitment to the universal … dimensions of law', the approach would therefore fall within 'convergence' rather than 'divergence' supporting approaches.[50] These are approaches which promote 'normative singularity' rather than being characterised by 'normative plurality'.[51] Here, the search is for *common* approaches to enforcement jurisdiction in light of harmonising instruments, thus taking the *converging* backdrop of public international law as the starting point.[52]

[2] Selection of State and Functional Comparisons

The United Kingdom (a non-federal common law state), the United States (a federal common law state), France (a non-federal civil law state) and Germany (a federal civil law state) have been selected in view of the two potential research outcomes.

First, to the extent that the practice, as between these national courts, is widespread, consistent, and representative, it ought to be regarded as constituting state practice – the first element in the definition of customary international law within the meaning of Article 38(1)(b) ICJ Statute. Whether the practice has crystallised as custom, for which the requisite *opinio juris* would need to be proven, is not the focus of this book. Various theories regarding the definition of custom have arisen in the literature.[53] According to Lepard, it is not even clear which evidence can and should be considered evidence of *opinio juris*. This point will be examined in relation to why it would be difficult to consider any 'common approach' identified by this work as evidence of custom. The focus of this book is instead on whether any identified state practice may be considered a source of a general principle of international law and, if so, on what theoretical basis. The theoretical foundation is the focus of Chapter 2.

Second, to the extent that the practice is both widespread, consistent and representative considering the relevant international legal principles and consistent with the normative approach developed in Chapter 2, this practice ought to be considered constitutive of a general principle of international law. The normative

---

49. In the UK, the Arbitration Act 1996, c. 23 (EAA) and State Immunity Act 1978, c. 33 (SIA). In the US, Federal Arbitration Act 1925 9 U.S.C. §§1-14 (FAA) and Foreign Sovereign Immunities Act 1976 28 U.S.C. 1330 (1976) (FSIA).
50. Neil Walker, 'Seven Species of Global Law' in *Intimations of Global Law* (CUP 2015) 56.
51. *Ibid.*
52. Some works have looked at convergence through the lens of particular actors; *see, e.g.,* Elaine Fahey, *On Framing Convergence of the EU with the International Legal Order* (Hart Publishing, 2020) (focusing on the EU as a global actor of convergence).
53. For one, there is not even an accepted theoretical understanding of *opinio juris*; *see, e.g.,* Brian D Lepard, 'General Sources of Evidence of Opinio Juris' in *Customary International Law. A New Theory with Practical Applications* (CUP 2010).

approach concerns the extent to which adjudicative jurisdiction may be considered a *manifestation* of enforcement jurisdiction. As mentioned, this general principle would relate to the lawful scope of international arbitral authority under international law and to the power which national courts may therefore exercise in respect of these bodies. For the reasons which will be given in the next section, these two determinations ought to be sufficient for the practice to constitute a general principle of international law within the meaning of Article 38(1)(c) ICJ Statute. The identification of the practice is the focus of Chapters 3-5.

The methodology falls within 'functional comparative' tradition (acknowledging many forms of functionalism).[54] This rests on the notion that laws may be compared if they are *functionally* equivalent, regarded as one of the core elements which functionalists agree upon, namely:

> function itself serves as tertium comparationis. Institutions, both legal and non-legal, even doctrinally different ones, are comparable if they are functionally equivalent, if they fulfil similar functions in different legal systems.[55]

From a functionalist perspective, the comparison of enforcement laws relies on *functional* (and thus not exact) comparators. Their equivalence may be determined through the effects of similar approaches for what they achieve rather than being based on the same concept. In this area, French courts call the recognition process 'exequatur' and German courts have distinct processes for recognition and execution (called 'Erkenntnisverfahren' and 'Zwangsvollstreckung'). Further, the source of the public international law norm on state immunity in monist states, such as Germany, is public international law itself rather than the state immunity laws which have been adopted by the dualist states, such as the UK and the US.

Acknowledging, however, that 'even the fact of commonality (to the extent it exists) does not have intrinsic normative force',[56] the 'public authority' approach developed in Chapter 2 is relied upon as the *centralis argumentum*. It both defines and justifies what is to come - the identification of enforcement principles in international arbitration. This is because only in so far as they are *consistent* with that theory, which has as its object the justification of adjudicative jurisdiction as a manifestation of enforcement jurisdiction, might they be considered a source of public international law. The public authority approach is, in other words, the justification for the practice as a source of public international law.

54. Michaels (n 48).
55. *Ibid.*, 342.
56. Jonathan Hill, 'Comparative Law, Law Reform and Legal Theory' (1989) 9 *Oxford Journal of Legal Studies* 103 https://doi.org/10.1093/ojls/9.1.101 (accessed 26 September 2025); Johannes P Verheul, 'Così fan tutte', in Katharina Boele-Woelki and Kokkini-Iatridou, D. (eds), *Comparability and Evaluation: Essays on Comparative Law, Private International Law and International Commercial Arbitration in Honour of Kokkini-Iatridou* (1994) 143-149.

[3] Application

Harmonisation has been defined above in section [F][1] and the national courts which will be analysed in terms of the extent of harmonisation have been identified in section [F][2]. To establish the extent of harmonisation between these representative courts, the functional comparative method entails two steps:

(1) First, concepts are identified which, across the courts under examination (UK, US, France, Germany), perform the same legal function within those systems, though they might be differently named. For example, a 'declaration of enforceability' in Germany is simply an enforcement order in the UK. These relate to three possible enforcement norms according to which the national courts of those states may regulate international arbitral authority: supervisory, recognition and review and execution jurisdiction.

(2) Second, the functional comparative doctrinal approach is employed to examine the extent of harmonisation of these enforcement forms between these national courts. As set out above, harmonisation is 'the process of ascertaining the admitted limits of international unification but does not necessarily amount to a vision of total uniformity'.[57] Functional comparisons are useful for identifying similarities and differences between case outcomes in this context, i.e., whether a court rendered the enforcement measure in a sufficiently similar context to a foreign court. This is an application of the traditional doctrinal method of analysis but for the purposes of comparing and identifying similarities and differences between different states.

National court decisions are only being considered in so far as they are representative, widespread, and consistent, which is the definition of state practice, the first element of customary international law, in accordance with applicable principles of international law.

(a) Consistent Nature

The 'consistent' nature of the practice is being determined according to whether any 'representative' common approaches exist in light of the relevant harmonising instruments. This aspect is related to whether the practice is 'representative' because it is centrally concerned with whether any approach 'in the public sphere' follows the same set of principles, generally found in harmonising laws and given effect through national court decisions as applied to international arbitration.

57. Menski (n 47) 39.

(b) *Representative Nature*

The 'representative' nature of the practice is being determined in accordance with the normative foundations developed in Chapter 2. Chapter 2 develops the 'public sphere' concept as the main lens through which relevant decisions are identified. The question is whether, considering a sufficiently large number of cases arising in the public sphere - which has been around 150 cases across the four different jurisdictions in respect of each aspect of enforcement (supervisory, recognition, execution) - any common approach can be distilled. Any common approach between national courts in the public sphere considering harmonising principles will be regarded as representative practice. Any countervailing approaches will be distinguished in Chapters 3-5 to further define any limitations on any common approach.

(c) *Widespread Nature*

The widespread nature of the practice is an interconnected aspect of representativeness. The chosen states have been selected as they are representative of different court approaches to decision-making authority globally (one federal common law, one non-federal common law, one federal civil law and one non-federal civil law state). The widespread nature of that practice will be illustrated by the *mere existence* of that practice in the public sphere. A representative shared approach which is consistent with harmonising norms and with no significant countervailing approach would consequently be considered widespread. Whether practice is empirically widespread is not being examined, except that a sufficiently large number of decisions in the public sphere are being considered a source of the norm (ca. 150-200 decisions per jurisdiction per chapter).

[4] Terminology: Rules, Principles and Norms

'Rules' and 'principles' will be used interchangeably with the concept of 'norms'. In accordance with Koskenniemi's approach, a 'rule' determines the outcome of any legal case definitively - for example, if a particular fixed fine would be due upon breach of a legal norm, then that outcome would be a legal 'rule'.[58] 'Principles' mean that any such legal 'rule' changes on a given set of facts, depending on the norms applicable. They bring out arguments in favour of one way or another and thus do not determine a solution conclusively.[59] This work will not seek to categorise the common approach as a 'rule' or 'principle'. Instead, the determined norm would *bind* states under public international law, since the central argument is that the approach amounts to a general principle of international law. For this reason, the terms 'rules', 'principles' and

58. As set out by Martti Koskenniemi, *From Apology to Utopia: The Structure of International Legal Argument* (CUP 2005) 37 in application of Ronald Dworkin's approach: Ronald Dworkin, *Law's Empire* (Belknap Press 1986), especially 87-88; Ronald Dworkin, *The Philosophy of Law* (OUP 1977) 43-60.
59. Koskenniemi (n 58).

'norms' will be used interchangeably in this book because they connote an approach which binds states rather than any designation as a 'rule' or 'principle' with any more nuanced meaning.

[G] IMPLICATIONS

Except for their application to international arbitral tribunals as a means for regulating the scope of their authority under public international law, as suggested in relation to *Abaclat* above, there are several possible implications of this work.

[1] Execution Jurisdiction in International Arbitration

The identification of a general principle of enforcement may assist parties to an arbitration in being able to more quickly establish court jurisdiction in fast-moving enforcement actions, in relation to execution against a state's assets. The *Yukos* dispute is a good example of the protracted nature of enforcement, especially when it comes to execution. The protracted nature of litigation across the globe concerning the enforcement of that award against Russia[60] has meant that there has been little success in terms of Yukos getting its hands on Russian assets. Identifying a general principle of international law on enforcement jurisdiction, if more widely recognised by international arbitral tribunals and national courts, ought to assist in harmonising an approach to enforcement in respect of commercial assets. This would narrow down the circumstances in which state immunity can be relied upon in the context of jurisdictional arguments.

Orthodox approaches in the arbitration literature consider whether immunity is impliedly waived by the arbitration agreement based on private party consent to that agreement.[61] Fox and Webb have stated that, based on such a consent-based analysis, there is no consistency relating to the circumstances in which a national court may exercise an enforcement power in respect of the international arbitral process.[62] According to them, 'there has been a considerable diversity of views among both jurists and courts as to how far a state can be assumed to waive immunity from execution in national courts in these situations'.[63] Thus, an analysis based on consent under the arbitration agreement does not assist in the circumstance of enforcement against

60. For context, the second largest award is USD 2.47 billion rendered in favour of Dow Chemical Company against Kuwaiti Petrochemical Industries Company.
61. Fox and Webb (n 8) 388-394 (in relation to arbitration); August Reinisch, 'European Court Practice Concerning State Immunity from Enforcement Measures' (2006) 17(4) *The European Journal of International Law* 803 https://doi.org/10.1093/ejil/chl027 (accessed 26 September 2025); Jeremy Ostrander, 'The Last Bastion of Sovereign Immunity: A Comparative Look at Immunity from Execution of Judgments' (2004) 22 *Berkeley Journal of International Law* 541 (focusing only on execution against assets); recently, Mees Brenninkmeijer and Fabien Gelinas, 'The Problem of Execution Immunities and the ICSID Convention' (2021) 22 *Journal of World Investment & Trade* 429 https://doi.org/10.1163/22119000-12340214 (accessed 26 September 2025) (focusing on ICSID).
62. Fox and Webb (n 8) 388.
63. *Ibid.*

assets, where parties might seek to seize multiple courts for enforcement with no clarity as to which ought to have jurisdiction in the circumstances.[64] In this context, since the international legal principle of immunity operates to exclude jurisdiction where the jurisdiction would be a breach of the foreign state's sovereignty, it is unclear whether - and if so, to what extent - national court enforcement jurisdiction ought to be excluded by this rule and/or principle.[65]

[2] Identification of State Immunity as a *Lex Specialis*

In disputes such as *Yukos*,[66] where immunity is often pleaded and/or argued as a bar to enforcement, it has been unclear whether the international legal principle of state immunity ought to operate as a rule or principle which excludes jurisdiction or whether it should operate as an exception to jurisdiction.[67] Private international law currently approaches the issue as being a question of whether an *otherwise* available immunity should be removed in order for the court to be able to exercise jurisdiction.[68] This does not consider the circumstances, if there are any, in which enforcement might operate as the *rule* and any given immunity as an exception.

Furthermore, this approach provides no certainty as to which type of enforcement proceedings and on which basis they may fall within the scope of the court's adjudicative jurisdiction and outside the (international) principle of state immunity. On the one hand, according to the international legal principle of state immunity, jurisdiction should only be available in so far as it does not breach the foreign state's sovereignty.[69] On the other hand, the New York Convention provides that arbitral

64. There are ongoing disputes in multiple jurisdictions in both the *Stati* (n 6) and *Yukos* (n 2) disputes.
65. Stoll (n 7) para. 1; similarly, Fox and Webb (n 8) 1 (described as a 'bar' from one state exercising its adjudicative or enforcement power over or in respect of another state); 84-86 (whether immunity is a rule or principle 'in its own right' or an exception to a 'pre-existing' jurisdiction); *See Arrest Warrant* (Merits) (n 27) [2]; e.g., *Arrest Warrant*, Sep. Op. President Guillaume (n 27) [1] (treating the court's jurisdiction as a question which arises prior to jurisdiction); but the extent to which state immunity might bar an enforcement power is unresolved: Fox and Webb (n 8) 82-85.
66. *See, Yukos Universal Limited (Isle of Man) v. The Russian Federation*, UNCITRAL, PCA Case No. 2005-04/AA227 (enforcement of the largest award in history is still pending), with disputes arising with regard to the scope of the Court's jurisdiction when a question of immunity is involved: *(1) Hulley Enterprises Limited, (2) Yukos Universal Limited, (3) Veteran Petroleum Limited v. The Russian Federation* [2021] EWHC 894 (Comm) (UK courts clarifying that they do not have the power under section 103(5) Arbitration Act 1996 to grant security in aid of recognition and enforcement proceeding before the Court has determined its jurisdiction in relation to principles of state immunity). *See, also e.g.*, the *Stati* dispute: *(1) National Bank of Kazakhstan (2) The Republic of Kazakhstan v. (1) The Bank of New York Mellon SA/NV, London Branch (2) Anatolie Stati (3) Gabriel Stati (4) Ascom Group SA (5) Terra Raf Trans Traiding Limited* [2020] EWHC 916 (Comm) (considering a referral from the Belgian court as to whether, *inter alia*, the Bank of New York Mellon had an 'attachable obligation' to the Republic of Kazakhstan, *see* [2]).
67. A perennial issue concerning the interaction between state immunity and adjudicative jurisdiction: Fox and Webb (n 8) 82.
68. Dicey (n 34) para. 10-002.
69. Fox and Webb (n 8).

awards should be 'recognised and enforced' irrespective of where they are made.[70] Moreover, the New York Convention does not cover the 'execution' aspect of enforcement – that is, once the award has been recognised, on what basis may the national court grant execution to enforce against assets? Indeed, Fox and Webb, in their seminal book on state immunity, have stated that one of the functions of immunity is 'as a method of allocating jurisdiction between states in disputes brought in national courts ... in the absence of any international agreement by which to resolve conflicting claims to the exercise of such jurisdiction'.[71]

The concept of *lex specialis* is well-established in public international law discourse, as one which resolves conflicts between potentially conflicting norms (here jurisdiction and immunity) by designating one as being part of a more 'special' and the other as part of a more 'general' set of rules or principles.[72] According to this: 'the maxim lex specialis derogate legi generali is a generally accepted technique of conflict resolution in international law. It suggests that whenever two or more norms deal with the same subject matter, priority should be given to the norm that is more specific'.[73] The identification of a common set of rules or principles would provide clarity as to when a national court may and/or ought to be able to exercise its enforcement jurisdiction in respect of the international arbitral process or award, *irrespective* of the international legal principle of immunity. Any such norms would 'allocate' jurisdiction between national courts where those jurisdictions may otherwise conflict.[74] Immunity would operate as a *lex specialis* – a more special rule or principle should norms conflict. In this context, the more 'general' set of rules or principles (*legi generali*) would thus generally apply to enable national courts to exercise enforcement powers in respect of the international arbitral process.

The International Law Commission identify in their Report on Fragmentation in International Law that *lex specialis* can be understood to arise in two main ways:

(1) first, it may cover a case where a specific rule should be read and understood 'within the confines or against the background of the general standard, typically an elaboration ... thereof'; or
(2) second, it can be 'understood more narrowly to cover the case where two legal provisions, both of which are valid and applicable, are in no express hierarchical relationship and provide incompatible direction on how on deal

70. The wording is that the Convention 'shall apply to the recognition and enforcement of arbitral awards made in the territory of a state other than where recognition and enforcement of such awards are sought'. Thus, the idea is that awards shall be recognised irrespective of where they are made because Contracting states agree to recognise them even if they were not made in their state (where recognition is sought).
71. Fox and Webb (n 8) 1.
72. Especially: International Law Commission, Doc A/CN.4/4/L.682, Fragmentation of International Law: Difficulties Arising from the Diversification and Expansion of International law (58th Session, 13 April 2006), especially paras 220-226, 251.
73. *Ibid.*, para. 251.
74. Fox and Webb (n 8) 1 (function 'iii' of immunity).

with the same set of facts. In such a case, *lex specialis* appears as a conflict resolution technique'.[75]

The sense in which *lex specialis* is understood in the present context is according to the second standard: it identifies a situation in which immunity might be considered ordinarily to apply – here, where a national court exercises enforcement jurisdiction – but is determined not to apply.

[3] Identification of Principles for Harmonisation of Adjudicative Jurisdiction

A public authority approach to analysing national courts as a source of international law develops the international legal literature on jurisdiction. The current body of literature on national courts has doubted their contribution to international law, instead focusing on how national courts might interpret prescriptive norms or adopt an 'international judicial function' from the perspective of the adoption of norms into national law.[76] The question considered is the extent to which national courts operate within the international legal sphere based on the perception that they only interpret prescriptive norms. What these authors may have overlooked is a perspective which considers adjudicative jurisdiction as a source of international law, as a conceptually distinct matter.

Taekema and Burg have stated how the use of legal philosophy can be used to enrich doctrinal work.[77] They describe several uses to which legal philosophy may be put in this context – one of which is 'argumentation analysis and construction'. This is the use of legal philosophy as the principal source, according to which one 'can help determine the plausibility of each argument and of the argumentation as a whole' by ensuring that an argument is logically valid and defensible. This work demonstrates uses of legal philosophy in such a way as to provide the normative foundation for the identification of state practice. Building on Von Bogdandy and Venzke's theory of public authority as a justification for adjudicative jurisdiction as a conceptually distinct source, expanding on their public law theory applied to *international* courts and tribunals to apply it to national courts as a source of enforcement jurisdiction.

75. Fragmentation Report, Doc A/CN.4/4/L.682 (n 72) [57].
76. *See*, especially the work of the *Leiden Journal of International Law* on the matter, e.g., Antonios Tzanakopoulos, 'Domestic Courts in International Law: The International Judicial Function of National Courts' (2011) 34 *Loyola Law International and Comparative Law Review* 133. *See*, also Roger O'Keefe, 'Domestic Courts as Agents of Development of the International Law of Jurisdiction' (2013) 26(3) *Leiden Journal of International Law* 541 https://doi.org/10.1017/s0 92215651300023x (accessed 15 November 2025) (considering national court contribution to be negligible on this basis, albeit from a traditional public international law perspective of adjudicative jurisdiction as interpretative of state laws. O'Keefe states: 'while domestic courts doubtless have occasion to pronounce on the law of jurisdiction of states; this is infrequent').
77. Sanne Taekema and Wibren Van der Burg, 'Legal Philosophy as an Enrichment of Doctrinal Research Part I: Introducing Three Philosophical Methods' (2020) *Law and Method* 1 https:// doi.org/10.5553/rem/.000046 (accessed 26 September 2025).

[4] Private International Law

According to traditional approaches in private international law, jurisdiction is generally based on the requirement of a link with a court's territorial jurisdiction in order for that jurisdiction to be exercisable in respect of particular subject matter or parties.[78] According to this, adjudicative jurisdiction concerns the extent to which the state may exercise jurisdiction in respect of a situation abroad according to its *internal* (or national) norms. When viewed as simply part of national law, this private international law norm justifies court jurisdiction based on this authorising principle found in national law.

Taking a broader approach to private international law as a possible manifestation of public international law, Goh has suggested that state immunity rules are allocative in nature in that they allocate jurisdiction between courts from a private international law perspective.[79] Indeed, current private international legal approaches to state immunity consider state immunity as a source or limitation of the court's jurisdiction from an *internal* perspective but not from a public international law perspective. For example, under section 1 of the State Immunity Act 1978 (SIA), a state is generally immune from UK jurisdiction 'except as provided for in the provisions of this Act'.[80] One such provision can be found in section 9, which states that an immunity is removed in respect of proceedings 'which relate to the arbitration'.

This private international law approach assumes that courts take different approaches depending on the principle of state immunity adopted under their national legislation.[81] From this perspective, there is limited clarity and no identified common approach as to which type of enforcement proceedings and on what basis may fall within the scope of adjudicative jurisdiction. It will be argued that these narrower private international law approaches overlook that national courts exercise forms of enforcement jurisdiction irrespective of the principle of state immunity and those decisions are a source of public international law.

[H] SUMMARY OF AIMS AND BOOK DESIGN

Moving beyond the orthodox position that arbitral tribunals operate outside of state structures, any enforcement norms would apply to govern the scope of their authority under public international law, i.e., the capacity of tribunals to act in accordance with international law. This question is answered in two stages: first, whether adjudicative

78. Dicey (n 34), e.g., para. 1-030.
79. Nelson Goh, 'Court-Ordered Interim Relief Against States in Aid of Arbitration: Sovereign Immunity, Waiver and Comity' (2017) 34(3) *Journal of International Arbitration* 679 https://doi.org/10.54648/joia2017032 (accessed 26 September 2025); similarly: Dicey (n 34) 9-002 (similarly acknowledging that the rules or principles in the State Immunity Act derive from the public international law principle 'par in parem non habet imperium' which means that a sovereign should not have jurisdiction over another sovereign).
80. State Immunity Act 1978, c. 33 (UK).
81. For example, Fox and Webb consider only whether an otherwise available immunity is waived based on the parties' consent to arbitrate and find there are differing approaches under national law: Fox and Webb (n 8) 388-394.

jurisdiction may be reconceived as a manifestation of enforcement jurisdiction at a theoretical or jurisprudential level, and second, how any such jurisprudential theory could be applied to determine a general principle of international law in international arbitration. Combining these two questions, the central question is whether international arbitral decision-making authority ought to be governed or regulated by public international law and, if so, what the rules are. Though the central focus of the work is on the second question, a core theme throughout the work is why international arbitral tribunal decision-making authority ought to be governed by public international law, a question principally developed in Chapter 6.

An answer to these questions would assist the practical matters described in relation to *Yukos*, where it has been difficult to reconcile the international legal principle of state immunity with enforcement jurisdiction. By clarifying whether, and if so, to what extent public international law would govern international arbitral authority, the international legal principle of state immunity would apply to limit the scope of this authority, thereby clearly defining the ambit of any enforcement norms.

The work is divided into seven chapters. Chapter 1 has introduced the topic and some of the contributions it seeks to make to international arbitration, public international law, private international law and legal theory, which will be expanded upon throughout the book. Chapter 2 builds a general theory of adjudicative jurisdiction as a manifestation of enforcement jurisdiction in public international law, applying it to identify relevant state practice arising in national courts in the UK. Chapter 3 expands to analysing the UK, US, French and German court practice in relation to supervisory jurisdiction, applying the theory to identify the scope of the principle as a source of international law. Chapter 4 does the same in relation to recognition and review jurisdiction. Chapter 5 does the same in relation to execution jurisdiction. Chapter 6 identifies further why the practice ought to be considered a general principle of international law considering competing theories, including the importance of regulation of international arbitral jurisdiction. Chapter 7 concludes the book by identifying its main contributions.

[I] CENTRAL QUESTIONS

The central questions of the work can therefore be summarised as follows:

(1) At a conceptual/theoretical level, can adjudicative jurisdiction be reconceived as a manifestation of enforcement jurisdiction, considering enforcement decisions by national courts in the area of international arbitration and state immunity? (Chapter 2).
(2) In accordance with the theoretical approach determined by Chapter 2, are there any public international law norms of enforcement jurisdiction in international arbitration and if so, what are they? (Chapters 3-5).
(3) Should any determined common approach be considered a 'general principle of international law' and if so, on what theoretical and/or practical basis? (Chapter 6).

Theoretically and methodologically, questions 1 and 2 of this book are 'moving': they are dependent on each other for the identification of any general principle of international law. In other words, only to the extent that the 'harmonised approach' identified by Chapters 3-5 accords with the underlying normative foundations established by Chapter 2, will it be argued that a general principle of international law has arisen. Those two aspects are necessary to prove the jurisprudential legitimacy and factual manifestation of any norm.

CHAPTER 2
Adjudicative Jurisdiction as a Manifestation of Enforcement Jurisdiction

Adjudicative jurisdiction has been overlooked as a source of the international law of enforcement jurisdiction, in part due to the traditional conception in international law that adjudicative jurisdiction is a mere facet of the state's prescriptive jurisdiction. This means national court decisions are only identified as interpreting the laws which a state has chosen to adopt, rather than making a more direct contribution to international law. This chapter identifies and situates the development of this new theoretical approach against the background of the key public and private international law literature. Based on public and private international law theory and practice, the chapter identifies how national court decisions may be considered a 'manifestation' of enforcement jurisdiction. This provides the central theoretical innovation of the book as a core thread for identifying state practice as a source of international law.

[A] INTRODUCTION

This chapter develops a novel approach to reconsidering adjudicative jurisdiction as a manifestation of enforcement jurisdiction rather than a mere facet of prescriptive jurisdiction. The traditional approach to adjudicative jurisdiction suggests that court contribution to international law is circumscribed by the state's consent to prescriptive norms, i.e., court powers to interpret the laws which the state has chosen to adopt. Adopting a broader approach to 'jurisdiction' as 'authority' – authority to decide in accordance with principle applicable to the scope of the court's authority (which may, as is argued in this book, be public international legal principles) – a new picture emerges. This chapter develops the central tenets of that approach, including identifying the international legal approaches which support it.

[B] *YUKOS* AND DECISIONS IN THE PUBLIC SPHERE

The UK court decisions in *Yukos* are exemplary of how adjudicative jurisdiction may be emerging as a manifestation of enforcement jurisdiction. An example of how this would apply to the practice under examination is the UK Commercial Court *Yukos* decision of 2014.[82]

Yukos had obtained an arbitration award, which was set aside at the seat of arbitration. Yukos then sought to recover sums due under the award and asked for the preliminary view of the UK court. The question for the Court was whether to give effect to the Russian setting aside decision and thereby decline to allow Yukos to pursue the recovery of sums pursuant to the award or reject that decision and recognise an Amsterdam Appeal Court decision giving leave to recognise the award. In an earlier decision, it found that the Defendant was 'estopped' (i.e., barred from relying on something contrary to what it had asserted in a previous action upon which the other party may have reasonably relied to its detriment) from denying that the decision of the Russian Court was the result of a partial and dependant judicial process.[83] The Court of Appeal then considered further preliminary issues, including whether the principle of 'ex nihilo nil fit' precluded the enforcement of awards in light of the Russian set-aside decision. This considered whether, if the award had been set aside in the Russian courts, there could exist an award to enforce. The Court found, in light of relevant principles of enforcement at common law, that even if the award were set aside at the seat, the ability of a defendant to rely on a foreign decision setting aside the award depends on 'ordinary principles applying to the recognition of foreign judgments'.[84] At common law, the award could still have legal effect even if annulled:[85] this was since the Russian decision had been against 'basic notions of honesty, natural justice and domestic concepts of public policy'.[86] By deciding to recognise the Dutch Court decision and to refuse to recognise the Russian set-aside decision, the Court thereby ensured that the enforcement procedure in its own courts could continue. In so doing, the *exercise* of the Court's jurisdiction in the public sphere, i.e., in respect of a foreign state, could be viewed as evidence of acknowledgement of its power to recognise the arbitral award - or indeed, as the case may be, to recognise the effect of a foreign decision recognising an award.

Taking the 2014 Yukos decision as an example of how UK courts are exercising enforcement powers 'in the public sphere', i.e., in respect of a state or an arbitration outside the territorial jurisdiction, the Court acknowledged its power to recognise a foreign court's setting aside decision in respect of an arbitration concerning a foreign state and did not regard immunity as excluding this form of enforcement.

The 2014 *Yukos* decision could be interpreted as being a direct consequence of the New York Convention, which, being a Treaty, obliges national courts to enforce

82. *Yukos Capital Sarl v. OJSC Rosneft Oil Co (No. 2)* [2014] EWHC 2188 (Comm).
83. *Yukos Capital Sarl v. OJSC Rosneft Oil Co (No.2)* [2011] 2 Lloyd's Rep 443 (per Hamblen J).
84. Yukos (2014) (n 82) [16].
85. Having effect *prima facie* under common law: Yukos (2014) (n 82) [12].
86. Yukos (2014) (n 82) [20].

foreign arbitral awards irrespective of where they are made and would thus seem to comport such an obligation on national courts.[87] However, there has been no clear practice to date which obliges national courts to enforce awards against foreign states where the state relies on the defence of state immunity to preclude such enforcement *on the basis of the New York Convention.* The literature on the interaction between enforcement of arbitration awards and state immunity in this context interprets jurisdiction as being based on the waiver of states to an immunity, for which no consistent practice emerges based on the New York Convention alone.[88] In the 2014 *Yukos* decision, the New York Convention was merely an instrument in light of which the Court considered the availability of its enforcement powers.[89] Similarly, as will be illustrated, the New York Convention is merely interpretative of the norms which the state chooses to adopt - that is, national arbitration laws giving effect to these enforcement norms. In this book, the New York Convention will thus be considered a harmonising instrument in light of which a national court may decide to grant an enforcement measure, or refuse to do so. This perspective invites a novel focus on national courts as a source of the norm rather than the adoption of any international legal norm into national law.

[C] GOING BEYOND TRADITIONAL APPROACHES TO ADJUDICATIVE JURISDICTION

According to orthodox approaches in international law, adjudicative jurisdiction is considered a mere facet of the state's prescriptive jurisdiction. 'Prescriptive jurisdiction' is a state's authority to adopt laws.

[1] *Trendtex*

Exemplary of this traditional approach is the *Trendtex* decision.[90] The Central Bank of Nigeria issued, through its correspondent, the Midland Bank in London, an irrevocable letter of credit in favour of the Claimant, a Swiss company, to pay for 240,000 tons of cement that the Claimant sold to an English company. Upon shipping of the cement, there was congestion at the port of discharge and the Central Bank declined to make the payments. The Claimant brought a claim to the UK Court for payments due in respect of the bank's breaches and repudiation of the letter of credit.

The English Court of Appeal decided, by majority, that under the principle of restrictive immunity, *jure gestionis*, according to which a foreign state may be impleaded before the acts of a foreign court for its commercial acts as distinct from acts

87. Article III.
88. Fox and Webb (n 8) 388-394; Reinisch (n 61) 803; Ostrander (n 61); recently, Mees Brenninkmeijer and Fabien Gelinas, 'The Problem of Execution Immunities and the ICSID Convention' (2021) 22 *Journal of World Investment & Trade* 429 https://doi.org/10.1163/22119000-1234 0214 (accessed 26 September 2025) (focusing on ICSID).
89. Yukos (2014) (n 82) [4], [12], [15]-[16].
90. *Trendtex Trading Corporation v. Central Bank of Nigeria* [1977] Q.B. 529.

of a governmental nature, it may be impleaded before the court and no immunity would apply because that norm had become part of international law.[91] Generally, the principle of immunity restricts the jurisdiction by one state in the territory of another state, where this would be a breach of the foreign state's sovereignty.[92] However, certain exceptions apply according to which states are deemed to waive the otherwise available immunity - for example, where they have consented with the state entity through a commercial contract, and the dispute arising relates to commercial assets. In that case, the state's immunity was not deemed to be breached because the decision did not interfere with that state's sovereignty. The Court found that it could exercise jurisdiction because the public international law norm of *jure gestionis authorised* it to do so, in that it had to follow the rule of international law, and thus the Court's decision was declaratory of that rule or principle.[93]

The decision illustrates the orthodox approach to treating adjudicative jurisdiction as an exercise of prescriptive jurisdiction rather than a feature of the state's enforcement jurisdiction. First, the UK Court was asked to pronounce on the rights and obligations of the Central Bank of Nigeria: it did not *enforce* the Central Bank's rights and obligations in any way. The exercise of the Court's jurisdiction resulted in a *decision,* whose object was not to ensure the Central Bank's compliance with international law. Second, by declaring its own jurisdiction based on the binding nature of the international legal principle of *jure gestionis,* the Court merely interpreted that norm as an internal aspect of its *state's* law, i.e., it was an interpretation of a prescriptive norm which the state had chosen to adopt. Thus, the *effect* of the decision was that it was interpretative of the prescriptive rule rather than an exercise of the state's enforcement power.

[2] Traditional Private International Law Approach

Major private international law texts conceive of jurisdiction *from the internal perspective* of its own laws.[94] The jurisdictional norm is based on the national law source which the state has chosen to adopt. Private international law texts ask whether a particular court may exercise jurisdiction over a situation that is not exclusively

91. *Ibid.*, 530 (in summary, that as per Lord Denning M.R. and Shaw L.J, international law now recognised no immunity from suit for a government department in respect of ordinary commercial transactions); further at 558F, 560H, 576G-H and 579G-H.
92. Stoll (n 7) [4] (based on *par in parem non habet imperium* which stipulates that a sovereign should not have jurisdiction over another sovereign); Fox and Webb (n 8) 4 (described as an exercise of 'sovereign authority' and being a 'bar' from enforcing a judgment against another sovereign state) and 23 (describing immunity as such in the civil context).
93. *Trendtex* (n 90) [534]-[535].
94. *See, e.g.*, Dicey (n 34) 1-028, 1-030 (determining whether there is a 'connecting factor' in terms of jurisdiction is always determined by the *lex fori* i.e., if brought in England, English law). For example, English law would define what domicile means for the purposes of a connecting factor based on domicile: 1-031.

domestic, for which a potential 'conflict' with the state's law may occur.[95] For example, if a British national domiciled in the UK had an accident while on holiday in Jamaica and a UK resident caused the accident, which court should decide the dispute?[96] Should it be the UK where it would be easier for the claimant to bring the claim; or Jamaica where the accident occurred; or the UK, because that was the place of the defendant's domicile too?

Private international law has traditionally been the domain for dealing with such questions, i.e., in the case of jurisdiction, designating the *lex fori* – i.e., the domestic law of the forum – as the forum which defines whether a dispute has links with one legal system or with another.[97] According to this, private international law texts analyse *how* the national court which is seized identifies the correct law by which to determine jurisdiction – being conflicts of laws' provisions adopted into *national* law.[98] It does not tend to tackle the underlying principled question of why one state ought to have jurisdiction rather than another over an international matter.

[D] A NEW APPROACH TO ADJUDICATIVE JURISDICTION AS A MANIFESTATION OF ENFORCEMENT JURISDICTION

Moving beyond traditional approaches, 'jurisdiction' is being defined in a wider sense than it is used in public international law discourse – that is, as *authority* of states to act within the framework of public international law.[99] That is, not merely the power of states to adopt a rule *within their territory* on the basis of the principle of sovereignty, but the principle that states may act, more generally, in international law and affect the legal relations between them.[100] This is an increasingly common definition of jurisdiction adopted in public international law discourse, given that jurisdiction is essentially 'normative' in nature.[101] Thus, it is a question not merely of a formal matter as to whether a particular state *has* jurisdiction in respect of a situation which is not purely of domestic concern, but the question of whether the state *should* have jurisdiction in accordance with public international law norms underpinning a state's capacity to adopt laws, i.e., authority in, or in accordance with, public international law.

95. Dicey (n 34) 1-001 and 1-003 ('conflict of laws' as being concerned with 'the law of England which deals with cases with a foreign element'; one question arising being, at para. 1-003, has the English court jurisdiction to determine the case?).
96. A similar problem occurred in relation to a British national injured on a Jamaican beach; *see*: *Owusu v. Jackson and Others* [2005] Q.B. 801.
97. Dicey (n 34) 1-030.
98. In the case of determining a jurisdictional 'connecting factor', for example, as being a question for the law of the *lex fori* – i.e., the forum state: Dicey (n 34) 1-030.
99. *See*, Bernhard Oxman, 'Jurisdiction of States' in Rüdiger Wolfrum (ed.), *The Max Planck Encyclopaedia of Public International Law*, Volume VI (OUP 2012) 547 explaining this distinction; Simma and Müller (n 1) 147.
100. This is how Oxman considers jurisdiction, being an exercise of authority by states vis-a-vis each other and in accordance with principles of international law: Oxman (n 99) 547.
101. Stephen Allen et al., *The Oxford Handbook of Jurisdiction in International Law* (OUP 2019) 4.

[1] Third Restatement

The Third Restatement on US Foreign Relations Law supports the approach of considering adjudicative jurisdiction as conceptually distinct from prescriptive jurisdiction.[102] The Third Restatement is regarded as an authoritative guide on state jurisdiction compiled from comparative law resources and provides a perspective from public international law.[103] This has added the additional category of 'adjudicative jurisdiction' as a form of jurisdiction which states exercise. In the previous versions of the Restatement, there was merely 'prescriptive jurisdiction' and 'enforcement jurisdiction'. 'Adjudicative jurisdiction' is defined as 'to subject persons or things to the process of [*the state's*] courts or administrative tribunals, whether in civil or in criminal proceedings, whether or not the state is party to the proceedings'.[104]

The conceptual distinction which is now made between adjudicative jurisdiction and prescriptive jurisdiction is significant. If adjudicative jurisdiction were a mere facet of the state's prescriptive jurisdiction, there would have been no need to add this additional category. This is acknowledged in scholarly work on the Third Restatement. For example, Olmstead points out that the additional category of 'adjudicative jurisdiction' in the *Third Restatement* does not just reflect an actualisation of prescriptive jurisdiction (i.e., an exercise of the 'law-making process' by the state through its courts under international law) but is rather the manifestation of a specific exercise of enforcement jurisdiction – i.e., the enforcement of a prescription through a judicial process.[105] As a definitional matter, this is reflected by the wording of 'jurisdiction to enforce' which is stated to be 'to induce or compel compliance or to punish noncompliance with its laws or regulations, *whether through the courts* or by use of executive, administrative, police, or other nonjudicial action'.

Moreover, under §431, which concerns 'jurisdiction to enforce', the relationship between prescriptive jurisdiction and enforcement jurisdiction is quite clear: a state may only enforce its *laws* if it has jurisdiction to prescribe such laws. However, no such limitation is prescribed under §421 in relation to jurisdiction to adjudicate. In this respect, it is stated that a state may exercise jurisdiction through its courts whenever this would be 'reasonable'. These grounds of reasonableness are expressly listed as the kinds of 'links' which are viewed as permissible under *private international law*; for example, if the person or thing is present in the territory. Thus, the Third Restatement seems to accept that a state need not have prescriptive jurisdiction to be able to exercise adjudicative jurisdiction.

---

102. Third Restatement (n 17). This is the precursor to the Fourth Restatement. Compare §401 from Third and Fourth Restatement which define the forms of jurisdiction in the same way. The Restatements are not official documents of the United States but were rather compiled by the American Law Institute, a private organisation constituted of law professors, judges and other law professionals, from comparative law sources. They are widely considered authoritative academic source on public international law rules or principles of jurisdiction; *see, e.g.*, usage by Ryngaert (n 15).
103. Third Restatement, para. 101 defines 'international law' as that dealing with the relations between states.
104. §421 Third Restatement; §401(b) Third Restatement; also §401(b) Fourth Restatement.
105. Cecil Olmstead, 'Jurisdiction' (1989) 14(2) *Yale Journal of International Law* 468, 469.

Accordingly, a distinction that may be drawn between the state's authority to enforce *law* for which it must have jurisdiction to prescribe and the principle that the state may *enforce its law* through its courts even if that state enforcing through its courts does not have jurisdiction to prescribe. Nothing excludes that this 'law' which the national court 'enforces' may include international law to the extent that international law is part of the law which the state seeks to enforce. Otherwise, the authors of the statement need not have added the additional category of 'adjudicative jurisdiction', which did not exist in the earlier draft of the Restatement. Adjudicative jurisdiction is considered under the statement as a conceptually distinct potential source of law from prescriptive jurisdiction.

[2] Scelle

Scelle's *dédoublement fonctionnel* theory conceived of the possibility that national courts may 'act' in the international legal sphere when they apply national legal norms.[106] According to this, when courts apply international law, they do not just 'apply' a law based on sovereign command, but it is the quality of the organ's function as an 'act' (of the state) which goes to the potential for its contribution to the international legal system. Put differently, being a state organ does not normatively exclude that the court *acts* as an 'international agent'. This international agency ought to be regarded as a further theoretical foundation for considering national court decisions as a source for public international law enforcement jurisdiction, especially in the current context where private international law norms are an alternatively relevant basis for jurisdiction.

Illustrative of how national courts may apply a national legal norm but at the same time potentially contribute to an *international* legal norm when exercising jurisdiction in the area under examination is the decision in *LR Avionics*.[107] An arbitration award had been rendered against the Federal Republic of Nigeria in a Nigerian arbitration. There was no connection to UK jurisdiction as a matter of public or private international law, i.e., neither of the parties were UK nationals or UK domiciled, and the law applicable to the arbitration was not UK law. The Claimant sought to register the award under section 101 EAA and the Nigerian judgment under section 9 Administration of Justice Act 1920 (AJA).[108] The Court had to determine whether it had jurisdiction under those provisions. Since the jurisdiction was being asserted against a foreign state, the question arising was whether the proceedings were deemed to 'relate to the arbitration' within the meaning of section 9 SIA, with the consequence that the Defendants were not immune from the enforcement proceedings.

106. Georges Scelle, *II Precis de droit de gens* (1932); further: Antonio Cassese, 'Remarks on Scelle's Theory of "Role Splitting" in International Law' (1990) 1 *European Journal of International Law* 210 https://doi.org/10.1093/oxfordjournals.ejil.a035763 (accessed 26 September 2025); Karin van Leeuwen, 'The Hague Academy as a Space of Encounter: How Scelle's 1933 Teachings on National Courts Landed in the Netherlands' (2024) 35(3) *The European Journal of International Law* 805, 806 https://doi.org/10.1093/ejil/chae049 (accessed 26 September 2025).
107. *LR Avionics Technologies v. The Federal Republic of Nigeria* [2016] EWHC 1761 (Comm).
108. *Administration of Justice Act 1920*, c. 81.

Section 9 provides that where a state has agreed in writing to submit a dispute which has arisen, or may arise, to arbitration, the state is not immune with respect to proceedings in the courts of the United Kingdom which 'relate to the arbitration'. The Court found that such proceedings to enforce an award under section 101 EAA are 'proceedings which relate to the arbitration' within the meaning of section 9.[109] Consequently, the UK Court ought to be regarded as recognising that its power to declare an award enforceable is within the scope of UK *international* adjudicative authority - and that this may be regarded as state practice, to the extent that there is sufficient widespread and consistent practice in the other representative states, which shall be examined in the following chapters. The exercise of *decision-making authority*, i.e., the power of national courts to decide, which, in effect, declared the award enforceable against the foreign state, can be seen as evidence that the Court did not consider the principle of state immunity as a bar to the jurisdiction.

As a formal matter from the internal perspective, the decision may be viewed as having its source in the national legal provision contained in section 101 EAA, which simply permits the national court to render the declaration of enforceability according to the national legislative rule and/or principle. At the same time, however, the national court can be seen to 'act' in the international sphere because it rendered a decision, despite there being no connection to its territory, i.e., in the public sphere, which had the effect of inducing the compliance of the foreign State with the arbitration award. In this case, since there was no connection to the UK jurisdiction as a matter of public or private international law, the decision itself might be evidence of an enforcement norm - i.e., the norm of recognising an award, which will be examined in greater detail in Chapter 4.

[E] PUBLIC AND PRIVATE INTERNATIONAL LAW SUPPORTIVE APPROACHES

From a traditional public international law perspective, adjudicative jurisdiction arises as a mere facet of prescriptive jurisdiction.[110] From this vantage point, adjudicative jurisdiction involves the recognition of a right or duty, exercisable by a court, to interpret and apply those municipal laws which a state chooses to adopt.[111] Consequently, it appears that this form of jurisdiction is principally concerned with the coordination of national law approaches to processes of adjudication[112] rather than

109. *See also*, *Svenska* (2006) (n 20) [117] (recognition and review proceedings do not attract immunity); *NML Capital Ltd v. Republic of Argentina* [2011] UKSC 31, [2011] 2 AC 495; further, *Dallah Real Estate and Tourism Holding Company v. The Minister of Religious Affairs, Government of Pakistan* [2010] UKSC 46.

110. Staker (n 15) 306; Shaw (n 15) 555 ff.; Akehurst (n 16) 145; *Oppenheim's* (n 15) 45.

111. Staker (n 15); Akehurst (n 16); Shaw (n 15); *Oppenheim's* (n 15).

112. Which, in a sense, would have no greater 'normative' force (i.e., the legal nature of the decision) than 'soft' principles of law governing the coordination of international courts and tribunals, a subject often analysed by scholars in the field of adjudicative jurisdiction: Yuval Shany, *Regulating Jurisdictional Relations Between National and International Courts* (OUP 2007) (from a public international law - theoretical perspective); Anne-Marie Slaughter, *A New World Order* (Princeton UP 2004) (from a global governance perspective).

with national courts making a more direct contribution to the development of international law. However, an approach which considers that national courts may directly contribute, rather than the norm being based merely on an interpretation of the prescriptive norm by the state, is supported by the literature as developed by the following sections. This provides the normative foundation for identifying a general principle of international law on enforcement jurisdiction, as may be emerging in representative national courts.

[1] *The Lotus*: The Foundation and Gaps

The traditional approach to prescriptive jurisdiction propounded in the *Lotus* decision is that a state is permitted to do all that it is not prohibited from doing.[113] However, the wider idea of 'jurisdiction' as being the authority of states to act under international law is encompassed and can be drawn from a more general statement in the *Lotus* decision as to sources in international law, where the Permanent Court of International Justice (PCIJ) stated:

> International law governs the relations between independent states. The rules of law binding upon states therefore emanate from their own free will as expressed in conventions *or by usages generally accepted as expressing principles of law* and *established in order to regulate the relations between these co-existing independent communities* or *with a view to the achievement of common aims.*[114]

The *Lotus* concerned the collision of a French and Turkish ship, resulting in the death of several Turkish sailors and passengers. Turkey exercised its criminal jurisdiction over the dispute, seeking to prosecute the French captain accused of the collision. Its jurisdiction to do so was challenged by France before the PCIJ. The parties both consented to the jurisdiction of the PCIJ. In deciding that Turkey *had not* acted in conflict with principles of public international law, the PCIJ elucidated the so-called *Lotus* principle. It found that since a state is permitted to do all that it is not prohibited from doing, then Turkey was permitted, in principle, to extend its criminal laws to the dispute. Thus, the '*Lotus* principle' stands for the proposition that in so far as a state's *prescriptive jurisdiction* is concerned – that is, a state's power to adopt laws – a state must generally point to a 'permissive' rule within national laws as the source of the rule. However, as the parties consented to the jurisdiction of the PCIJ, the question of adjudicative jurisdiction was not at issue. Consequently, the decision itself does not speak to whether there are any rules or principles of international law related to adjudicative jurisdiction as a distinct form of jurisdiction compared with prescriptive jurisdiction, i.e., whether there are lawful forms of adjudicative authority independent of any prescriptive norms.[115]

113. S.S. Lotus (*France v. Turkey*) (Judgment) [1927] PCIJ (ser A) No. 10 [46].
114. *Ibid.*, [44].
115. In *Lotus*, the Court acknowledged that a basis for its jurisdiction was a Treaty which the parties had signed. According to the wording of the question asked by the Court (below in this footnote), the decision should properly be regarded as an analysis of the principle of prescriptive jurisdiction relating to whether Turkey could extend its *laws* (i.e., prescriptive

The *Lotus* decision is important for a second reason. The PCIJ stated that in relation to enforcement jurisdiction:

> Now the first and foremost restriction imposed by international law upon a State is that – failing the existence of a permissive rule to the contrary – it may not exercise its power in any form in the territory of another State. In this sense jurisdiction is certainly territorial; it cannot be exercised by a State outside its territory except by virtue of a permissive rule derived from international custom or from a convention.[116]

This approach relates to the traditional view of enforcement jurisdiction – this form of jurisdiction is regarded as only 'not prohibited' if it is 'permitted' according to a rule of international custom or from a convention. This approach can be distinguished from this work, which considers whether there are any *lawful* forms of enforcement which are neither prohibited nor permitted but rather lawful based on the tacit consent of courts. Such an approach appears not to be excluded on the basis of *The Lotus* as that decision did not decide the question of enforcement jurisdiction but rather prescriptive jurisdiction, and in any event recognised more generally that norms may developed according to the tacit consent of states.[117]

[2] Lawfulness of Authority and Judge Simma

Whether a state may exercise jurisdiction according to some *permissive* rule, based on a formal, consent-based rule or principle, is distinct from the question of whether, as a matter of international law, there are any norms which govern the scope of a state's *lawful* authority. This approach, though not expressly set out there, may be regarded as in-keeping with statements in the *Lotus* decision itself, in particular with regard to 'usages' as potentially expressing principles of law: 'the rules of law binding upon states emanate from their own free will as express ... *by usages generally accepted as expressing principles of law*'.[118]

Judge Simma is one proponent of this wider idea of 'jurisdiction' as 'authority', being the jurisdiction of states to act in accordance with each other and international law, rather than merely a specific exercise of their sovereignty. In his criticism of the

power) over the dispute. In so far as adjudicative jurisdiction is concerned, the decision could be viewed as an elucidation of the *principle* of prescriptive jurisdiction, but this would not have been a necessary analysis, given there was a basis in a Treaty for analysing the scope of Turkey's prescriptive power. Thus, this aspect of the decision could also simply be viewed as an interpretation of the discrete treaty norm. At the relevant page, the Court asked: 'Has Turkey, contrary to Article 15 of the Convention of Lausanne of July 24th, 1923, respecting conditions of residence and business and jurisdiction, acted in conflict with the principles of international law – and if so, what principles – by instituting [criminal proceedings] ... in pursuance of Turkish law against M Demons' assuming therefore that the PCIJ had adjudicative jurisdiction (*Lotus* (n 113) [2]).

116. *Lotus* (n 113) [45].
117. *Ibid.*, [44].
118. *Ibid.*, [46].

Lotus decision,[119] Simma explained that the so-called *Lotus* principle - according to which a state is permitted to do all that it is not prohibited from doing - does not speak to the question of the *legality* of jurisdiction.[120] To state that something is not prohibited does not mean it is logically therefore permitted. According to this view, there ought to be jurisdictional rules or principles in between these two levels - permissive and prohibitive - according to which a state may *lawfully* exercise jurisdiction.

It is useful to compare the orthodox international law approach, according to which adjudicative jurisdiction is a facet of prescriptive jurisdiction, with the approach to be developed here. The latter approach considers how *exercises* of decision-making authority, or simply stated, decisions by national courts, may be regarded as a source of norms of public international law relating to enforcement jurisdiction *irrespective* of the adoption of a particular prescriptive rule and/or principle. Under traditional public international law conceptions of jurisdiction, only 'permissible' grounds of authority are considered a source of adjudicative jurisdiction - that is, norms which *authorise* a national court to exercise jurisdiction on the basis of a prescriptive norm.[121] This appears to apply the '*Lotus* principle' according to which a state is permitted to do all that it is not prohibited from doing.[122] According to this approach, jurisdiction is simply defined by the rules or principles which a state chooses to adopt. Instead, considering jurisdiction more widely as the authority of states to act in their relations with each other, under international law, the acts of courts - in so far as they are reflective of the norm - become significant as a potential source.

[3] Kaushal and Von Bogdandy and Venzke

Kaushal explains that since a national court is located at the intersection between the state and the law, then an exercise of its jurisdiction 'is a reference back to law's authority and thus an expression of sovereign legitimacy'.[123] Similarly, Von Bogdandy and Venzke ask the question of how *international* courts may be critiqued as to their legitimacy. Before such concerns can be addressed, they ask the question of how international courts can be conceived as bodies with legitimacy. They claim that the best approach is to view them as bodies of *public* authority - namely, bodies capable of rendering *legal* decisions.[124]

Whilst this approach can be criticised from a few perspectives, including its artificial creation of a 'public' central organ in international law which does not exist - generally equivalent to the sovereign state within national legal systems - it provides

119. Accordance with International Law of Universal Declaration of Independence in Respect of Kosovo (Advisory Opinion) [2010] ICJ Rep 403 (Declaration of Judge Simma) [8].
120. *Lotus* (n 113) [46].
121. According to the 'orthodox' approaches mentioned above, e.g., Staker (n 15) 306-334; Shaw (n 15) 555 ff.; Akehurst (n 16) 145; *Oppenheim's* (n 15) 456.
122. *Lotus* (n 113) [44].
123. Asha Kaushal, 'The Politics of Jurisdiction' (2015) 78(5) *Modern Law Review* 759, 761 https://doi.org/10.1111/1468-2230.12143 (accessed 26 September 2025).
124. Von Bogdandy and Venzke (n 31) 17.

a useful starting point for national court authority as a source of international law. The reason is that since jurisdiction in the public sphere engages a national court at the *source* of its authority,[125] then at the same time as rendering a decision, a national court may exercise a lawful or legitimate form of authority. In so far as such a decision is in accordance with international law, this may be evidentiary of state will in respect of a particular subject matter. Should a sufficient number of states engage in the same practice, this may be evidence of the first element, being state practice, which is necessary for a finding of customary international law within the meaning of Article 38(1)(b) ICJ Statute.[126] In this regard, the national courts, being representative of differing public law approaches to authority, are therefore being regarded as representative of state practice, in so far as those decisions are also consistent and widespread in light of harmonising norms applicable to the scope of their enforcement jurisdiction.

[F] HARMONISING PRINCIPLES

This chapter introduced the idea that jurisdiction is being used interchangeably with decision-making authority or the authority of national courts to act in accordance with each other and any applicable public international law norms. This conception is closely tied to the idea that jurisdiction is 'normative'.[127] The question of whether a state has jurisdiction based on sovereignty – such as by way of application of a jurisdictional norm in a treaty – differs from whether an exercise of authority ought to be deemed lawful in accordance with norms underpinning authority under public international law. This will be developed further in relation to the concepts of 'sovereign equality' and the 'international rule of law' and how these might *justify* why an exercise of decision-making authority by national courts may be consistent with public international law.

[1] Common Interests' Approach

An international legal concept which supports reconsideration of adjudicative jurisdiction as a manifestation of enforcement jurisdiction is the 'common interests' approach, which is a concept which Villalpando shows may underlie inter-state relations and legitimise the authority of judicial organs within it.[128]

---

125. Kaushal (n 123) 759 ('it is immediately apparent that law has a foundational relationship to jurisdiction: [since] jurisdiction is a reference back to law's authority and thus an expression of sovereign legitimacy').
126. Developing new theories for customary international law has been a central focus of the International Law Commission, e.g., Report of the International Law Commission, Sixty-eight session (2 May-10 June and 4 July-12 August 2016) [UN Doc A/71/10], Chapter V identification of customary international law, especially, Part III, conclusions 4-8.
127. Allen et al. (n 101) 4.
128. Santiago Villalpando, 'The Legal Dimension of the International Community: How Community Interests Are Protected in International Law' (2010) 21(2) *European Journal of International Law* 387 https://doi.org/10.1093/ejil/chq038 (accessed 26 September 2025).

Villalpando speaks of the 'omnipresence' of community interest. Common interests shared by states underpin inter-state relations and legitimise organs that claim they are acting on the community's behalf.[129] The very concept of an 'international community' must be criticised because it relies on the idea of some centralising organ or superstate which is somehow 'above' national legal orders. The realities of the international legal order are far more complex, and their relationship to national legal orders is more nuanced. However, the idea that there are some common interests which states share is a useful perspective for understanding how national court decisions may protect such interests, even if the obligation they protect may not be expressly stated by the prescriptive rule.

Consent to arbitration has not necessarily been sufficient to establish the authority of national courts to enforce the arbitral award.[130] Compared with permanent international courts and tribunals, whose jurisdiction tends to be established on the basis of a treaty or constitutive instrument, the jurisdiction of international arbitral tribunals can be established through various means – including private party agreement, institutional rules and bilateral and multilateral treaties. Even under arbitrations based on treaties, the legal event necessary to invoke the jurisdiction of the arbitral tribunal is a breach of the treaty in addition, of course, to party consent under that treaty. The treaty itself is not the legal basis for national court jurisdiction in support of the arbitral process or arbitral award.

When considering how the arbitral process is enforced, or how states induce parties' compliance with that process under international law, it thus becomes important to consider national court decisions for how they may contribute to any harmonised public international legal norm. This question pertains to which principles of public international law justify or underpin authority, such that decision-making authority can be considered a source of the international law on jurisdiction in its own right? Those principles will be considered in the next sections.

[2] Sovereign Equality

One common aim or principle underpinning authority which may justify *lawful* exercises of adjudicative jurisdiction as a source – here, of enforcement jurisdiction – is 'sovereign equality'. As Kelsen explains, whilst 'sovereignty' is the authority of states as subjects under international law, sovereign equality does not flow directly from that sovereignty but is instead inherent in the quality of states as equals under international law.[131] 'Authority' is not the same as 'legal capacity' or the authority of states as subjects of international law. Instead, it is concerned with a state's capacity to act in accordance with or to adopt public international law norms. To the extent that states

129. *Ibid.*, 388.
130. Fox and Webb (n 8) 388 ('if the arbitration is to be held in the forum state (or to apply forum state law) then waiver of immunity to the jurisdiction at least to the extent of the supervisory powers over arbitration of the forum court may be *implied*' (does not say direct)).
131. Hans Kelsen, 'The Principle of Sovereign Equality of States as a Basis for International Organization' (1944) 53(2) *The Yale Law Journal* 207, 208 https://doi.org/10.2307/792798 (accessed 26 September 2025).

exercise authority with each other and any applicable principles of international law, this might be regarded as underpinned - or justified - by the principle of sovereign equality.

Take, for example, the 2014 *Yukos* decision, the facts of which have already been recounted.[132] There, the Court set aside an award and recognised the Dutch Court's decision *in view of the aim of enforcement* which is a principle protected in the New York Convention. Article I(1) New York Convention provides that contracting states shall recognise and enforce arbitral awards made in the territory of a state other than the state where such awards are made. Section 101 English Arbitration Act 1996 (EAA)[133] gives effect to Article I(1) New York Convention, providing that contracting states shall recognise and enforce New York Convention awards 'in the same manner as a judgment or order of the court to the same effect'. In the Amsterdam Court decision recognising an award that had been set aside in Russia, the Court had already found that it would not be compelled to recognise the Russian court's decision. This was on the basis that the award could be recognised as enforceable under the *same applicable principle,* giving effect to Article I(1) New York Convention.[134] Finding that it would follow the Amsterdam Court's decision in this regard - and refuse to recognise the Russian set-aside decision - the UK Court could thus be considered ensuring that a foreign decision supporting enforcement of the arbitral award was recognised.

As will be further explained, the principle of enforcement found in the New York Convention is not the source of the court's jurisdiction but contains harmonising principles in light of which such decisions are made, including in relation to supervision, review and recognition and execution jurisdiction. To the extent that national courts ensure that the aim of enforcement is met, then such a decision would be justified by the international law principle of sovereign equality. That would be to the extent that other courts follow the same approach in similar circumstances and considering any applicable harmonising principles. On that basis, jurisdiction may be interpreted to not be a breach of the international principle of state immunity, but rather a lawful exercise of decision-making authority in accordance with the principle of sovereign equality, which is of common interest to all states.

[3] International Rule of Law

The 'international' rule of law is another justificatory principle for the practice, provided that it is defined so as to not merely include the two 'traditional' elements of the rule of law, being law and justice. 'Formalist' conceptions of the rule of law accept a narrower approach to international authority, which is more closely equated to the 'national rule of law'.[135] These authors, such as Watts, Chesterman and Nollkaemper,

132. *Yukos* (2014) (n 82); *See* section [B] of this chapter for the relevant facts.
133. Considered in light of any recent amendments by the Arbitration Act 2025 (c. 4).
134. Amsterdam Court of Appeal, Case Number 200.005.269/01, *Yukos Capital S.à r.l. v. OAO Rosneft* [3.4]-[3.5].
135. *See*, Arthur Watts, 'The International Rule of Law' (1993) 36 *German Yearbook of International Law* 15; Simon Chesterman, 'An International Rule of Law' (2008) 56 *American Journal of*

define the 'international' rule of law in the same way as the 'national' rule of law, comprising only the two elements of law and justice. According to this, judicial bodies are 'legitimate', i.e., constituted on a legally justifiable basis, where they exercise authority in accordance with the scope of authority conferred upon and with any moral principles which might be applicable to the authority. This national legal conception of the 'rule of law' excludes any *wider* rules or principles of law that might apply to regulate or constrain the authority of judicial bodies under *public international law* when the national rule of law is elevated to the international legal level.

McCorquodale rightly points out that to equate the international with the national rule of law is a 'false comparison'.[136] He states that the additional element necessary to make the rule of law workable at the international law level is 'effective implementation'. As pointed out by Cassese in his commentary on Scelle's *dédoublement fonctionnel* theory, seeing as no sovereign at the international law level enforces international law, then there must be a wider enforcement principle to ensure that the rule of law is heeded at the international law level.[137] Enforcement is an inescapable element of every functioning legal system. Whilst he notes that 'the activities of the international dispute settlement system are ... an important part of the international rule of law in that they help to create a web of discourse about and for international law' and how such a 'web' might 'assist the compliance-pulling power of international law', it is not examined how national courts themselves may assist in such a 'compliance pull' in accordance with the international rule of law. Consequently, the international rule of law is being understood as a principle which underpins whether an exercise of authority by one court is consistent with another and with international law.

Therefore, when considered at the international level, the 'rule of law' ought to encompass not merely the aspects of law and justice but also effective implementation.[138] From this perspective, it becomes possible to see how national courts, on behalf of states, may ensure effective implementation enforcement jurisdiction.

It is useful to compare the traditional approach to adjudicative jurisdiction – which considers adjudicative jurisdiction as a specific application of the prescriptive norm – to this approach to understand how it differs. On the one hand, the traditional perspective tends to explain how one national court gives effect to a rule of international from the perspective of *that particular* legal system. This perspective rests on the court's interpretation of the legislative rule or principle which the particular state has chosen to adopt. On the other hand, an 'international rule of law approach' allows international lawyers to view national courts as bodies or agents of international law rather than focusing on a perspective based on an interpretation of national laws.

Comparative Law 331 https://doi.org/10.5131/ajcl.2007.0009 (accessed 26 September 2025); and more recently, André Nollkaemper, *National Courts and The International Rule of Law* (OUP 2011) 3-4.

136. Robert McCorquodale, 'Defining the International Rule of Law: Defining Gravity' (2016) *International and Comparative Law Quarterly* 277, 290. https://doi.org/10.1017/s0020589316000026 (accessed 26 September 2025).
137. *Ibid. See also*: Cassese (n 106).
138. McCorquodale (n 136) 303.

According to this approach, national courts would then be able to collectively give effect to international law norms and develop them.

Illustrative of the first approach is the *Trendtex* decision. As already explained in section [C][1] of this chapter, Lord Denning merely declared what the international law rule was, recognising this as a matter of UK law. This was merely a decision, therefore, which reflected acknowledgement of the international legal principle as part of the court's national laws.

Compare this to the example of *Yukos* already given. On its face, the decision itself said little about the enforceability of international arbitral authority: it merely recognised the effect of the decision of the Amsterdam Court. From the internal perspective of the UK legal system, the decision could thus be seen as having its source in the recognition and enforcement of judgments as a matter for the internal private international law norms of the state. However, from the international perspective adopted herein, the *exercise* of authority – in so far as it gave effect to an *international* principle of enforcement – may be regarded evidence of the norm to the extent that there is similar widespread, representative and consistent practice in light of harmonising norms on jurisdiction. In this sense, national courts may be considered conduits of the international rule of law because they ensure the effective implementation of this principle. It is the *national court* itself which is the source of this practice rather than the *decision* in the sense described through analysis of the *Trendtex* decision, that is adjudicative jurisdiction as merely declaratory of the prescriptive norm. This is an important conceptual distinction from traditional approaches, which only consider the content of the decisions themselves rather than their functional effects, i.e., the fact that they result in enforcement of an arbitral process or award.

[G] PRIVATE INTERNATIONAL LAW

New approaches to jurisdiction in private international law also support the emergence of adjudicative jurisdiction as a manifestation of the state's enforcement powers. Knop, Michaels, and Riles, in their article on international law in domestic courts, have argued that the discipline of private international law has been overlooked as a lens through which to examine the treatment of international law by national courts.[139] Private international law is often understood as a method or discipline following a particular policy rather than a discipline in its own right.[140] Mills highlights the approach of private international law to questions of jurisdiction and its potential relevance in the sphere of public international law regulation.[141]

139. Karen Knop, Ralf Michaels and Annelise Riles, 'International Law in Domestic Courts: A Conflict of Laws Approach' (2010) 103 *Proceedings American Society of International Law* 269, 270 https://doi.org/10.1017/s0272503700034297 (accessed 26 September 2025).
140. *Ibid.*, 272. Stating that 'conflict-of-laws' approach may be a way forward in the field of international law in domestic courts for the reason that 'the reality of overlapping jurisdictions – has been the very raison-d'être of conflicts doctrine since inception in the field'.
141. Alex Mills, *The Confluence of Public and Private International Law: Justice, Pluralism and Subsidiarity in the International Constitutional Ordering of Private Law* (CUP 2009).

[1] Private International Law as a Source of Public International Law: Theory

According to Knop, Michaels and Riles, what is overlooked when viewing private international law as a method or policy is that the principles developed by it may be (incorrectly) viewed as merely a sovereign expression of a public international law rule or principle.[142] From this internal perspective, private international law is viewed as *the* source of the national court's jurisdiction. Thus, public international law has nothing to say on the matter since the question of jurisdiction is resolved by the provision in national law.

Mills has argued that an overly positivistic approach to international law has allowed for the subjugation of private international law as a body confined to the regulation of international private legal interests within the scope of state sovereignty and thus by the internal state.[143] However, Mills acknowledges that private international law employs an 'international regulatory function' when viewed as part of public international law. From this perspective, it might be considered whether, where private international law is viewed as part of public international law, it is declaratory of the public international law rule or principle.

[2] Decisions to Consider

In the traditional conflicts of laws textbook, Dicey addresses whether any particular form of immunity fulfils the requirements in the UK State Immunity Act 1978 (SIA) rather than the *prior question* of whether a jurisdiction may be available *regardless*, in principle, of the application of an immunity.[144] This is understandable given that the focus on traditional private international law texts is on conflicts of law rules which are found in national law.[145] From this perspective, national laws tend to adopt an approach where immunity is the rule, and a particular exception has to be established for that immunity to be removed.

For example, the capacity of national courts to establish they have jurisdiction over claims *in rem* - i.e., the question of whether a national court has jurisdiction in respect of particular property - is said to rest on the location of that property within the jurisdiction based on a provision to this effect adopted into national law, i.e., the private international law norms of the forum court. Similarly, whether a national court has jurisdiction *in personam*, i.e., its power in respect of particular parties to the dispute, is approached as a question of whether 'a claim [can be] positively ... brought against a person to compel him [or her] to do a particular thing, e.g. the payment of a debt or damages for a breach of a contract ... or to compel him [or her] not to do something e.g. when an injunction is sought'.[146] This approach provides for a link to

142. Knop, Michaels and Riles (n 139) 272.
143. Mills (n 141).
144. *See, e.g.*, Dicey (n 34).
145. Dicey (n 34) 9-019.
146. Dicey (n 34) 1-079-1-080.

the jurisdiction as the justification for jurisdiction, with the identification of that principle being *national law*. However, it does not consider on what principled basis the state *ought* to be exercising jurisdiction considering any public international law norms.

In the area of enforcement of arbitration awards and state immunity, the UK provision in section 9 SIA holds that where a state has agreed in writing to submit disputes to arbitration, the state is not immune 'as respects proceedings in the courts of the United Kingdom which relate to the arbitration'.[147] Looking at any court decision from the perspective of its application of the prescriptive norm enshrined in the Act, the decision merely *interprets* the rule or principle which the state has chosen to adopt. However, from the perspective of considering the court's *exercise* of jurisdiction as a source of any enforcement norm, a more complex picture arises according. Here, national courts are called upon to determine the interaction between the international legal principle of state immunity, which is given effect within a state's national laws, and the scope of an enforcement aspect of their adjudicative jurisdiction.

For example, in the 2005 decision in *Svenska Petroleum*,[148] the Swedish Claimant, Svenska Petroleum, sought to enforce against the Defendant state's (Lithuania's) assets in the UK, with the Defendant raising various state immunity defences. Morison J had given Svenska permission to enforce the final award under section 101 English Arbitration Act (EAA).[149] Section 101 gives effect to Article I(1) New York Convention. Section 101 EAA provides that contracting states shall recognise and enforce New York Convention awards 'in the same manner as a judgment or order of the court to the same effect'. Thus, this places an obligation, in principle, on courts to enforce arbitral awards even if they are rendered in a foreign state, in accordance with Article I(1) New York Convention. In the 2004 *Svenska* decision before Morison J, Lithuania had applied to set aside the award in addition to reserving its right to contest the Court's jurisdiction on the basis of its immunity from the adjudicative jurisdiction of foreign courts as enshrined in section 1 SIA.[150] This provides the general principle that a state is generally immune from the jurisdiction of the courts [of the United Kingdom] except where so provided in the provisions of the SIA. Svenska argued that such enforcement proceedings fell outside the scope of this principle of state immunity and within the scope of section 9 SIA, which provides a state is not immune from proceedings which 'relate to the arbitration'. The contention that recognition and enforcement proceedings fall within section 9 SIA was also raised in the 2005 proceedings.

The approach of the Court as regards to the question of whether recognition and enforcement falls within section 9 SIA demonstrates a few important aspects. First, the New York Convention was not the source of the court's authority to decide, but rather section 101 EAA to which it gives effect. Second, the Court also had to decide according to relevant principles of immunity as to whether it could exercise such jurisdiction, including the interaction between section 101 EAA and section 9 SIA. Thus, using

147. Section 9(1) SIA.
148. *Svenska Petroleum v. Government of Lithuania* [2005] EWHC 2437.
149. *Arbitration Act 1996* (UK), c. 23.
150. *Svenska* (2005) (n 148) [6].

Svenska as one source for the type of decisions considered in this book, *national court decisions* are the principal source for any enforcement norms under consideration and the New York Convention is one harmonising instrument. Further, by considering whether it could recognise the arbitration award in light of section 9, the principle enshrined therein was another source of the court's jurisdiction to decide. However, this private international law rule, which allows the court to consider whether consent to arbitrate brings the dispute within the scope of section 9 SIA, is not the source of the public international law norm of enforcement. However, a decision based on that section may be a source of the norm, since section 9 may enshrine one justifying principle in light of which the decision is made.

[3] Decisions Which Must Be Excluded

There are some decisions where courts have exercised jurisdiction based on the private international law rule, but the decision ought to be *excluded* from any common approach. This can be examined through an example - *EM v. Republic of Argentina.*[151]

NML had obtained a valid money judgment against the Republic of Argentina. It applied for a discovery order from a US Court, which would compel two non-party banks to comply with *subpoenas duces* - particular orders in the US courts for the production of evidence - to seek information about Argentina's assets outside the United States. Argentina challenged the action stating that it infringed its sovereign immunity by compelling disclosure about its assets abroad in breach of §§1602 *et seq.* of the Foreign Sovereign Immunities Act 1976 (FSIA). The Court first considered this matter to arise as a question of its subject matter jurisdiction - that is, whether the Court could exercise jurisdiction in respect of the subject matter in the dispute - here, being the disclosure order. Additionally, as a matter of *reasoning*, the Court questioned whether the order would implicate Argentina's immunity. According to this reasoning, in so far as such an order would be permitted under the FSIA, it is viewed as a rule or principle which would *authorise* enforcement jurisdiction. The Court stated in this regard: 'the district court's power to order discovery to enforce its judgment does not derive from its ultimate ability to attach the property in question but from its power to conduct supplementary proceedings, involving persons indisputably within its jurisdiction, to enforce valid judgments'.

This statement is important for two reasons. First, it acknowledges that discovery cannot be ordered in all cases, but those which merely relate to the enforcement of an already valid judgment against a sovereign. Moreover, it considers that the FSIA *confers* a power on it to grant the order in this regard. Thus, the instrument, which as a matter of national law gives effect to the public international law on state immunity, may also be regarded as *authorising* the court to exercise jurisdiction in respect of the foreign state. In other words, the FSIA is treated, from the sovereign's internal perspective, as a *justification* or *authorising act* for the exercise of jurisdiction.

151. *EM Ltd. v. Republic of Argentina*, 695 F. 3d 201 (2d Cir. 2012).

Whether the decision is correct as a matter of principle or not, it follows a generally defensible course of reasoning, relying on whether the jurisdiction could be justified based on the FSIA which gives effect to the international principle of state immunity. The provision of private international law - here in the FSIA - could be viewed as the authorising act which provides evidence that the state regards the exercise as binding as a matter of law. However, this ought to be *only* to the extent that the court's authority is also consistent with the *public international law* norm.

In that decision, the Court failed to acknowledge that ordering discovery *beyond* the territorial application of the FSIA, i.e., in respect of a foreign state, without express authorisation, would ordinarily require express consent. A discovery order, by its nature, would compel or induce the compliance of a foreign state to do something. The general rule is that absent express consent of the foreign state, this would be a breach of the public international law rule or principle that enforcement jurisdiction is prohibited unless the foreign state consents to the rule. In that decision, the Court merely considered that because there was a valid judgment, it ought to be able to order a discovery order that extended *beyond* US territorial jurisdiction without identifying the consensual basis for state jurisdiction. Consequently, decisions must be checked for whether the exercise of jurisdiction is consistent with the principle underpinning the public international legal norm.[152] Otherwise, they ought to be regarded as an impermissible extension of the state's enforcement jurisdiction beyond its territory - often described in the literature as an extraterritorial exercise.

Thus, while private international law norms may properly be regarded as a source of the public international law norm, this should only be to the extent that the jurisdiction is otherwise consistent with public international law norms applicable to the scope of court jurisdiction.

[H] ADJUDICATIVE JURISDICTION AS A MANIFESTATION OF ENFORCEMENT JURISDICTION

This section examines theoretical approaches to authority which support the conception that adjudicative jurisdiction ought to be regarded as arising as a manifestation of enforcement jurisdiction. The section also demonstrates how those theoretical lenses can be used as a methodological tool to support the validity and defensibility of the norm under examination.[153]

---

152. Similarly: *Republic of Argentina v. NML Capital Ltd*, 573 U.S. 134 (2014); Further: 'Republic of Argentina v NML Capital, Ltd' (2014) 128 *Harvard Law Review* 381 (the Court ordered extraterritorial asset enforcement on the basis that it was 'not prohibited' by the FSIA. However, it did not *justify* why this would be consistent with the international legal principle of immunity, i.e., why it would not breach the foreign State's sovereignty). Thus, like EM, it ought to be regarded as an *impermissible* exercise of enforcement jurisdiction. The decision in *Republic of Argentina* will be examined in further detail in Chapter 5.
153. Considering Taekema and Burg's approach: *see* Taekema and Burg (n 77) and Chapter 1[G][3].

[1] Kant

Kantian philosophy is a useful lens for understanding the inherency, or lack of inherency, of national court decisions. In *Metaphysik der Sitten*, Kant attempts a systematisation of principles of his moral philosophy, which he argues can be used to distinguish different types of legal acts - for example, what is just or right and what is merely lawful.[154] It is not in this wider sense that the work is being considered here, but rather for what it says about the *inherency* of acts as distinct from the object or thing to which they are said to relate.
Since *Metaphysik der Sitten*, a prevalent idea in Western legal philosophy and discourse has been that for an act to be enforceable as of right, such act may be referential to no particular underlying purpose or norm but may instead be based on *practical necessity*.[155] No particular desire or purpose is assumed by the agent itself, but simply as a consequence of its act, the norm or purpose may be assumed by the act itself.[156] In this regard, Kant defines 'desire' as 'practical desire', meaning that the desire towards a thing or object is not inherently bound to the object itself.[157] However, that desire to do an act, though not founded in the object or thing itself, may be the basis for the legal act.[158]

This theory ought to assist international lawyers in understanding how national court decisions can be interpreted as evidence of state will - at the same time, as being evidence of an exercise of state power, decisions may be evidence of law.[159]

Another example is how Kant distinguishes *Wille* (freedom) from the concept of *Willkür* (freedom of choice). Whilst freedom of choice is a desire which is not merely based on an action but also on a *reason* for choosing to act in a certain way, freedom itself is said to be fundamentally grounded in practical necessity itself (*praktische Vernunft*) and therefore has *no inherent quality*.[160] At the same time, in his application of practical necessity to law, Kant accepts that 'freedom' is the basis for law itself.

---

154. Immanuel Kant, *Die Metaphysik der Sitten* (17th edn, Insel-Verlag Wiesbaden 2014); for example, in relation to private law, from 353; for property law, from 370.
155. *Ibid.*, 316-317.
156. *Ibid.*, 316 (defining 'desire' as 'practical desire' meaning that the desire towards a thing or object is not inherently bound to the object itself). However, that desire to do an act, though not founded in the object itself, may be the basis for the legal act (p. 317) (Kant calls this 'freedom of choice' or *Willkür* which will be explained further below).
157. Kant (n 154) 316.
158. *Ibid.*, 317.
159. 'State will' being evidence of the type of tacit consent which might therefore underpin a source of international law: Kant (n 154) 316; according to Report of International Law Commission, Sixty-Third Session, Annex A, A/66/10, 308, 338, at 307, para. (v), theories and approaches to the formation of customary international law are also important for determining and examining its content. Thus, this does not exclude that theoretical approaches may be useful in examining the formation of customary international law (here, state practice).
160. Kant (n 154) 317 ('Das Begehrungsvermögen nach Begriffen, sofern der Bestimmungsgrund desselben zur Handlung in ihm selbst, nicht in dem Objekte angetroffen wird, heist es ein Vermögen, nach Berlieben zu tun oder zu lassen. Sofern es mit dem Bewusstsein des Vermögens seiner Handlung zur Hervorbringung des Objekts verbunden ist, heist es Willkür ... Das Begehrungsvermögen, dessen innerer Bestimmungsgrund, folglich selbst das Belieben in der Vernunft des Subjekts angetroffen wird, heißt der Wille').

These conceptions about the inherency of authority (or the *lack* of any inherent quality) are useful for understanding national court acts as a source of international law. If a Kantian approach is adopted in respect of the activities of national courts as a source, this would mean that national court 'acts', though not necessarily having any *inherent* quality, could from this perspective be conceived as being a source of public international law. According to this, an exercise of authority by a national court is not to be referred to a broader purpose. Instead, when that act is viewed together with other similar acts, from a *practical necessity* perspective, it may be evidence of law.

An example of how the act of a national court exercising jurisdiction might be considered law in international arbitration is the *Yukos* decision, already set out above.[161] Having obtained an arbitration award, certain preliminary matters came before a UK Court as to the enforceability of an award. A Russian Court had set aside the award whereas the Amsterdam Court of Appeal had recognised it, despite that annulment decision. The question for the Court was whether to give effect to the Russian decision and thereby decline to allow Yukos to pursue the recovery of sums pursuant to the award or reject that decision and recognise the Dutch Court's enforcement decision. The UK Court decided to recognise the Dutch decision by finding that the Defendant was estopped from relying on the Russian court's decision to annul the award (and in particular, that it was the result of a 'partial and dependant' process). As a result, the *effect* of the national court decision may be said to have ensured the continuing enforceability of the arbitral award even though the way the Court went about doing this was to *refuse* to recognise the validity of a foreign court decision (rather than recognise the award itself).

On one level, it can be said that the national court decision would not have the same *inherent* quality as a decision rendered to directly recognise and enforce an award – for example, based on Article I New York Convention. Nonetheless, the effect of the Court's act in refusing to recognise the Russian decision, and thereby agreeing with the Netherlands Court, indirectly supported the recognition of the award. Thus, considering national court decisions as 'acts' which might ensure compliance with proceedings and/or awards may allow for a broader set of national court practice to be considered a source of public international law because they would not necessary rely solely on a principle contained in a formal legal instrument such as the New York Convention. This fits with the wider aims of this work, which is to consider whether there are *any* enforcement norms arising in this area, given the lack of appraisal of 'enforcement jurisdiction' in public international law in general –[162] thus implying that the broadest possible approach should be taken to identify these. This would include not merely interpretations of New York Convention principles by state courts but also the full extent of national court decisions which may develop or contribute to any enforcement norms in respect of the international arbitral process. The court decisions examined

161. *Yukos* (2014) (n 82); relating to the point of issue estoppel: Yukos (2011) (n 83).
162. Especially in light of the current lack of exploration of 'enforcement jurisdiction' (Chapter 2, in relation to the *Lotus* (n 113) at [E][1] and given the focus on applying the 'public sphere' concept to identify these (Chapter 1[E] and [F]).

thus often encompass decisions considered in light of national arbitration laws as well as state immunity laws.

This Kantian perspective applied to national courts means that their *acts* or *exercises* of jurisdiction in the public sphere, could be evidence of jurisdictional norms, to the extent that this approach is shared in the public sphere, with the other representative courts and otherwise in accordance with international law. It is not generally disputed in international legal discourse that the *decisions* of national courts may contribute to the development of a rule of international law, in so far as they are *declaratory* of that rule.[163] However, what is being claimed here is that the *acts* of national courts themselves – i.e., particular exercises of adjudicative jurisdiction – may themselves be constitutive of the positive law rule or principle on enforcement jurisdiction. Put differently, when a court *decides* to exercise jurisdiction over a foreign state, though there may be no prescriptive law which obligates the court to exercise jurisdiction, the act of exercising jurisdiction itself may be evidentiary of a principle. This could be evidence of state will and state practice where other courts render enforcement measures according to the same purpose, or on the same basis.

Taking into account the widest scope of national court decisions as a source of tacit consent to the enforcement norm, this analysis ought to apply whether or not the national court intended to ensure enforceability of the award. From its own sovereign perspective, the court may have just been applying the law which the state has adopted. However, the *effect* of the decision may still be to contribute to public international law to the extent that the decision amounts to a lawful exercise of enforcement authority in the public sphere, consistent with harmonising principles.

[2] Kelsen

Without subscribing to a monist approach to international law,[164] given that the approach adopted in this work applies across both monist and dualist states, Kelsen's *Grundnorm* theory is useful for understanding how national court decisions ought to be conceived functionally (i.e., according to their legal effect) as enforcement.[165] Monism is the theoretical perspective that international and national law are part of the same system rather than requiring the separate adoption of laws by the state to give effect to the international legal norm.[166] It is possible to use Kelsen's approach as a lens for examining national courts as a source without subscribing to monism as a necessary prerequisite for identifying the norm.

According to Kelsen's theory, every legal concept or body of law derives its legal validity from some *basic* norm – with the name of the theory, '*Grundnorm*', meaning fundamental or basic in German. Thus, legal principles or concepts not only belong to

163. According to orthodox approaches, as demonstrated by *Trendtex* (n 90); Chapter 2[C].
164. François Rigaux, 'Hans Kelsen on International Law' (1998) 9 *European Journal of International Law* 325 https://doi.org/10.1093/ejil/9.2.325 (accessed 26 September 2025) (Kelsen is widely regarded as a 'monist').
165. *Ibid.*
166. Anthony Aust, *Modern Treaty Law and Practice* (CUP 2007) 187.

a body of law but also derive their validity or existence as law from some basic norm which governs them. This assists in understanding how private international law rules which, when viewed as *part* of public international law, may be declaratory of the public international law norm.

Take the case of *Kuwait Airways* as a paradigm example, in which a costs decision following judgment was made.[167] Kuwait Airways Corporation had applied for damages against the Iraqi Airways Company and the Republic of Iraq after obtaining a judgment in its favour in 2002 for expropriation of its aircraft following the Iraqi invasion of Kuwait.[168] The Court stated in its costs decision that, in principle, its jurisdiction was restricted under section 1 SIA 1976 which, being reflective of the principle of state immunity in customary international law, states: 'a state is immune from the jurisdiction of the courts of the United Kingdom except as provided in the following provisions of this Part of this Act'. Accordingly, a court is restricted according to the principle of state immunity, as given effect in section 1 of the Act, to exercise jurisdiction unless a specific exception applies. Nonetheless, the Court found that since the Republic of Iraq 'funded, supervised and controlled the litigation', it had jurisdiction, under section 3 of the Act, which applies to 'commercial activities' for which a state is *not* immune from the jurisdiction of foreign courts. Accordingly, the court could render a decision and award Kuwait Airways costs. Granting costs in that decision is a form of enforcement jurisdiction since it induces the compliance of a foreign state to pay a sum, regardless of state immunity, thus going beyond a mere decision, as was explained by reference to the *Trendtex* decision. One might ask how this form of jurisdiction ought to be distinguished from a decision such as the earlier one in which the UK court declared Kuwait's *entitlement* to damages. Whereas in the 2002 decision, the UK court only declared Kuwait's obligation to pay, in the later decision, the court actually enforced that claim against Kuwait and ordered the payment of damages (and the costs consequences of that) which thereby became enforceable against it (at least within UK jurisdiction).

Whilst from the Court's sovereign perspective, the private international law rule was formally the source of jurisdiction, when this is viewed as a source of public international law, the significance of the private international law norm changes. The Court, in basing its decision on section 3 SIA, thereby *justified* its jurisdiction on the ground that this was *not* excluded by the international legal principle of immunity. On the one hand, this may be regarded as a mere exercise of the court's prescriptive power – here, the principle of *jure gestionis* given effect to in the state's national laws. On the other hand, viewing the jurisdiction, based on this private international law rule, as a source of a public international law norm, its significance is different. From this perspective, *jure gestionis* is merely one principle which justified the Court's exercise of jurisdiction in the public sphere, i.e., in respect of the foreign state. Since the decision effectively sought to induce Iraq's compliance through a decision on damages, it may be regarded as a form of enforcement. Far from being the authority for the jurisdiction,

167. *Kuwait Airways Corporation v. Iraqi Airways Company* [2008] EWHC 2039 (TCC).
168. The judgment can be found at *Kuwait Airways Corporation v. Iraqi Company* [2002] EWHC 1626 (Comm).

the private international law rule in the SIA was only one justification for the exercise of jurisdiction.

This fits with Kelsen's idea that, while norms derive their validity from a pre-existing norm, those 'new' norms may create more specific applications of the governing norm for concrete cases.[169] On the one hand, immunity was the governing norm according to which the Court rendered an enforcement measure in respect of commercial activities. On the other hand, from the public international law perspective, this private international law rule could also be viewed as giving shape to a *new* norm according to which the Court was permitted to exercise enforcement jurisdiction in respect of commercial activities. Kelsen's theory takes public and private international lawyers away from considering private international law norms as belonging to their own discrete body of rules or principles. Instead, it becomes possible to consider these norms as deriving their legal validity from the public international law to the extent that the exercise of jurisdiction is justified by the adoption of, or tacit consent to, a public international law rule and/or principle.[170]

[I] CONCLUSION

Both from public and private international law perspectives, as well as according to theoretical approaches, adjudicative jurisdiction may be treated as a manifestation of public international law norms on enforcement jurisdiction.

Traditional international legal approaches only consider adjudicative jurisdiction as a facet of the prescriptive jurisdiction of the state. This approach overlooks norms of public international law, which may be developing as an aspect of the tacit consent of states in their court decisions, even if an express norm has not been adopted in legislation. This chapter has developed a theoretical basis according to which such an approach is possible. This is for the purpose of determining what the *lawful* scope of enforcement aspects of adjudicative authority is in international arbitration. By 'lawful', it is meant that the exercises of authority by national courts are consistent with international legal principles underpinning authority, including sovereign equality and the international rule of law, as well as any principles applicable in the area, such as the international legal principle of state immunity. According to this wider perspective of 'jurisdiction' as 'authority', adjudicative jurisdiction may thus be considered a direct source of international law rather than needing to rely - at least not solely- on an interpretation of the prescriptive norm which the state has chosen to adopt. In this context, national courts - as the principal public organs with decision-making authority - may be viewed as the source of any such norms.

169. *See*, Scott Veitsch, Emilios Christodoulidis and Lindsay Farmer, *Jurisprudence: Themes and Concepts* (2nd edn 2012) 119 (while the new norm follows the same logic of authorisation by the general governing norm which provides it with its validity, the new norm might be a specific application of that norm in a new concrete case).

170. This also builds on Mills' approach (n 141) consider public and private international law as being related or deriving from the same body of law; however, it applies this idea in a very specific way for the purposes of identifying enforcement norms in this discrete area.

As explained in Chapter 1, the range of public authority 'acts' which are being considered a source of enforcement jurisdiction, in light of harmonising instruments, includes three situations: (1) where there is no connection between the court's jurisdiction and the arbitration dispute; (2) where the court exercises jurisdiction irrespective of the international legal principle of state immunity which would otherwise be applicable to enforcement jurisdiction; (3) where the exercise of jurisdiction in the public sphere based on a private international law norm is also evidence of the public international law rule. The interrelationship between these examples has been introduced in Chapter 1 and explored through this chapter: they are examples of where the court, which may, from Kaushal's perspective, be seen to be acting at the source of the state's authority, renders an enforcement measure irrespective of the *potential* to breach the foreign state's sovereignty. The international legal principle of state immunity would place the main limitation of the scope of enforcement jurisdiction from a public international law perspective. However, if, in a sufficient set of decisions, national courts exercise jurisdiction in the public sphere, and this is otherwise justifiable under public international law, this practice ought to be regarded as underpinned by tacit consent.

To be clear, 'national court' is not being equated with 'state', nor is it necessarily being treated as an 'agent' of the state, as some works have done.[171] Instead, the question is whether the acts of national courts, or decisions defined more widely so as to encompass not merely decisions for what they state but their effects, may be constitutive of any public international law rules or principles. Whether or not the national court is conceived as an organ or agent of the state for these purposes is immaterial to the analysis being carried out, which concerns the extent to which adjudicative jurisdiction is a *manifestation* of any public international law norms.

171. *See, e.g., Reparation for Injuries Suffered in the Service of the United Nations, Advisory Opinion,* ICJ Reports 1949, p. 179 (national courts may also be responsibility on behalf of states as their organs or agents); O'Keefe (n 76).

Part II

Harmonising National Court Approaches to Enforcement Jurisdiction

[A] INTRODUCTION TO CHAPTERS 3, 4 AND 5

In her recent work on general principles of international law, Saunders found that the function and type of any 'general principle' are determined by the author's choice, or determination, of the 'jurisprudential legitimacy' (or legal basis) for the rule or principle.[172] Consequently, while Chapter 2 focused on the normative legitimacy of the norm, the following chapters focus on identifying and describing what the content of the norms are, which accords with this perspective.

This is directed towards identifying, in accordance with the perspective developed by Chapter 2, widespread, representative, and consistent national court practice. That would constitute 'state practice' – the first element in the definition of customary international law within the meaning of Article 38(1)(b) ICJ Statute. To the extent that representative national courts consistently exercise their decision-making authority in the public sphere, in a widespread and consistent manner *and* in accordance with the normative perspective demonstrated by Chapter 2, this ought to be regarded as forming a general practice underpinned by the tacit consent of states.

The concept of harmonisation is being utilised as a lens for both identifying and comparing national court practice as a source of any norms of enforcement jurisdiction.[173] Harmonisation is defined as 'the process of ascertaining the admitted limits of international unification but does not necessarily amount to a vision of total uniformity'.[174] The methodology section defines what is meant by 'widespread', 'representative' and 'consistent', but to repeat the important aspects:

172. Saunders (n 46) 6.
173. Methodology, Chapter 1[F][1].
174. Menski (n 47) 39.

(1) Whether the practice is 'representative' is concerned with whether a sufficiently large number of representative cases arise 'in the public sphere' as illustrative of any common norms considering harmonising instruments. To the extent that they contradict these approaches, countervailing approaches will be distinguished. Provided there are no significant countervailing approaches, or they can be distinguished as a matter of principle or law, the practice will be regarded as sufficiently 'representative'.
(2) Whether the practice is 'consistent' is determined by the extent of any 'representative' court practice in the public sphere considering harmonising instruments.
(3) Whether the practice is 'widespread' is concerned with whether there is a sufficient set of practice between the chosen representative national courts.[175]

The degree of commonality between the chosen representative[176] national court approaches is determined by applying the functional comparative approach.[177] This will identify whether, considering harmonising instruments, any consistent national court practice in the public sphere arises as a source of any such norms. As set out in the introduction and developed in Chapter 2, practice 'in the public sphere' encompasses at least two types of decision: (1) where there is no connection between the court's territorial jurisdiction and the arbitration dispute; and (2) where one party is a foreign state. This forms the basis for tacit consent to any rule or principle of international law relating to enforcement jurisdiction. A third approach will be considered, namely: (3) where, based on the private international law rule or principle, the decision is also declaratory of the public international law norm. This chapter will begin to develop how each of the three aspects is illustrative of the public international law norm, to be further developed in Chapters 4 and 5.

175. Methodology, Chapter 1[F][2].
176. The reasons for the choice of the UK, US, France and Germany has been set out at: methodology, Chapter 1[F][2].
177. The details of this are set out in the methodology section of this study; Methodology, Chapter 1[F][2].

CHAPTER 3

Supervisory Jurisdiction

Supervisory jurisdiction is the first enforcement norm which national courts are developing in the public sphere as a source of the international law. Against the background of harmonising instruments, including the New York Convention, national laws (arbitration and state immunity laws) and any relevant procedural laws, this chapter identifies the extent and scope of this practice across four representative states (UK, US, France and Germany). The practice arises in respect of two forms: relief which supports the discrete arbitral proceeding, and relief which supports the functioning of the arbitration process more generally. Further, the Chapter distinguishes particular forms of relief in respect of which special requirements arise, including anti-suit injunctions and disclosure.

[A] INTRODUCTION

'Supervisory jurisdiction' encompasses any measures which support the international arbitration proceeding or assist the enforcement of the arbitration agreement, including interim injunctions, setting aside of the award, stays and enforcement of peremptory orders granted by arbitral tribunals. According to the arbitration literature, it is the court at the seat of the arbitration which generally ought to have supervisory jurisdiction.[178] There are obvious reasons for this choice, including the fact that the *lex arbitri* – being the procedural law applicable to the arbitration – is generally the law of the seat. This designation of choice of procedural rules was included as the default

178. Gary Born, *International Commercial Arbitration* (3rd edn, Kluwer Law International 2021) Chapter 17 (analysing interim relief available according to approaches under national laws as the starting point); Blackaby et al. (n 22) para. 7.05.

position in the UK by the new Arbitration Act 2025.[179] In *U & M Mining*, a UK Court considered whether the parties were entitled to go to a Zambian Court for relief in relation to an LCIA arbitration in London. The Court stated that any court which is not the seat may *only* 'exceptionally' grant interim 'if for practical reasons, the application can only sensibly be made there and so long as the proceedings are not simply an attempt to outflank the arbitration agreement'.[180] This chapter does not seek to challenge the practical assumption that parties should pursue interim relief at the seat as the first port of call; instead, it looks at those circumstances where courts other than those at the seat have been seized and analyses those as a source of the scope of the arbitral tribunal's enforcement jurisdiction in the public sphere. The circumstances in which such a power is being regularly exercised will also be examined in the final part of the chapter.

There are several situations where it would be useful for *any* national court, irrespective of any link to the arbitration, to be able to grant supervisory relief. This includes where the arbitral tribunal is not yet constituted and therefore only the national court is able to order the relief; where the arbitral tribunal is otherwise under some incapacity and therefore unable to grant the relief; where, due to the type of measure, only the national court has power to grant it; or where the case is one of 'urgency' such that the arbitral tribunal cannot act swiftly enough.[181]

From a state immunity perspective, the scope of the court's power has only been considered to the extent that states have agreed -expressly or impliedly - to waive immunity by virtue of their private agreement to arbitrate.[182] This chapter considers the alternative approach - that supervisory jurisdiction is available irrespective of state immunity, analysing national court decisions as the direct source of international law rather than being exclusively based on their interpretation of the prescriptive norm which the state has chosen to adopt.

[B] OBJECT AND PURPOSE OF SUPERVISORY JURISDICTION

Born defines provisional or interim measures of protection as measures which are 'designed to protect parties or property during pendency of international arbitral proceedings'.[183] This aim is reflected in the object and purpose of national arbitration

179. Under section 1(2), inserting in section 6, section 6A, which states at (1) that '(1) the law applicable to the arbitration agreement is: (a) the law that the parties expressly agree applies to the arbitration agreement, or (b) where no such agreement is made the law of the seat of the arbitration in question'.
180. *U & M Mining v. Konkola Copper Mines* [2013] EWHC 260 (Comm) [63]; Similarly, finding a stay should only be granted in exceptional circumstances where the UK is not the seat: *Excalibur Ventures LLC v. Texas Keystone Inc* [2011] EWHC 1624.
181. This circumstance is foreseen in section 44(3) EAA, which provides this expressly as a basis upon which a United Kingdom court may, at its discretion, order such measures as it 'thinks necessary' to remedy any such urgency. But it is otherwise unclear as to whether a national court may, more generally, be seized to render such relief regardless of any link with the jurisdiction.
182. *See, e.g.*, Fox and Webb (n 8) 388.
183. Born (n 178) 2601.

laws and the UNCITRAL Model Law, which has been adopted by 93 of a total of 126 jurisdictions, including Germany.[184] This provides for an obligation on national courts to issue interim relief in respect of international arbitrations regardless of any link to the court's territory:

> a court shall have the same power of issuing an interim measure in relation to arbitration proceedings, *irrespective of whether their place is in the territory of this state.*[185]

Comparable powers can also be found in those representative states which have not adopted the UNCITRAL Model Law, and which are under examination, being the UK, US and France. As per section 2(3) EAA read in conjunction with section 44 EAA, 'court powers exercisable in support of arbitration proceedings' are available 'even if the seat of the arbitration is *outside* England and Wales or Northern Ireland or no seat has been designated or determined'. Article 1449 French Civil Procedure Rules (CPC) (as amended in 2011) is silent as to the basis upon which the French *Tribunal de Grande Instance* has jurisdiction to order interim measures, providing merely that the existence of the arbitration agreement does not exclude the court making orders for the 'taking of evidence or provisional or conservatory measures'.[186] Similarly, the US Federal Arbitration Act (FAA), though it does not expressly provide power to courts to order interim measures, is also relevant in so far as its principles have been interpreted as a source for these powers by national courts.

The following identifies: the power to support the arbitral proceeding; the (wider) power to support the functioning of the arbitral process; requirements of the jurisdiction which limit the circumstances in which it may be exercised in the public sphere; and features of the practice which support why the rule ought to be regarded as a general principle of international law, including how countervailing approaches ought to be distinguished.

[C] POWER TO SUPPORT THE ARBITRAL PROCEEDING

Supervisory measures may be rendered by national courts to support the international arbitral proceeding as well as, more broadly, its functioning. There are three strands of national court practice which illustrate this:

---

184. Status: UNCITRAL Model Law on International Commercial Arbitration 1985, with amendments (2006), UN Doc A/40/18 ('UNCITRAL Model Law') (including Germany though excluding the other states herein examined). This statistic was identified on 11 November 2025, and is updated at the following link: https://uncitral.un.org/en/texts/arbitration/modellaw/commercial_arbitration/status (accessed 26 September 2025).
185. Article 17J UNCITRAL Model Law.
186. *Code de Procedure Civile,* Consolidated version January 2018, as amended by Decree No. 2011-48 of 13 January 2011.

(1) The first is where the national court exercises a supervisory form of jurisdiction in the *public sphere*.[187] Without any link to the jurisdiction, the justification for decision-making authority cannot be the private international law norm and thus *calls for explanation*. The central argument is that, pursuant to this practice, adjudicative jurisdiction ought to be considered a source of the international law on enforcement jurisdiction; here, the court's power to order supervisory relief ('the first strand').

(2) The second is where, as a matter of *reasoning*, the court accepts the availability of the applied-for supervisory relief in the public sphere. Due to the shared reasoning of these representative courts, usually based on the private international law rule, this practice ought to be also regarded as a source of the international law norm on supervision ('the second strand').

(3) The third is where the court considers whether it has jurisdiction in the public sphere and either determines that such jurisdiction is not limited by the principle of state immunity, or the reasonable inference is that the jurisdiction is not so limited. By considering that such jurisdiction is *not* so limited by the international legal principle of state immunity, this reasoning might be further considered a source of the norm ('the third strand').

To the extent that the practice is otherwise representative, widespread and consistent, tacit acceptance by national courts to the rule can be regarded as underpinning it. Considering the perspective that adjudicative jurisdiction may normatively be considered a manifestation of enforcement jurisdiction set out in Chapter 2, the central argument is that this practice therefore ought to be considered a source of international law.

[1] Exercises of Decision-Making Authority in the Public Sphere ('The First Strand')

(a) US

Exemplary of the US approach is the decision in *Toyo Tire Holdings*.[188] Toyo Tire applied for the reversal of a decision by a district court which found that a preliminary injunction could not be granted when parties agree to arbitrate and a party seeks interim relief from the court. The preliminary injunction concerned an order to prevent Continental Tire from taking certain steps in an arbitration under the ICC Rules. The ICC has its seat in France; it is stated in Article 43, for example, that 'any claims arising out of or in connection with the administration of the arbitration proceedings by the court' shall be governed by French law and settled by the Paris Judicial Tribunal in

187. The 'public sphere' concept is set out in the Chapter 1[E][1]; for its application in terms of the methodology adopted, *see* Chapter 1[F].

188. *Toyo Tire Holdings of Americas, Inc v. Continental Tire North America Inc and Others*, 10-55145, 609 F.3d 975 US (9th Cir. 2010).

France.[189] The Court issued interim relief in respect of parties to an ICC arbitration, stating expressly that such relief aimed to preserve the 'meaningfulness of the arbitral process'.[190] Finding that under Article 23 ICC Rules, preliminary injunctive relief may be granted by the US national court, the Court stated that:

> Toyo seeks an injunction to preserve the status quo until the arbitral panel can consider and rule upon Toyo's application for interim relief pending the arbitration panel's final decision ... in cases such as this, judicial interim relief may be necessary to preserve the meaningfulness of the arbitral process.[191]

Toyo Tire was an American company. From a private international law perspective, the 'link' to the jurisdiction which enabled the court to exercise 'subject matter' and 'personal' jurisdiction was the fact that one of the companies was situated in the US. In these cases, there is at least a basis for the court's subject matter jurisdiction in the arbitration agreement, according to which the court at least has a *prima facie* right to exercise jurisdiction under the New York Convention to grant interim relief.[192] However, the foundation of the national court's power to *decide* in respect of the particular state is more ambiguous based on a traditional approach:[193] there was no connection between the Court and the arbitration dispute.[194]

The basis for court jurisdiction was stated to be Article 23(2) ICC Rules, which did not preclude the grant of interim relief 'in appropriate circumstances' before the matter is transmitted to the Arbitral Tribunal. The 'appropriate circumstances' were regarded as being where the interim relief 'is necessary to preserve the status quo and the meaningfulness of the arbitration process - provided the requirements for granting injunctive relief are otherwise satisfied'.[195] One of those requirements was, as decided in the previous case of *Simula*,[196] that there was a serious question to be tried on the claims put forward and that, in this case, there was an 'adequate showing of irreparable

189. Article 43 ICC Rules.
190. *Toyo Tire* (n 188) p. 981. Interim relief, more generally, is considered in arbitration texts according to whether the particular court, under its national laws, may grant the measure, or in light of the UNCITRAL Model Law; e.g., Born (n 178) 2606.
191. *Toyo Tire* (n 188) p. 979.
192. *See*, further, e.g., *Mitsui Co Ltd v. Delta Brands, Inc*, Civil Action No. 3:04-CV-1070-L (N.D. Tex. 20 May 2005) (a request to compel an ICC arbitration (with the seat outside the jurisdiction) was founded at least *prima facie* on the ground that there was an agreement to arbitrate and one of the parties. However, the separate question of the source of the power to compel the arbitration is not the New York Convention, but is to be considered in light of principles contained therein). An order to compel the arbitration to proceed is an exclusively US mechanism under section 4 Chapter 1 FAA or section 206 of Chapter 2 FAA in relation to New York Convention awards.
193. That is, under private and public international law, which generally considers the need for a 'link' to the jurisdiction: *See* Chapter 2[C][2].
194. As is the orthodox approach, e.g., according to the 'seat theory'; e.g., Born (n 178) 2205-2282 (these are considered 'neutral competent courts' which are therefore well-placed to support the arbitral process). This norm might also perform an allocatory function, as a rule or principle of private international law, in so far as it determines which court should have jurisdiction (as distinct from any other court); *see* Goh (n 79) and Chapter 1[G][4].
195. *Toyo Tire* (n 188) p. 981.
196. *Simula, Inc. v. Autoliv, Inc.*, 175 F.3d 716 (9th Cir. 1999).

harm'.[197] Finding against the District Court's denial of a preliminary injunction and in favour of the Appellant based on the dicta in *Simula*, the Court exercised its jurisdiction in the public sphere in respect of a tribunal *outside the Court's territorial jurisdiction*.

By the mere exercise of this particular form of authority in the public sphere, the national court can be seen to have recognised that the exercise of jurisdiction falls within its general competence to decide on the matter of interim relief (or any other form of supportive relief).

The practice is representative of US practice with regard to the general availability of supervisory relief, where defined to include preliminary injunctions, orders to compel the arbitration to proceed and the power to set aside the arbitration award and stays.[198] Pre-judgment attachment and measures relating to compelling witness attendance and evidence will be considered separately below as an exception arising in US practice but ought not to detract from the general availability of the stated forms of supervisory relief. Exceptions in relation to pre-judgment attachment and compelling evidence arise due to nuances within US laws, which will be considered further below.

(b) UK

Exemplary of this approach in the UK courts, as well as the broader types of supervisory relief which can be taken into account as evidence of the norm, is the decision in *Pearl Petroleum*.[199] A Swiss company applied to a UK Court for an order of enforcement of a peremptory order rendered by a London Court of International Arbitration (LCIA) tribunal against the Kurdistan Republic of Iran.[200] 'Peremptory orders' are a particular interim order issued by arbitral tribunals to ensure compliance with their orders. UK courts have the power to enforce them according to section 42

197. *Toyo Tire* (n 188) p. 978.
198. *See, e.g.*, further *Mitsui* (2005) (n 192); *See PAO Tatneft v. Ukraine*, 301 F. Supp.3d 175 (United States District Court, District of Columbia, 2018) (in this confirmation decision, stays are considered and had been granted in respect of proceedings against Ukraine, though the stay of a recognition and enforcement proceeding was ultimately rejected for reasons other than state immunity. This form of supervisory relief is considered further below in relation to inherent powers of courts as a source of the international legal principle); further, *Hardy Exploration & Production (India), Inc. v. Government of India, Ministry of Petroleum & Natural Gas*, Civil Action No. 16-140 (United States District Court, District of Columbia) (considering a stay may, in principle, be granted in light of principles related to the general objectives of arbitration). Interim relief, more generally, is considered in arbitration texts according to whether the particular court, under its national laws, may grant the measure, or in light of the UNCITRAL Model Law, e.g., Born (n 178) 2606.
199. *Pearl Petroleum Company Limited, Dana Gas PJSC and Crescent Petroleum Company International Limited v. The Kurdistan Regional Government of Iraq* [2015] EWHC 3361 (Comm); similarly, US courts review orders granted by arbitral tribunals: *Banco de Seguros del Estado (Uruguay) v. Mutual Marine Office, Inc. (US) and others*, 344 F.3d 255 (2nd Cir. 2003), especially [19]-[20] (in deciding whether to affirm orders by the international arbitral tribunal relating to pre-judgment security, the Court found that the arbitrators did not exceed their authority by doing so, thereby reviewing the availability of pre-judgment security in respect of a corporation wholly owned by a state).
200. Constituted under the London Court of International Arbitration (LCIA) Rules (current edition in force as of 1 October 2020). As per Article 16.2, the default seat of the arbitration is in London which means courts there have jurisdiction to order supportive measures, in principle.

EAA. It was common ground that the Respondent was a separate entity within the meaning of section 14 SIA, with the outstanding issue on immunity being whether the proceedings relate to anything done by the Respondent in the exercise of its sovereign authority in circumstances such that the state would be immune from jurisdiction within the meaning of section 14(2)(b).

Considering the issue of state immunity as a *separate* issue to jurisdiction, the Court found it had jurisdiction to make a section 42 EAA order to enforce the peremptory order, stating that, under section 40(2) EAA, the proper and expeditious conduct of arbitral proceedings included 'complying with ... any order ... of the tribunal'.[201] Thus, by virtue of finding it had jurisdiction vis-à-vis a foreign state, with immunity not limiting *that* power, the Court implicitly accepted – through the rendering of a decision *in the public sphere* – that this form of supervisory relief was available irrespective of immunity. Moreover, this approach appears to also be consistent with the approach of the Court, considering first that there was a power in general to make an order under section 42 of the Act, and then separately considering whether, notwithstanding that power, the Respondent had immunity pursuant to the SIA. The Court thus separately considered whether the Respondent could benefit from state immunity by virtue of proceedings relating to anything done in the exercise of its sovereign authority but this did not affect the jurisdictional analysis. Finding the Respondent's actions pertained to an exercise of a *separate* entity's authority but not of the state of Iraq, the Court found that state immunity was not so engaged.[202] Thus, had immunity been available, it was separate from the question of whether jurisdiction was available.[203]

The Court accepted the Claimant's submissions in respect of jurisdiction, finding that it had jurisdiction to make an order for the purpose of the 'proper and expeditious conduct of the arbitration', which is available to the arbitrators under section 41 EAA by default and to the enforcing court under section 42.[204]

This approach, in so far as it is representative of UK practice relating to supervisory jurisdiction as a lawful form of enforcement jurisdiction, is representative of the UK approach more generally in relation to supervision: measures which support the arbitral proceeding are generally available in the public sphere, including interim measures,[205] freezing injunctions, anti-suit injunctions, enforcement of peremptory orders and ordering of security.[206] Concerns arise over the type of available injunctions

201. *Pearl Petroleum* (n 199) [24](iv).
202. *Ibid.*, [36]-[37].
203. *Ibid.*, considering especially the structure of the decision and the conclusions at [53].
204. *Ibid.*, [21] and [26].
205. In respect of which the power to grant interim relief is available pursuant to section 44 EAA.
206. Similarly, and in relation to further types of supervisory relief: *BNP Paribas S.A. v. Open Joint Stock Company Russian Machines AS* [2011] EWHC 308 [34] (relating to anti-suit injunctions, the Court found these were available in accordance with the court's inherent power under section 37 Senior Courts Act 1981 (c. 54)); recently, *Deutsche Bank AG v. RusChemAlliance LLC* [2023] EWCA Civ 1144; *Mobil Cerro Negro Limited v. Petroleos De Venezuela S.A.* [2008] EWHC 532 (UK), especially [18]-[19] (freezing injunction available in accordance section 44 EAA and section 37 Senior Courts Act 1981 (c. 54) which authorises UK court power to grant supervisory forms of relief regardless of where the seat of the arbitration is); *Soleh Boneh International Ltd v. Water Resources Development (International) ltd, Government of the Republic of Uganda and*

in respect of states in light of the *UK P&I* decision,[207] but it is suggested below that this decision was wrong in light of the developing international approach and should be distinguished based on the cases of *Deutsche Bank*[208] and *Unicredit.*[209] Supervision is available in certain respects when compelling witness evidence is concerned, which shall be considered further below.

Contrasted with the US exception in relation to pre-judgment attachment, to be explained further below, there is no exception in relation to pre-judgment attachment in the UK, which is regarded as a lawful form of supervision in the UK regardless of state immunity. In *Mobil Cerro Negro,* the arbitration was commenced before the ICC in New York and concerned the alleged exploitation of oil resources in Venezuela by its national oil company, PDV.[210] PDV applied to set aside an order by the Court granting a temporary worldwide freezing injunction (WFO). Even though the Court ultimately set aside the Order, it found that it had the power to grant such a freezing order in principle pursuant to section 44 EAA and section 37 of the Supreme Court Act (SCA). Had Mobil been able to show a good arguable case that PDV's conduct in relation to its assets was unjustified and that the matter was urgent such that there was a 'real risk of dissipation', the jurisdiction could be exercised.[211] Consequently, the decision is evidence that pre-judgment attachment is regarded as a lawful form of supervision, available, in principle, irrespective of immunity. By accepting that the power was available, jurisdiction based on section 44 EAA and section 37 SCA emerges as a manifestation of the public international law norm. There are of course restrictions on when that power ought to be exercised, depending on nuances within national laws, which is a separate question of when the otherwise lawful supervisory measure can be granted, considered in the 'limitations' section below. Post-judgment attachment is a matter of execution jurisdiction and thus will be considered in Chapter 5.[212]

(c) Germany

The German approach in the public sphere is straightforward as German civil procedural law adopts the UNCITRAL Model Law *verbatim*. Since Germany is a civil law country, the source of jurisdiction is therefore found in the applicable legal code; here being the civil procedural code. According to §1033 *Zivilprozessordnung* (the German Code of Civil Procedure, 'ZPO'), in conjunction with §1025(2) ZPO, a German Court expressly has the parallel right to order interim relief irrespective of where the arbitral

---

National Housing Corporation [1993] 2 Lloyd's Rep 208 (security was awarded in respect of enforcement against arbitral award, including a finding that such security was not an injunction within the meaning of section 13(2)(a) SIA).

207. *UK P&I Club NV v. Venezuela* [2022] EWHC 1655 (Comm).
208. *Deutsche Bank* (2023) (n 206).
209. *Unicredit Bank GmbH v. Ruschemalliance LLC* [2024] EWCA Civ 64 [41].
210. *Mobil Cerro* (2008) (n 206) especially [18]-[19].
211. *Ibid.*, [35]-[38].
212. Considering the application of the test for a WFO following the rendering of the arbitration award: *ArcelorMittal* (2019) (n 32); *see* Chapter 1[D].

proceeding takes place or what law it applies.[213] §1033 ZPO provides that preliminary measures may be taken as security with regard to the subject matter in an arbitration. §1025(2) ZPO states that this section applies, including where the venue of the arbitral proceedings is abroad. German courts have consistently exercised jurisdiction in the public sphere on that basis, recognising the availability of such measures as an aspect of their state's adjudicative jurisdiction.[214] This includes not only interim relief and security but also pre-judgment attachment, for which it has been stated that the international jurisdiction of German courts is undisturbed in respect of arbitrations abroad because, according to §919 ZPO, the court at the place where the asset is arrested is the court with jurisdiction (provided other jurisdictional requirements are met).[215] This provision has extended to support arbitrations abroad regardless of immunity, provided there are otherwise grounds for attachment, which would generally be the case where the foreign court or tribunal has decided that enforcement would be frustrated without the possibility of attachment.[216]

(d) France

On the face of its own Civil Procedure Rules, the position in France might be regarded as more difficult to identify in the public sphere. Again, France is a civil law country, which means the source of the court's power is generally situated in the applicable code of procedure, here being France's Civil Procedural Rules (CPC). On the express wording of Article 1505 CPC, the President of the *Tribunal de Grande Instance* has general jurisdiction to order interim measures only when there is some connection to France or one of the parties is exposed to a risk of denial of justice. As will be developed in the next section, it is thus important to take the *reasoning* of courts into account. This provides further support for the jurisdiction as a source of shared norms with French courts, even if there is no express provision for a French court's international supervisory competence.

Illustrative of this approach from a French perspective is the *Arab Republic* decision in the French Court of Appeal.[217] An award was rendered against Egypt under the ICC arbitration rules. Egypt moved to set the award aside based on Articles 1504 and 1502 Nos 1 and 5 CPC (now Articles 1518 and 1520 Nos 1 and 5). Article 1518

213. *Zivilprozessordnung* (ZPO), adopted on 30 January 1877, as amended on 21 October 2011, published: Bundesgesetzblatt Teil I, 9 December 2005, Volume 72, pp. 3202-3378, ISSN: 0867-3411.
214. *See, e.g.*, District Court of Braunschweig ('LG Braunschweig'), 4 August 2015, SchiedsVZ 2015, 292-294 [81] (expressly stating such measures are available pursuant to §1033 ZPO in respect of foreign arbitration awards); Ben Steinbrück, *Die Unterstützung ausländisches Schiedsverfahren durch das staatliche Gericht* (Mohr Siebeck 2009) (analysing interim relief as one power which a court may exercise in respect of the arbitral process, though not considering exercises 'in the public sphere' as a discrete matter); developing the comparative perspective from the UK-German perspective: Satya T Mouland, 'Comparing the Role of the Courts in English and German Arbitration Law' (2016) *ELSA Law Review* 169.
215. *See*, C 257/75 Amtsgericht Hamburg-Harburg, Decision of 9 July 1975, 612.
216. *Ibid.*
217. Cour d'Appel, 12 July 1984, *Arab Republic of Egypt v. SPP Ltd (Middle East) Ltd*, 23 ILM 1048 (1984).

provides that the only means of recourse against an award made in France is an action to set aside, and Article 1520 sets forward the particular grounds upon which such an award can be set aside, though these are quite narrow.[218] The Court considered, *inter alia*, that Egypt had 'legitimate reasons for defending [its] case on the merits, even before arbitrators whom it deemed to lack jurisdiction, in order to attempt to mitigate the prejudice which might result from an award against it', thereby taking into account the fact that Egypt had defended its case on the merits did not necessarily mean it had submitted to the arbitral tribunal's jurisdiction.[219] An aspect of the court's reasoning concerned state immunity and whether, if Egypt did not submit to arbitration, it had not waived its immunity. This was not determinative of the question of consent to arbitrate, however, as the court found there was no arbitration agreement (irrespective as to the question of immunity, which was considered separately). In so doing, the *reasoning* of the Court shows French courts support arbitrations by reviewing the foreign state's capacity to enter into arbitration agreements irrespective of immunity.[220] Even if it did not *positively* render a measure of interim relief in respect of the state, the French Court accepted its power to exercise a form of supervisory authority to support the arbitral proceeding in the public sphere - here, in the form of reviewing the arbitration agreement in the context of setting aside proceedings.[221] Although this form of jurisdiction can and should separately be considered an aspect of the court's review jurisdiction (as below in Chapter 4), it also ought to be regarded as part of the court's supervisory authority. Review powers entail court power to support or refuse to support jurisdiction based on the *agreement* and not just refusing to enforce the award.

Further, the fact that French courts do not generally grant interim relief in the public sphere does not mean supervision is not a *lawful* form of enforcement exercisable in respect of the international arbitral process. Even if French courts do not formally grant interim relief based on national legal provisions, their reasoning as regards supporting the arbitration process can be interpreted as evidence of the norm as set out in the next section.

218. The widest is where the award would breach 'international public policy' but this is typically only established where there are 'manifest, effective and concrete' breaches of the international legal order, ordinarily only established by activities such as fraud or money laundering. *See, e.g.*, CA Paris, 21 February 2017, *Kyrgyz Republic v. Mr Belokon*, Case No. 15-01650.
219. *Arab Republic* (n 217) [7].
220. This power derives from the court's power, in its national law, to set aside the award. The harmonising principle in the New York Convention in Article III(1)(e) is that an award may be refused recognition and enforcement where the award 'has been set aside or suspended by the "competent" authority of the country in which, or under the law of which, the award was made'; *see, e.g.*, Jean Rouche, Gerald H Pointon and Jean-Louis Devolvé, *French Arbitration Law and Practice: A Dynamic Civil Law Approach to International Arbitration* (2nd edn, Wolters Kluwer 2009) 212.
221. Similarly: *Republic of Ecuador v. Chevron Corporation*, 638 F.3d 384 (2d Cir. 2011) (US Court reviewed capacity of Ecuador to enter into arbitration agreement pursuant to a bilateral investment treaty between the United States and Ecuador). This is a power generally available in accordance with Article II New York Convention, one of the exceptions being where a Court finds the agreement is 'null, void, inoperative or incapable of being performed'.

[2] Private International Law: Common Reasoning ('The Second Strand')

The French decision in *Fitzpatrick* shows how the court's reasoning for jurisdiction in the public sphere, based on the private international law rule, can be considered a source of the public international law norm.[222]

The Republic of Equatorial Guinea applied to the French Court calling for the suspension of arbitral proceedings and a protective measure in respect of an 'imminent danger' after Fitzpatrick obtained an ICC award against it. While the arbitration was under the ICC Rules (with its seat in France), it took place against a foreign state and thus can be regarded as 'in the public sphere'. The question for the French Court was whether it would find it had jurisdiction under Article 809 CPC (now Article 873 CPC) to grant interim relief in respect of an ICC.[223]

Article 809 CPC provides the tribunal with the power to order protective measures 'to restore (the parties) to (their) previous state as required, either to prevent imminent damage or to abate a manifestly illegal nuisance'. In its reasoning for not granting the measure, the Court stated the arbitral tribunal had already been seized, and thus, no such 'imminent danger' could be proven. However, the Court recognised that conservatory measures (*mesures conservatoires*) are intended to guarantee the execution of the arbitral tribunal's future decision. Thus, if there was such an 'imminent danger' that the arbitration could not proceed or that the parties' rights were in imminent danger, the reasoning suggests that court jurisdiction ought to be available on this basis. Even though, from the Court's perspective, the source of the rule was Article 809 CPC, from the public international law perspective adopted here, the reasoning of the court which interprets this provision may be declaratory of the rule. In this regard, the reasoning of the Court indicated that such measures would be available to support the arbitral *process*.[224]

---

222. Tribunal de grande instance de Paris (Réf.) 29 March 2010, *République de Guinée Équatoriale v. Société Fitzpatrick Equatorial Guinea Ltd.*, Rev. arb. 2011, Issue 2, 499.
223. *Ibid.*
224. Similarly: Cour de Cassation, 4 July 2007, *République du Congo v. Groupe Antoine Tabet*, Rev. arb. 2008, Issue 3, 441 (regarding an ICC award rendered against a foreign state - here Congo - the Court found that parties can seek annulment of any such award which has the effect of staying any arbitration proceedings where the arbitral tribunal has not ordered provisional execution of the award. Thus, the concept goes both ways and also may have the effect of halting arbitral proceedings when an award is not valid); Germany: LG Braunschweig, 4 August 2015 (n 214) [65] (security measures available in the public sphere, based on §1033 ZPO); UK: *Ecobank Transnational Inc v. Tanoh* [2015] EWCA Civ 1309 (considering whether to grant an anti-enforcement injunction against a foreign state based on the High Court power to grant injunction, including questions related to 'comity' on whether the 'agreement of the parties ... is respected'); US: *Aggarao v. MOL Ship Management Co Ltd*, 675 F. 3d 355 (4th Cir. 2012) [31] (the Court reviewed as a matter of discretion whether it should exercise an inherent power to grant an injunction to preserve the status quo so that an arbitral award rendered in the Philippines may not be a 'hollow victory').

[3] Consideration in the Public Sphere Irrespective of Immunity ('The Third Strand')

Sometimes the reasoning of courts needs to be considered a source for any harmonised approach because the outcome does not contribute on the basis of any express national law rule, but the reasoning may be illustrative of it. The *wider* approach taken by this book - considering adjudicative jurisdiction as a manifestation of enforcement jurisdiction - is useful from this angle because it is not dependent on the relevant aspect of the decision being adopted in the state's national law. Rather, the decision might develop the *international* legal rule or principle to the extent that the exercise of adjudicative jurisdiction is declaratory of the norm considering harmonising instruments, while the national law is distinct.

The French *Soguipêche* decision demonstrates how this might assist in situating the international legal principle of immunity as an exception to this practice.[225] As explained in the introduction, the international legal principle of immunity may be regarded as being breached where an extension of court authority is regarded as infringing the foreign state's sovereignty. State immunity, as stated, is the main principle of international law which restricts or limits court enforcement jurisdiction. However, the practice expanded upon in this chapter shows that supervisory jurisdiction does not breach that principle, being available irrespective of state immunity. Practice regarding when state immunity would apply to exclude jurisdiction in this context also further supports the rule.

In *Soguipêche*, a French Court considered whether it would, like the Quimper Commercial Court before it, order the attachment of certain vessels in security for an arbitration claim subject to an ICSID arbitration with no connection to French territorial jurisdiction. The Court ultimately decided that, under the rules to which the parties consented (ICSID), national court supportive jurisdiction was not available. This was due to the application of Article 26 ICSID, which provides that consent to ICSID should be deemed to exclude 'any other remedy'. This has been interpreted widely by scholars and further national courts in other jurisdictions as implying an exclusion of the supervisory jurisdiction of national courts.[226] This particular exception relating to ICSID will be considered further below. However, for our purposes here, the *reasoning* of the Court is still illustrative of representative court practice to the effect that immunity *does not generally exclude* the court's power to supervise an arbitral process outside its jurisdiction.

The Court reviewed the question of whether the said vessels could be attached pursuant to the arbitration to which the foreign state was party.[227] Thus, even though

225. Rennes Court of Appeal, 26 October 1984, *Société Atlantic Triton v. République populaire revolutionnaire de Guinee et société Soguipêche*, Appeal No. 84-17.525.
226. Christoph H Schreuer with Laurence Malintoppi, August Reinisch and Anthony Sinclair, *The ICSID Convention: A Commentary* (2nd edn, CUP 2009) 351; Campbell McLachlan, Laurence Shore and Matthew Weiniger, *International Investment Arbitration: Substantive Principles* (2nd edn, OUP 2017) para. 1.04; *E.T.I. Euro Telecom International NV v. Republic of Bolivia, Empresa Nacionale De Telecomunicaciones Entel SA* [2008] EWHC 1689 (Comm).
227. *Soguipêche* (n 225).

the measure was not, in fact, granted – for special reasons relating to parties' specific consent under ICSID – through its reasoning *in the public sphere,* the Court did not regard such power as being excluded by the international legal principle of state immunity. Immunity is not regarded as applicable to the question of the Court's jurisdiction, though it should be noted that the company in respect of which attachment was sought was a company with a 'legal identity separate from that of the State of Guinea' in that it engaged in commercial activity. However, this was considered a separate legal question, being a *lex specialis* rather than excluding the consideration of whether the measure could be granted.

Even though the decision did not ultimately result in the Court granting the measure in question in *Soguipêche*, it may still be regarded as a source of the rule, since it was not the international legal principle of immunity which excluded the jurisdiction but rather specific consent under the ICSID Convention. This is representative of a wider approach regarding decision-making authority in the public sphere, which considers whether supervisory relief would be available, irrespective of the international legal principle of immunity. According to these decisions, immunity is consistently interpreted so as not to apply to this form of enforcement.[228]

The question of whether the state is engaged in a commercial, rather than a sovereign activity, and thus whether jurisdiction should be excluded based on state immunity – which, it is being argued, is a *lex specialis* question – falls outside the scope of this work. The general principle being established here is that courts have a general jurisdiction to grant supervisory measures as a matter of principle irrespective of state immunity. Questions of state immunity and whether an immunity nevertheless applies to *exclude* jurisdiction ought to be treated as an exception to the general rule herein being described. This would provide greater conceptual clarity as to the interaction between enforcement jurisdiction and immunity in the area of international arbitration.

[4] Supportive Academic Sources

According to Goh, state immunity, as with other rules of foreign relations, is allocative rather than exclusionary in nature and underlying these rules is an inquiry as to which forum has jurisdiction and to the proper scope of relief.[229] Goh draws on the work of McLachlan for the proposition that private international law rules are allocative in nature.[230] Taking that a step further, to the extent that immunity has been *consistently*

228. Further: Cour de Cassation (Civ. 1re), 8 July 2015 *Société Ryanair et Société Airport Marketing Services Ltd v. Syndicat Mixte des Aeroports de Charente (SMAC)*, Appeal No. 13-25.846 [8] (expressly acknowledging that annulment proceedings must comply with requirements of French law *irrespective of where the award is made* due to the principle that exequatur (recognition) extends to foreign awards pursuant to Article 1516 CPC, which includes the power to set aside awards) (France); *Pearl Petroleum* (n 199) (immunity not considered limiting the scope of the jurisdiction) (UK); *Banco de Seguros* (n 199) (US); LG Braunschweig, 4 August 2015 (n 214) (Germany).
229. Goh (n 79).
230. Campbell McLachlan, *Foreign Relations Law* (CUP 2014).

treated as *not* limiting the court's supervisory jurisdiction, it may also be regarded as allocating jurisdiction between the courts in the public sphere.

Major textbook authors in international arbitration state that the very function and purpose of interim and other measures of supervisory relief is to support the arbitration.[231] As Lew puts it, court supervision does not undermine the principle of consent to arbitration but rather facilitates the arbitration.[232] This is perhaps most obviously demonstrated by the widespread use of anti-suit injunctions which are brought in order to restrain parties from arbitration proceedings where court proceedings are pursued in contravention of the arbitration agreement. Further, during the arbitral proceeding, the national court may review whether the arbitration agreement can be enforced to determine whether it should stay its proceedings, or rather defer back to the arbitral process. Given the need for such measures – in their various forms – it is thus hardly surprising that states, through their national courts, have consistently granted such measures in the public sphere irrespective of whether there is a connection to their own territorial jurisdiction. Thus, this form of jurisdiction is also consistent with principles underpinning international arbitration, being the facilitation and support of the process through rendering measures which the tribunal may not be able to grant.

[D] A WIDER POWER? SUPPORTING THE ARBITRAL FUNCTION

As distinct from the narrower purpose of supporting the discrete arbitral proceeding, consistent, widespread and representative national court practice emerges relating to the court's power to support the arbitral functioning more widely.[233] This is distinct from the power to support the arbitration proceeding because it does not merely support the parties' discrete rights to the arbitration by preserving the status quo,[234] but the court is obliged to step in where a failure to do so would prevent the proper *functioning* of the arbitral process.

[1] Staying Proceedings Pursuant to Inherent Powers

A 'stay' is a mechanism of civil procedure in the UK and US which permits a court to stop or pause in their tracks, court proceedings commenced in breach of the arbitration

231. Lew, 'Does National Court Involvement Undermine ...?' (n 30) 497.
232. *Ibid.*, 490 'national court involvement in international arbitration is a fact of life as prevalent as the weather', particularly drawing on the measures herein discussed at: 496, and 514-535; similarly: Yves Derains and Eric A Schwartz, *A Guide to the ICC Rules of Arbitration* (2nd edn, Kluwer Law International 2005) 294-295; Born (n 178) 2638-2639 (recognising the 'overlapping' jurisdiction with national courts to grant interim relief).
233. This principle is also cited in the arbitration literature, as relating to the function of interim protection, as being to provide 'effective ... judicial protection' by ensuring that the 'parties' dispute [is not] unnecessarily exacerbated during the pendency of the dispute'. Born (n 178) 2605; citing *Opinion of Advocate General Tesauro, The Queen v. Secretary of State for Transp., ex parte Factortame Ltd*, Case No. C-213/89, [1990] E.C.R. I-02433, [18] (E.C.J.).
234. As in cases such as *Mitsui* (2005) (n 192) (order to compel would have only been possible to 'preserve the status quo' of parties).

agreement. This power can be found, for example, in section 9 EAA in the case of UK jurisdiction. The availability of this power may be regarded as supporting the process of the arbitration more broadly, rather than merely the discrete rights of parties to the dispute.[235]

In *Sea Spray Holdings,*[236] Sea Spray initiated proceedings in the New York State Supreme Court against Buyers and a third party and thereby applied for a stay of proceedings in the New York State Supreme Court. Although there was a connection to US territorial jurisdiction, with the arbitration occurring under the American Arbitration Association (AAA) Rules, this link to the jurisdiction did not form part of the reasoning as to why the Court should exercise jurisdiction to support the functioning of the arbitration. Instead, the Court relied on its 'inherent' power to stay proceedings which derives from the court's power to regulate its own jurisdiction.

The question arising for the Court was whether it should stay proceedings under the FAA or conversely should recognise that the Buyers were not a party to the arbitration and consequently its rights and obligations should be determined by the Court. In finding that there was no merit to Sea Spray's claim, the Court exercised its inherent authority to stay proceedings under section 3 of the FAA. The Court found, under the applicable principles of New York Law on the commitment to arbitrate and contractual principles, that Sea Spray's interest fell within the broad scope of the arbitration agreement.[237]

In any event, this power to stay proceedings, as being based on the inherent power of US courts, has been recognised in the public sphere in the 2018 *PAO Tatneft v. Ukraine* case.[238] Even though the Court denied the request for a stay pending the outcome of parallel proceedings in France, the US Court recognised that its inherent powers to stay proceedings would be available in principle (and thus not limited by state immunity).[239]

(a) Inherent Powers of Courts as a Source

The basis for the Court's jurisdiction in the *Sea Spray Holdings* decision was its 'inherent authority to effectively manage its docket', which was stated to be 'incidental to the power inherent in every court to control the disposition of the causes of its docket with economy of time and effort for itself, for counsel, and for litigants. How this can best be done calls for the exercise of judgment, which must weigh competing interests and maintain an even balance'.[240] This has been described as 'case management

235. *See, e.g., Hulley Enterprises Ltd et al v. The Russian Federation,* 211 F. Supp. 3d 269 (D.D.C. 2016) (US); further: *Aggarao* (n 224) [31] (the Court reviewed as a matter of discretion whether it should exercise an inherent power to grant an injunction to preserve the status quo so that an arbitral award rendered in the Philippines may not be a 'hollow victory').
236. *Sea Spray Holdings v. Pali Financial Group, Inc and others,* 277 F. Supp. 2d 323 (S.D.N.Y. 2003).
237. *Ibid.,* [14].
238. *PAO Tatneft* (2018) (n 198).
239. *Ibid.,* [51].
240. *Citing Landis v. North Am. Co.,* 299 U.S. 248, 254-255, 81 L.Ed. 153, 57 S.Ct. 163 (1936).

powers' of courts.[241] Practice based on the inherent powers of courts ought to be considered a source of the practice, despite the connection to territorial jurisdiction because such powers derive from the public authority of courts to manage their docket and other case management powers. Further, in these instances, adjudicative jurisdiction is not dependent on the prescriptive rule which the state has chosen to adopt but is concerned with an inherent exercise of authority.

Perhaps the most obvious example arising in the UK and US courts is where the court exercises an inherent power to 'stay' proceedings.[242] However, inherent jurisdiction is also the basis for authority in the case of interim injunctions: for example, on the basis of section 37 SCA 1981, a UK High Court may order an interim injunction 'in all cases where it appears to the court to be just and convenient to do so'.[243] This derives from an 'inherent' power of the courts because it emanates not merely from the legislative power laid down by Parliament in section 37 but also from the old equitable power available to courts to regulate their powers where the legislature did not provide for such.[244] While the power might formally originate in a statutory source, its substantive content relates to the circumstances in which the court finds it ought to grant that power including, for example, whether it is 'just and convenient' that the measure be granted.

Consequently, authority derived from the courts' inherent powers may be considered an exercise of the *public* power of the courts, being concerned with their right to regulate proceedings and thus not with whether the state has consented to the norm adopted into national law.[245]

(b) Private International Law Approaches in Civil Law States

French and German courts do not recognise inherent powers to stay proceedings because stays do not generally exist in civil law countries. Where they render decisions based on a private international law norm, however, that norm may arise as a manifestation of a comparable rule which has the effect of preserving a party's rights and thereby maintaining the status quo in proceedings.

For example, in the 4 August 2015 decision before the Braunschweig High Court, which is representative of the civil law approach, a German Court granted provisional

241. *See, e.g., Minister of Finance and Malaysia Development Board v. International Petroleum Investment Company and Aabar Investments PJS* [2019] EWCA Civ 2080 [54]-[55]. More particularly in relation to stays, available under CPR r. 3.1(2)(f): *Excalibur* (n 180) [67].
242. *See*, especially, *Channel Tunnel Group Ltd v. Balfour Beatty Construction Ltd* [1993] A.C. 334 [53] (UK) (the facts of which are to be set out further below in 'preservation of contractual rights'); *Sea Spray Holdings* (n 236) (US).
243. Senior Courts Act 1981 (c. 54).
244. *See, e.g.*, most recently, in the Family law context: *UL v. BK (Freezing Orders: Safeguards: Standard Examples)* [2013] UKHC 1735 (Fam) [9] and [14] (though 'inherency' may not give the court a *wider* power than legislature confers, it is still clearly one *source* of the jurisdiction and thus makes up part of its substantive content).
245. *See, e.g., BNP Paribas S.A. v. Open Joint Stock Company Russian Machines* [2011] EWHC 308 (Comm) [34] for an example of inherent powers being exercises for the grant of an injunction based on the court's power in section 37 SCA 1981 and (in a more limited way) under section 44 EAA; *Channel Tunnel* (n 242).

relief to prevent the Respondent to the arbitration from breaching a term of the contract which was subject to an ongoing arbitration involving the preservation of the Appellant's rights to its own sugar beet.[246] An arbitration took place in Belgium, which had been granted and in respect of which a recognition (exequatur) proceeding was already pending pursuant to §§1062 ff. ZPO. The Appellant applied for an interim injunction preventing the Respondent from selling the goods to third parties in breach of the agreement subject to the arbitration. A German Court - despite having no connection to the Belgian arbitration (apart from the German nationality of one of the parties) - was seized to grant the relief. The jurisdiction was constituted based on §1033, which provides that measures of interim relief are generally available regardless of whether Germany is at the seat of the arbitration. This approach is also widely reflected in French practice where the objective of supervisory relief has been to *support* the arbitral process regardless of any link to the court's jurisdiction.[247]

Even though the jurisdiction may be conceived as being founded in the private international law rule enshrined in §1033, which authorises the court's jurisdiction as a matter of national law, taking this reasoning as evidence of the rule or principle, the *exercise* of authority serves the purpose of supporting the arbitral proceeding in the public sphere.

[2] Setting Aside Jurisdiction

A further example of supporting the functioning of the arbitration, rather than merely the discrete proceeding, is where the court reviews the validity of the arbitration agreement while deciding whether to set aside the award or not. In so doing, the court reviews the substantive jurisdiction of the arbitral tribunal. Although this power also falls within the court's review jurisdiction, considered in the next chapter, it might also be regarded as being a facet of the court's power to support the functioning of the arbitral proceeding in determining whether the arbitration agreement is valid or not. In addition to the French approach considered above in relation to the *Arab Republic*, it is useful here to consider common law approaches.

Illustrative of the common law approach is the decision in the 2020 *PAO Tatneft v. Ukraine*.[248] The UK Commercial Court considered whether it was able to set aside an arbitration award in respect of which leave had been granted to enforce by Teare J and which had not been overturned on the basis of state immunity by Butcher J.[249] Butcher J had already considered whether a state immunity argument could be made, it being argued by PAO Tatneft that the state had lost its right to rely on state immunity due to

246. LG Braunschweig, 4 August 2015 (n 214).
247. Similarly: Cour Dapos; appel de Paris (Pôle 1 - Ch. 1), 27 October 2011 No. 11/11104 (the court's supportive power derives from Article 1493(2) (now Article 1469(2) CPC) On that basis, the 'juge d'appui' ('support judge') had authority in 'its mission of assistance and cooperation as a state judge'. A refusal to do so would be a denial of justice and breach of 'international public policy'); *Arab Republic* (n 217) (France).
248. *PAO Tatneft v. Ukraine* [2020] EWHC 3161.
249. *Ibid.*, [4]-[5].

the applicability of section 9 – that the state had submitted to the arbitration.[250] Finding that Ukraine was estopped from raising an illegality argument that should have been raised before Butcher J in the state immunity application, the Court ultimately declined the application to set aside.[251] The arbitration took place under the UNCITRAL Rules and was brought by Tatneft, a Russian oil company, under an arbitration agreement in a BIT between Ukraine and Russia. Ukraine raised state immunity as a possible defence to jurisdiction on the basis that it had not submitted to the (UK) jurisdiction within the meaning of section 9 SIA; however that defence had clearly failed in the earlier application before Butcher J.[252]

Finding that it did not even need to consider the question of state immunity in the setting aside application, the Court found that it is a 'universally accepted and fundamental rule of international arbitration', namely that there is discretion under section 103(2) to enforce an award in accordance with the New York Convention. In this regard, the Court found that the 'decision to enforce the award' was in accordance with this generally recognised legal principle, and thus, the Court would exercise its discretion. State immunity did not become an issue, and waiver did not need to be considered due to this universally accepted principle, whereby an award should be enforced and this 'does not depend solely on English law'.[253] Accepting that while Ukraine did of course have a right to challenge the Court's jurisdiction based on immunity,[254] the state immunity challenges were dismissed on grounds *other* than those related to the court's general jurisdiction to set aside the award, being considered a question distinct from, and unrelated to, the court's general jurisdiction to recognise and enforce an award (or set it aside) under section 103 Arbitration Act.[255]

The Court in the 2020 decision referred to the supervisory nature of its jurisdiction, stating, 'the English courts favour supporting international arbitration by making it straightforward to have awards recognised and enforced internationally, unless a good reason to do otherwise is shown. This is the intention of the New York Convention of the 1996 Act, which give effect to it. Accordingly, the public interest demands challenges to enforcement be resolved efficiently and without unwarranted delay'.[256]

The approach in *PAO Tatneft* supports the notion propounded in this chapter: that supervisory jurisdiction ought to be, and is being, regarded as a lawfully exercisable form of enforcement jurisdiction irrespective of state immunity. Since there are consistent decisions in the public sphere to this effect, this ought to be regarded as falling within the court's international adjudicative jurisdiction.[257]

250. *Ibid.*, [80] as per Butcher J's decision in [2018] 2 Lloyd's Rep 403 [109].
251. *PAO Tatneft* (2020) (n 248).
252. *Ibid.*, [58].
253. *Ibid.*, [84].
254. *Ibid.*, [66].
255. *PAO Tatneft* (2018) (n 198), compare [2] and [3].
256. *PAO Tatneft* (2020) (n 248) [72].
257. *Arab Republic* (n 217) (France); *PAO Tatneft* (2020) (n 248) (UK); *Deutsche Telekom AG (Germany) v. Republic of India, Kammergericht* [Court of Appeal], Berlin, 12th Civil Chamber, Case No. 12 Sch 7/21, 26 January 2023 [37] (the Court had to be satisfied there were no grounds for annulment under Article V New York Convention when considering whether an award

[3] Anti-suit Injunctions: A Special Case?

It is difficult to reconcile the decision in *UK P&I* with decisions in the public sphere.[258] In that decision, an anti-suit injunction was refused based on principles underpinning state immunity, even where the dispute was submitted to arbitration and proceedings were commenced in breach of that agreement. This section attempts to reconcile that decision with other decisions in which anti-suit injunctions have been granted in the public sphere.

(a) **RusChemAlliance***: General Principle Supporting Anti-Suit Injunctions*

In *Deutsche Bank v. RusChemAlliance*, the UK Court considered whether it could grant an anti-suit injunction to restrain proceedings pursuant to foreign arbitration rules (here, an ICC Arbitration in Paris).[259] The subject matter of the dispute – a guarantee issued by a German bank in favour of a Russian company – was governed by English law. The Court found in those circumstances that there was a sufficient connection to the English courts to grant the relief under section 37 SCA, being the source of the power in English law, which was said to have gone beyond section 44 EAA.[260]

Section 37 SCA provides the UK High Court may order an interim injunction 'in all cases where it appears to the court to be just and convenient to do so'.[261] This derives from an 'inherent' power of the courts because it emanates not merely from the legislative power laid down by Parliament in section 37 but also from the old equitable power available to courts to regulate their jurisdiction where the legislature did not provide for such.[262] According to that provision, the court has a more general power to

---

could be recognised as enforceable, which arose irrespective of immunity which was not raised in proceedings); *Bahrain Telecommunications Co v. Discovery Tel*, 476 F. Supp. 2d 176 (District Court of Connecticut, 2007) p. 182 (in an LCIA Arbitration, the US supporting the availability of interim relief to 'maintain the status quo', although ultimately did not grant the interim relief for reasons other than jurisdiction and immunity).

Further: *Infrastructure Services Luxembourg v. Kingdom of Spain* [2023] EWHC 1226 (Comm) (UK High Court finding that the ICSID Convention and the Energy Charter Treaty both qualified as submission to UK jurisdiction, and thus immunity did not preclude jurisdiction to set aside (except that the extent to which tribunal jurisdiction can be reviewed was limited under the ICSID Convention)): [69]; *Energoalians SARL v. République de Moldavie*, Cass civ 1, 28 March 2018, 16-16568 (French Court of Cassation set aside award rendered against Moldova on the basis that the acquisition of a right to claim money arising from a debt linked to an electricity supply contract cannot constitute an 'investment' under the Energy Charter Treaty. Immunity did not arise as a defence).

258. *UK P&I Club* (2022) (n 207).
259. *Deutsche Bank* (2023) (n 206).
260. Though an initial appeal ground, whereby the appeal could have been pursued based on section 44 was not pursued, it is not conclusive whether such an anti-suit injunction would also be available under section 44 EAA, but the question is presumably unimportant where the power would be available in any event under section 37 SCA 1981.
261. Senior Courts Act 1981 (c. 54).
262. *See, e.g.*, most recently, in the Family law context: *UL v. BK* (n 244) [9] and [14] (though 'inherency' may not give the court a *wider* power than legislature confers, it is still clearly one *source* of the jurisdiction and thus makes up part of its substantive content).

grant an injunction, including when arbitration proceedings are 'not on foot or proposed' to preserve that proceeding.[263]

Importantly for this work, the Court also found that the 'natural forum' being the seat was no bar to the UK court granting the injunction because, as per well-developed case law, by granting the anti-suit injunction, the UK courts are seeking to uphold and enforce the parties' contractual bargain as set out in the arbitration agreement.[264] Finding that it could grant the anti-suit injunction, the English court found that it was the 'proper forum' to grant an anti-suit injunction on the basis, *inter alia*, of the jurisdictional nexus founded in the English law governing clause. Since the governing law was English law, the Court would be able to grant the injunction to enforce the promise in the arbitration agreement:

> [38] The English court, faced with an English law governed contract containing a promise by a party not to do something and a threat by that party to do the very thing he has promised not to do, will readily and usually enforce that promise by injunction ...
>
> [39] Hence the court will usually grant an ASI to enforce an arbitration agreement unless there is good reason not to: see The Angelic Grace at 96 col 2 per Millett LJ, 97 col 1 per Neill LJ.

Mr Justice Males found that since the question of whether an interim anti-suit injunction could be granted was one concerning jurisdiction, then the gateway criteria set out in paragraph 3.1(6)(c) of Practice Direction 6B of the English Civil Procedure Rules (CPR) had to be satisfied (being the relevant criteria in this case). Since the bank only had to satisfy the criteria that it had a 'good arguable case' and England was the 'proper place for bringing the claim', the Court found that an anti-suit injunction could be granted.[265]

The Court indeed pointed to anti-suit injunctions as being part of the 'supervisory' or 'supporting' jurisdiction of the UK courts as set out in the *West Tankers*[266] and *Enka*[267] decisions. Thus, the leading practice suggests that there must be a connection in terms of at least the applicable law to the dispute, as being the forum state's law, for an anti-suit injunction to be available. Hence, the court will generally enforce an arbitration agreement 'unless there is a good reason not to'.[268] The Court also recognised that since the French court would not grant an anti-suit injunction, the choice was between the claim being entertained or not being brought at all.[269]

263. In reliance on *Ust-Kamengorsk Hydropower Plant JSC v. AES Ust-Kamengorsk Hydropower Plant LLP* [2013] UKSC 35 [48], the position put forward by Bright J is maintained: *Deutsche Bank* (2023) (n 206) [16].
264. *Deutsche Bank* (2023) (n 206) [38].
265. *Ibid.*, [34]-[35].
266. *West Tankers Inc v. Ras Riunione Adriatica di Sicurtá SpA (The Front Comor)* [2007] 1 Ll Rep 391.
267. *Enka Insaat ve Sanayi AS v. OOO 'Insurance Company Chubb'* [2020] UKSC 38, [2020] 1 WLR 4117.
268. *Deutsche Bank* (2023) (n 206) [39].
269. *Ibid.*, [41].

This application of this principle – that anti-suit injunctions should generally be available powers of courts, even outside the arbitral tribunal's general jurisdiction – was based on the 'general principle' that an injunction should restrain breaches of negative contracts 'almost as of right' which is a well-established principle of English law.[270] The power to grant anti-suit injunctions in the public sphere is also established based on an inherent power in the US courts.[271]

The UK courts have also established that where a final rather than an interim injunction is sought, it is relevant to further consider whether the law governing the arbitration agreement is actually English law rather than there being a 'good arguable case' that it is English law when deciding whether it is 'just and convenient' to grant the measure.[272] On the basis that the arbitration agreement was governed by English law,[273] the Court similarly affirmed the same principles as in *Deutsche Bank* in *Unicredit*.[274] The Supreme Court found in *Unicredit* that the UK Court could grant an anti-suit injunction to restrain the pursuit of court proceedings in Russia in breach of an arbitration in Paris. There was a good arguable case that the claim fell within one of the relevant gateways, being that the contract was governed by English law and that England was the proper place to bring the claim being the forum where the case could be 'suitably tried in the interests of all the parties and for the ends of justice'.[275] This concept derives from the private international law concept of the 'appropriate forum' or *forum non conveniens*, thus demonstrating how a decision based on the private international law norm can form the justification for the public international law rule.

(b) UK P&I Club*: Red Herring or Genuine Exception?*

By way of contrast, in the decision in *UK P&I Club NV*,[276] the Court of Appeal found that since anti-suit injunctions – at least *final* anti-suit injunctions – are more 'coercive' in nature, they therefore fall within a category of injunctive relief, which is excluded against states under section 13(2)(a) SIA, including in respect of a state's non-sovereign activities.[277]

The case arose out of the loss of a Venezuelan navy patrol vessel, 'The Resolute', in early 2020, resulting in a collision with an ice-classed cruise liner engaged in tourism in Antarctica. The Resolute was insured by the first Claimant, UK P&I Club NV. While

270. *Ibid.*, [39].
271. Similarly (US): *Sea Spray Holdings* (n 236) (a Court exercised its 'inherent power' under section 3 FAA to stay proceedings related to an arbitration under the American Arbitration Association (AAA) Rules); *Hulley Enterprises* (2016) (n 235) (the stay is said to 'stay' proceedings derived from its 'incidental to the power inherent in every court to control the disposition of the causes on its docket with economy of time and effort for itself, for counsel, and for litigants'); Further (UK): *Mobil Cerro* (2008) (n 206) especially [18]-[19] acknowledging availability of freezing orders under section 37 (though not granting the measure due to the requirement of a 'real risk of dissipation' not being proven).
272. *Unicredit* (2024) (n 209) [41].
273. *Ibid.*, [65] and [70].
274. *Unicredit* (2024) (n 209).
275. *Ibid.*, [36]-[37].
276. *UK P&I Club NV v. Venezuela* [2023] EWCA Civ 1497.
277. *Ibid.*, [9], [50].

Venezuela sought to have its claims litigated in the courts of Dutch Curaçao and Venezuela, UK P&I applied to the UK Court for an anti-suit injunction on the basis the claims were in breach of an arbitration clause in the contract of insurance with The Resolute's owners.

The ground for application for anti-suit relief was that Venezuela's claims in substance were claims to enforce the terms of the contract of insurance between the Dutch Club as insurer and its members, initially before the High Court.[278] There was the separate matter of whether under Venezuelan law there existed a direct claim against the Clubs, borne out of the law and independent of the contract of insurance,[279] Venezuela not being a party to the arbitration agreement. Nonetheless, both the High Court and the Court of Appeal did accept that the claims were materially the same and therefore fell within the arbitration clause, to which Venezuela had consequently consented pursuant to section 9 SIA.[280]

Venezuela sought to rely on section 13(2)(a) for the assertion that it had immunity from injunctive relief. UK P&I contended that if an anti-suit injunction were not granted, it would engage their right to a fair trial enshrined in Article 6 European Convention on Human Rights (ECHR) by prohibiting them from accessing the court in order to ensure Venezuela could not advance its claims before the courts in breach of contract.[281] The Court of Appeal affirmed the High Court's finding that section 13(2)(a) engaged Article 6(1) ECHR, and that it fell within the range of possible rules consistent with international standards.[282]

Section 13(2) provides:

> (2) Subject to subsections (3) and (4) below –
> (a) Relief shall not be given against a state by way of injunction or order for specific performance or for the recovery of land or other property … .

Article 6 European Convention of Human Rights provides:

> [i]n the determination of his civil rights and obligations … everyone is entitled to a fair and public hearing within a reasonable time by an independent and impartial tribunal established by law.

The Court of Appeal affirmed the decision of the High Court in respect of a reading down of section 13(2)(a), as precluding anti-suit injunctions *both* in respect of sovereign and non-sovereign activities, *because* section 13(2)(a) pursues a legitimate domestic objective by proportionate means in accordance with Article 6 ECHR.

The Court of Appeal stated:

> Once it is understood that an anti-suit injunction is a *coercive remedy* which is part of the court's enforcement jurisdiction, it can be seen that the policy of making states immune to them is justified and rendered proportionate by: (i) the international sensitivity and comity mentioned by Lord Lloyd-Jones at [84] in General

278. *UK P&I Club* (2022) (n 207) [6].
279. *Ibid.*, [29].
280. *Ibid.*, [87]; *UK P&I Club* (2023) (n 276) [4].
281. *UK P&I Club* (2022) (n 207) [89].
282. *UK P&I Club* (2023) (n 276) [41]-[43].

> Dynamics, (ii) the policy of not wanting to threaten states with coercive action and the potential of criminal and financial sanctions, and (iii) the ability to declare that those seeking an anti-suit injunction were contractually entitled to have their dispute determined (as in this case) by arbitration.

It appears that the Court here is making a distinction between adjudicative and enforcement jurisdiction, applying an approach to enforcement which would regard immunity as the 'rule' and enforcement (here anti-suit injunctions) as the exception. This is on the basis that section 13(2)(a) 'prohibits ... coercive orders against states'. This would seem therefore to apply to orders which would *compel* a state to take certain action in support of the arbitral proceeding, including document disclosure, as set out in Article 24.1 UN Convention on Jurisdictional Immunities of States and their Property and as set out at paragraph 108 of the Court of Appeal's judgment. This decision appears to suggest that anti-suit injunctions may also fall within that category on the basis that they are more coercive in nature.

The consequence of this finding is that Sir Geoffrey Vos MR sitting in the Court of Appeal found that the High Court judge was right to refuse to grant the Clubs a permanent anti-suit injunction restraining Venezuela from pursuing proceedings against them in Venezuela and Dutch Curacao, notwithstanding acceptance by both parties that Venezuela had submitted the relevant disputes to arbitration within the meaning of section 9 SIA.[283]

In light of this study, the findings of the UK Court of Appeal in *UK P&I* are inconsistent with the harmonising approach between representative national courts' decisions on supervisory jurisdiction, irrespective of state immunity, in relation to international arbitral proceedings. However, it is important to take the decision into account for what it says about permanent anti-suit injunctions as a special exception to the otherwise developing practice and consider whether that view would be justified considering the principles underpinning state immunity in international law.

The decision suggests that where the form of supervisory relief is more 'coercive' in nature, in that it is backed by criminal or financial penalties which can be enforced by the state for failure to comply, then they are less likely to fall within the concept of 'supervisory jurisdiction' within the meaning of this chapter.[284] However, in accordance with the approach taken by this work, anti-suit injunctions – including permanent ones – arguably ought not to be regarded as 'coercive' in nature where they are made pursuant to a valid arbitration agreement and therefore perform the function of inducing the compliance of parties with the arbitration agreement to which they consented. On this basis, *UK P&I* may be considered misconceived as it fails to take into account the underlying principles of consent which justify the jurisdiction of courts to supervise in the first place, including by granting anti-suit injunctions. The Court could be said to have enabled foreign proceedings to continue in breach of the arbitration agreement.

283. *Ibid.*, [4].
284. Being available in respect of the international arbitration (whether seated in the exercising court's state or abroad) regardless of state immunity.

Even though the effect of the decision may be to imply that anti-suit injunctions are generally not available in respect of states, whether the dispute concerns sovereign or non-sovereign activities, the Court refused to lay a firm line in the sand with regard to whether there is a 'settled view' in customary international law as to orders for injunctions and specific performance against states in proceedings relating to their non-sovereign activity.[285] Instead, the judgment finds that Article 6(1) ECHR is satisfied because section 13(2)(a) lays 'within the range of possible rules consistent with current international standards'.[286] Therefore, in one view, it does not decide the issue central to this work, which is whether consistent and widespread practice emerges concerning whether supervisory powers are generally available *in respect of arbitrations*, as this issue is not considered in the judgment. However, the *effect* of the decision was of course *not* to affirm a without notice anti-suit injunction granted by HHJ Pelling sitting as a High Court Judge in the [2021] EWHC 595 decision in the same matter because section 13(2)(a) would prohibit such injunction.

A conclusion permitting the availability of anti-suit injunctions as not being the type of coercive relief against states within the meaning of section 13(2)(a), but being a permissible extension of adjudicative jurisdiction, could arguably have been reached based on section 9 SIA. To reiterate, this provision states that where a State has agreed in writing to submit a dispute to arbitration, the State is not immune as regards proceedings which 'relate to the arbitration'. The decision does not appear to consider this provision when making its decision based on section 13(2)(a) alone; even though Venezuela had not formally 'agreed in writing' to arbitrate, it was accepted that it had submitted to the jurisdiction. Perhaps the decision could have been distinguished from *Unicredit* and *Deutsche Bank* on the basis that Venezuela had not consented to arbitrate, but no such distinction was made.[287]

Compared with the *Unicredit* decision considered above, the UK Court found it did have an inherent power to grant a final anti-suit injunction in respect of an arbitration seated outside the jurisdiction where there was a serious issue to be tried on the merits, a good arguable case that the claim 'fell within one of the relevant gateways' (there, that English law governed the dispute) and that England was the 'proper place to bring the claim'.[288] It is difficult to see why a different approach should apply to states where the governing law is English law, *and* additionally (as in *Unicredit*), the governing law of the arbitration is English law, where the purpose is to induce compliance of the parties with the arbitration agreement and disputes are considered to fall within the arbitration agreement.

Of greater concern, perhaps, is the indication by the Court that, under section 13(2)(a), this could extend to other injunctions and not merely anti-suit injunctions, which are more coercive in nature.[289] In so far as anti-suit injunctions are concerned, which are backed by criminal or financial penalties which can be enforced by the state

285. *UK P&I Club* (2022) (n 207) [115].
286. *Ibid.*, [116].
287. *Ibid.*, [87].
288. *Unicredit* (2024) (n 209) [38], [60] (governed by English law); [78] (England was appropriate forum to bring claim).
289. *UK P&I Club* (2023) (n 276) [59].

for failure to comply, it is perhaps more understandable why final anti-suit injunctions might be regarded as falling within the types of relief which section 13(2)(a) was supposed to capture and therefore as a matter of policy, should be a form of relief which is excluded by state immunity.

(c) Interim Conclusions

Taking all these considerations into account, the best view is that *UK P&I* should be read, in the arbitration context, as an exception in light of *RusChemAlliance* and *Unicredit*. Where anti-suit injunctions are pursued against states, the dicta in *UK P&I* suggests that section 13(2)(a) can be relied on to exclude state immunity and therefore now amounts to an exception within UK jurisdiction. However, it has been suggested that *UK P&I* incorrectly interpreted section 13(2)(a) in circumstances where it had been accepted that the disputes fell within the arbitration agreement and therefore the anti-suit injunction sought to enforce the contractual bargain between the parties.

Based on section 9, the availability of supervisory relief should be supported following principles set out in *Unicredit Bank GmbH* and *Deutsche Bank AG* since those proceedings 'relate to the arbitration', but this question was not considered in detail in the Court of Appeal's judgment. The consequence is that the decision in *UK P&I* introduces more confusion as to the categories of supervisory relief which be available in respect of international arbitrations, given that the Court did not decide that permanent anti-suit injunctions would never be available, but rather appeared to find that a state would have a defence to such injunctions based on Article 6 ECHR. The decision is perhaps best read as an exception which arose due to Venezuela's lack of submission to arbitration and/or given the application of Venezuelan law to the discrete question, though unfortunately, the Judge did not distinguish the point on this basis.

One solution, considering the growing general principles being illustrated in relation to arbitration, is that section 13(2)(a) would be to not exclude anti-suit injunctions from the scope of a court's supervisory jurisdiction in relation to arbitration proceedings. This would follow on the basis that such powers, properly considered, fall within *adjudicative* jurisdiction rather than enforcement jurisdiction, to which the restrictive doctrine on immunity does apply. Therefore, in respect of non-sovereign or commercial activities, the anti-suit injunction should have been available. That would be in-keeping with the findings of this study, that, properly viewed, supervision is an enforcement aspect of adjudicative jurisdiction, which supports the international arbitral process rather than enforcement jurisdiction in the sense of coercing certain action. This is because the effect of such relief is to induce compliance with the international arbitral process.

This work thus directly challenges the finding of the Court of Appeal at [7] of *UK P&I*, where it affirmed the High Court's finding that 'different states adopted different practices as to whether they regarded injunctions as part of their adjudicative or part of their enforcement jurisdiction'.[290] Instead, this book demonstrates that where an international legal approach is adopted to jurisdiction, supervisory powers in respect of the arbitration process plainly are enforcement aspects of *adjudicative* jurisdiction and fall to be recognised as such due to widespread, representative and consistent practice by national courts. This is because, at least in so far as supervision is concerned, these aspects of enforcement support the arbitration process, including the parties' consent to arbitrate.

[4] Exceptions Concerning the Taking of Evidence

While UK, US and German courts have allowed at least limited support in compelling the attendance of witnesses and securing document production in relation to arbitrations outside the territorial jurisdiction, the approach of French courts is more limited. Consequently, powers concerning the taking of evidence do not constitute a generally exercisable power by courts in respect of international arbitral tribunals according to the representative courts.

(a) Securing the Attendance of Witnesses

Pursuant to section 43 and section 44 EAA, UK courts have the same powers in aid of arbitration as they do in respect of UK court litigation, and those matters include the taking of evidence of witnesses and the preservation of evidence.[291] Section 2(3) EAA provides specifically that UK courts can secure the attendance of witnesses 'even if the seat of the arbitration is outside England and Wales'; this applies to both securing the attendance of witnesses under section 43 and more general measures of support under section 44. This has now been clarified by the Arbitration Act 2025, through the introduction of the phrase that orders under section 44 can be made 'whether in relation to a party or any other person' by section 9(2) of the 2025 Act.

The UK Court of Appeal has clarified in *A and B v. C, D and E* that ordering a non-party to an arbitration to give evidence is a power available pursuant to section 44(2)(a) EAA, including in aid of arbitral proceedings located outside UK jurisdiction.[292] The tribunal was in New York, but the non-party was resident in the UK. Overturning Foxton J's decision that section 44 was not broad enough to encompass powers against third parties, the Court of Appeal found section 44(2)(a) is clearly directed towards obtaining evidence of individuals who are not parties to the arbitration. The Court found this would include foreign-seated arbitrations pursuant to section 2(3). Foxton's decision had relied on decisions in *Cruz City*[293] and *DTEK Trading*,[294] in which section 44 was stated not to be broad enough to encompass

290. *Ibid.*, [7]. Repeated by the Court of Appeal at [48] of its Judgment: *UK P&I Club* (2023) (n 276) [48].
291. Section 84(2)(a) and (b) EAA.
292. *A and B v. C, D and E* [2020] EWCA Civ 409, particular [35]-[36].
293. *Cruz City I Mauritius Holdings v. Unitech Limited* [2014] EWHC 3704 (Comm).
294. *DTEK Trading SA v. Mr Sergey Morozov and another* [2017] EWHC 94 (Comm).

powers in respect of non-parties. The Court of Appeal stated that it wished to leave the issue of whether those decisions were correctly decided to any appeal.[295] While *Cruz City* dealt with the question of whether an injunction could be granted against non-parties, *DTEK Trading* was concerned with whether an order to preserve and allow a third party to inspect documents under section 44 would be allowed in the circumstances. Consequently, the Court of Appeal's decision is limited to the taking of evidence from third parties rather than the preservation of evidence and inspection by them. However, the Court did note that the decisions in *Cruz City* and *DTEK Trading* were concerned with the interpretation of service out provisions on a non-party pursuant to the relevant civil procedure rules.[296] In-keeping with Merkin and Flannery's criticism of those decisions, that the comments concerning section 44 were only *obiter* but clarification would be desirable, those decisions appeared ripe for appeal, at least prior to the Arbitration Act 2025.[297] The introduction of the new wording in section 44(1) EAA, pursuant to section 9(2) of the 2025 Arbitration Act, to the effect that preservation orders are now available in respect of third parties, appears to have put this issue to bed.

German courts recognise that they have powers to assist in the taking of evidence, but only those powers which the tribunal is 'not empowered to perform'.[298] This power has been identified as being available in relation to an arbitral tribunal outside the jurisdiction (e.g., under the ICC in Zurich), and thus, an exercise in the public sphere is regarded as permissible.[299] In Germany, it is recognised therefore that since arbitral tribunals cannot compel witnesses to attend, German courts can do so, provided those witnesses are located within the particular court's (usually regional) jurisdiction. This principle applies irrespective of where the arbitral tribunal is located.[300]

French and US court practice, however, has excluded the securing of attendance of witnesses in respect of arbitral tribunals. French courts cannot compel witnesses to attend because no such power exists in the CPC.[301] Some US practice has illustrated that courts will not consistently order the attendance of witnesses based on the 'private' nature of the arbitral institution. In *National Broadcasting Company*,[302] the US Court of Appeals concluded that courts do not have powers to assist discovery in connection with private arbitral tribunals, as well as to subpoena witnesses (with §7 FAA, which does permit court assistance, said to be available only where the

295. *A and B v. C, D and E* (n 292) [27].
296. *Ibid.*, [9].
297. *Ibid.*, [27].
298. Section 1050 ZPO.
299. High Court of Thüringen, 4 Sch 03/06 (8 August 2007).
300. *Ibid.*
301. *See, e.g.*, Janet Walker and Douglas S Jones, 'Practical Insights on Default of a Party or Absence of a Party or Witness: France', Practical Insights on Arbitral Procedure (Kluwer, 2024) (the extent to which courts can intervene is to draw an adverse inference regarding the non-attendance of witnesses when asking whether to overturn the award according to due process). The power of witnesses to be sworn in and to take testimony is with the arbitral tribunal, not the court: Article 1467 CPC.
302. *National Broadcasting Co. v. Bear Stearns Co.* 165 F.3d 184 (2d Cir. 1999).

arbitration is in the United States).[303] While accepting that such a power would arise in principle before the tribunal itself, the Court rejected the notion that this could extend to a private arbitration tribunal, whose purpose was in part to exist outside the public realm of the courts and only on the basis of private party consent.[304]

The fact that US and French courts are not willing to secure the attendance of witnesses does not mean that this should not be a power *generally* available before national courts as a lawful aspect of supervisory jurisdiction. The practice does not, for example, state that securing the attendance of witnesses is not possible due to an *international* legal principle such as state immunity. For the reasons thus far put forward in this book, there is no reason for excluding national court assistance on such a basis, where such assistance is limited to the specific documents requested, which reflects the more limited approach of the other courts examined.[305]

Given the purpose of supervisory jurisdiction is to assist the tribunal, this would be perfectly consistent with the parties' consent to the arbitration *and* would be in-keeping with the object and purpose of supervisory jurisdiction thus far illustrated, which is to support rather than overstep the jurisdiction of the tribunal.[306] Given some disparate practice exists, harmonisation would be timely and ensure greater consistency of application by other national courts, at least by providing that such a power would not be excluded or limited by the international legal principle of state immunity. Should the rules be accepted as a general principle, they would be subject to any applicable national procedural laws.

(b) Power to Order Disclosure During Arbitral Proceedings

Except in relation to ICSID and US practice, the examined courts have consistently recognised that there is a power to order production of documents in respect of an international arbitration, though this power tends in practice to be exercised in a more

303. *Ibid.*, p. 75. *See, National Broadcasting* in *ZP Automotive US, Inc. v. Luxshare, Ltd.*, 596 U.S. 619 (Supreme Court of the United States) §4.
304. *Ibid.*, pp. 74-76. While there was a shift in approach suggesting that national courts could grant discovery assistance in respect of an arbitral tribunal constituted under a BIT as such tribunal proceeding could be considered a 'proceeding in a foreign or international tribunal' under §1782 in *Fund for Protection of Investor Rights in Foreign States Pursuant to 28 U.S.C § 1782 v. Alixpartners LLP*, 5 F.4th 216 (United States Court of Appeals, 2nd Cir. 2021); This approach seems to have returned to the more restrictive approach in *National Broadcasting*, 596 U.S. 619 (n 303) in which it was considered that only a governmental or intergovernmental adjudicative body constitutes a 'foreign or international tribunal' under §1782, and not an arbitral tribunal, whether constituted to determine state to state disputes, or private commercial disputes.
305. *See, e.g., BNP Paribas* (2003) (n 245).
306. *See* the arbitration literature earlier illustrated which would support this: Lew, 'Does National Court Involvement Undermine ...?' (n 30) 490 ('national court involvement in international arbitration is a fact of life as prevalent as the weather', particularly drawing on the measures herein discussed at: 496, and 514-535); similarly: Derains and Schwartz (n 232) 294-295; Born (n 178) 2638-2639 (recognising the 'overlapping' jurisdiction with national courts to grant interim relief).

limited manner, in respect of 'specific documents'.[307] Courts also have differing approaches as to whether such disclosure is possible in relation to third parties.

According to the UK approach, there is a power to seek production of documents from a non-party to the arbitration under section 43 EAA.[308] This power first arose under the 1950 Arbitration Act, section 12(4), which empowered the Court to issue a *subpoena ad testificandum* or *duces tecum*, to compel a witness within the jurisdiction. This power may also be exercised in the public sphere, especially given that it was stated in *South Tyneside Borough Council* that '[b]y its nature, a witness summons seeks to compel production from a non-party to the proceedings in question'.[309] Gross J went on to state that 'the object of a witness summons is to obtain production at trial of specified documents; accordingly, the witness summons must specifically identify the documents sought, it must not be used as an instrument to obtain disclosure and it must not be of a fishing or speculative nature'.[310]

German courts allow for the disclosure of documents, provided three requirements are met: there must be a specific connection between parties, the obligated party must be able to provide the requested information without undue hardship, and the entitled party must have a justifiable uncertainty about the existence or scope of its right.[311] For example, such a power might be available in respect of a third party in the national court, which would not however be available before the arbitral tribunal. Pursuant to §1050 ZPO, this power is available regardless of whether the seat of the arbitration is in Germany, provided that the parties so request it and where the tribunal is not itself able to provide such assistance.[312]

French approaches to document requests tend to be more limited, with the power of determining the materiality and relevance of the production of documents generally falling within the jurisdiction of the tribunal rather than the courts. Even though that power is largely with the tribunal, the tribunal itself may authorise the request of a party from the state courts (from the *President of the Tribunal Judiciare*) to obtain an order against third parties to obtain evidence held by them.[313]

In addition to excluding the attendance of witnesses, the US Court of Appeals in *National Broadcasting Company* clarified that production of documents, or discovery, would be precluded for the same reasons.[314] The decision was based on a provision in section 1782 Title 28 United States Code, which comprises Federal Law[315] and only permits production in a proceeding 'in a foreign or international tribunal'. While not excluding an international arbitral tribunal constituted under a public international law

307. *BNP Paribas* (2003) (n 245) [5]-[6]; *South Tyneside Borough Council v. Wickes Building Supplies Ltd* [2004] EWHC 2428 (Comm) [23] (per Gross J).
308. *BNP Paribas* (2003) (n 245) [9]-[10]; *A and B v. C, D and E* (n 292) [70].
309. *South Tyneside* (n 307) [23] (per Gross J); *A and B v. C, D and E* (n 292) [70].
310. *South Tyneside* (n 307) [23].
311. Section 142 ZPO.
312. The wording of 1050 states that these are the conditions for the taking of evidence. However, §142 ZPO also needs to be satisfied in respect of any disclosure request.
313. Nadia Darwazeh and Constance Malleville, 'Practical Insights on Document Production: France', Practical Insights on Arbitral Procedure (Kluwer, 2023).
314. *National Broadcasting Co.* (n 302).
315. 28 U.S.C. §1782.

instrument, the Court found that private commercial arbitrations would be excluded from such jurisdiction.

For the same reasons set out above in relation to state immunity, there is no reason to preclude disclosure, provided it is adequately circumscribed in accordance with ordinary principles of procedure applicable to arbitral tribunals. Such powers of supervision ought not to be regarded as breaching the foreign state's sovereignty nor unduly encroaching on consent underpinning the arbitral process but rather supportive of the enforcement of the international arbitral process.[316] Such powers, especially if recognised as being part of international law, would help allow for the disclosure of documents in relation to foreign-seated arbitrations and arbitrations where states are a party irrespective of state immunity.

[E] LIMITATIONS ON THE SCOPE OF SUPERVISORY JURISDICTION

The common approach shows how supervisory measures may *generally* be granted by any national court *because* it is being recognised as an aspect of its adjudicative jurisdiction in the public sphere. Nonetheless, the availability of such jurisdiction in *any* national court may give rise to issues of conflicting jurisdictions where multiple courts seek to assert authority over the same dispute – a problem traditionally dealt with by private international law.[317] This is important in view of the risk of overbroad assertions of the general ground of jurisdiction by parties, resulting in several overlapping and competing jurisdictions.[318] This issue has been linked in the field of private international law to the problem of 'forum shopping', i.e., where parties, by use of the private international law of a forum state, seek to apply to the court with the most favourable law for it.[319] This risk would arise seeing as this practice permits a national court to exercise jurisdiction regardless of any link to the jurisdiction.

This section deals therefore with any limitations on the jurisdiction in the public sphere. It is important to note that these additional requirements do not apply in every circumstance of supportive jurisdiction. While not restricting the fact that the power to grant various forms of supervisory relief is generally available and lawful as a matter of international law, national courts may impose additional restrictions on when those powers are in fact exercised.

316. Lew, 'Does National Court Involvement Undermine …?' (n 30).
317. Dicey (n 34) 1-003 (the very purpose of the field of 'conflict of laws' is to deal with cases with a 'foreign' element where the application of multiple laws or multiple jurisdictions may conflict).
318. This issue arises in the sphere of private international law; *see*, especially Dicey (n 34) 1-003 (the very purpose of the field of 'conflict of laws' is to deal with cases with a 'foreign' element where the application of multiple laws or multiple jurisdictions may conflict).
319. *See, e.g.*, Dicey, Morris and Collins, *The Conflict of Laws* (15th edn, Sweet & Maxwell 2012) 30-174 (one example of 'bad' forum shopping is said to be where there are multiple jurisdictions available, and the debtor uses this to shield or move assets).

[1] Arbitral Tribunal Not Yet Constituted or Unable to Act

The first harmonised principle is where the arbitral tribunal is not yet constituted. Indeed, US practice recognises that, at least where the court has no connection to the dispute, interim relief ought to be granted where the arbitral tribunal is unable to act. This is exactly what occurred in the seminal decision of *Toyo Tire Holdings*.[320]

The facts have already been recounted.[321] As mentioned, a preliminary injunction was granted in respect of an ICC arbitration proceeding to 'preserve the meaningfulness' of the arbitration without there being any link to the US forum. On appeal, a US Court concluded that it was precisely because the arbitral tribunal was not yet constituted that it might be necessary to grant interim relief to maintain the meaningfulness of the arbitration.[322] Further decisions in the other representative jurisdictions also identify the failure of the tribunal to act in a timely manner, or where it is not yet constituted, as a justification for the jurisdiction.[323] Section 44(3) EAA limits the powers of courts to preserve evidence or assets to cases of 'urgency' so as to ensure that the powers of the arbitral tribunal are not usurped.

Another example is the taking of evidence in German and French court proceedings. §1050 ZPO expressly provides that it is for the arbitral tribunal to conduct the taking of evidence and that a party 'may request that a court provide assistance in taking evidence by performing any other judicial acts for which the arbitral tribunal is not authorised'. Similarly, the tribunal may authorise a request of a party from the state courts (from the *President of the Tribunal Judiciare*) to obtain an order for obtaining evidence.[324]

Consequently, one reason for supervisory measures, which seek to preserve the status quo or meaningfulness of the arbitration, may be where the arbitral tribunal is not constituted or unable to grant the measure in question.

[2] Risk of Assets Going Unsatisfied or Being Dissipated

A second shared limitation on international supportive jurisdiction is where there is a 'real risk' that the assets under the award will go unsatisfied or be dissipated. This ground principally arises in the area of freezing injunctions, which tend to be granted

320. *Toyo Tire* (n 188).
321. *Ibid.*
322. *Ibid.*
323. Similarly, *Cetelem S.A. v. Roust Holdings Limited* [2005] EWCA Civ 618 (UK), especially at [37] (the purpose of section 44 is to give the court powers where the arbitral tribunal is unable to act effectively, while the wording of section 44(3) makes clear that these powers of the courts are not supposed to usurp the arbitral process); LG Braunschweig, 4 August 2015 (n 214) (in the very title of the decision it is stated that the measure pursues to aim of 'security' of the claim arising out of the arbitral award pending recognition of such an award. This is reflective of the aim stated in §1033 ZPO, and serves the purpose of preventing dissipation where orders seeking preservation of assets are sought); *Soguipêche* (n 225) [1] (France) (on the basis of the risk of dissipation of assets, the measure requested here was to attach vessels; this was available seeing as the Court contemplated the measure in respect of a foreign state, merely not exercising its power due to specific consent under ICSID).
324. Darwazeh and Malleville (n 313).

following the rendering of the arbitration award. Though these measures may also be considered an aspect of the court's execution function, they may also arise in the context of seeking to freeze assets pending the award being rendered.

The test applied by the UK courts can be demonstrated by the *Mobil Cerro* case.[325] The dispute arose out of an oil development which the Respondent, the Bolivarian Republic of Venezuela, pursued on a joint venture basis with the Appellant Venezuelan state-owned entity. Upon nationalisation of Mobil's interests in those projects, Mobil applied to arbitrate the dispute before ICSID. While the dispute was ongoing, Mobil applied for a 'Mareva injunction' under section 44 EAA – a special type of injunction to freeze assets in view of assets at risk of dissipation outside of UK jurisdiction, which would be subject to any award. Considering an application to set aside the freezing order, the Court stated that it would be satisfied that the test for a good arguable case is met provided that the Claimant can demonstrate that transfer of assets outside the jurisdiction would make enforcement of any judgment more difficult.[326] Doubt as to the creditworthiness of the Defendant would not be sufficient to demonstrate such a risk.[327] Instead, a 'real risk', at least according to the UK approach, requires the demonstration of the risk of 'dissipation', which must involve a risk impairing the claimant's ability to enforce a judgment or award. To demonstrate this, it is necessary to show that enforcement *in the UK* would be impaired.[328] However, it is not necessary to prove intention on the part of the Defendant to frustrate enforcement, provided that, objectively, this would be the effect.[329]

The requirement that assets need to be at risk of dissipation has been identified through the analysis of a number of sources. This includes: as a matter of interpretation of the applicable private international law norm,[330] in the reasoning of courts as to when measures should be granted,[331] and considering approaches which hold

325. *Mobil Cerro* (2008) (n 206) [37]; *Ninemia Maritime Corp v. Trave Schiffahrtsgesellschaft GmbH (The Niedersachen)* [1983] 1 W.L.R. 1412, 1422.
326. *Mobil Cerro* (2008) (n 206) [38]; further, *U & M* (n 180) (there was a real risk of dissipation where it could be inferred that KCM's liquid assets 'would be dealt with other than in the ordinary course of business with a view to making enforcement of awards more difficult').
327. *Mobil Cerro* (2008) (n 206) [36].
328. *Ibid.*, [40].
329. *Holyoake v. Candy* [2017] 2 AER (Comm) 513 [34] (there must be a 'real risk', judged objectively, that a future judgment would not be met because of unjustifiable dissipation of assets ... Solid evidence will be required to support a conclusion that relief is justified, although precisely what this entails in any given case will necessarily vary according to the individual circumstances).
330. In the case of Germany, §1033 ZPO: LG Braunschweig, 4 August 2015 (n 214) (as considered above, the relief available in respect of the germplasm in order to prevent a breach of the agreement).
331. In the case of the US: *Bahrain Telecommunications* (n 257) (In respect of an LCIA arbitration, Court accepted that provisional relief must be available according to the principle underlying the notion of a provisional remedy – that is of 'the preservation of the status quo – namely the parties' financial status quo pending issuance of a final judgment').

jurisdiction to be available irrespective of immunity where the requirement is considered as a background requirement of the jurisdiction.[332]

In addition, in the US, the requirement of irreparable harm may need to be proven and requires a 'course of conduct in relation to assets, actual or feared' and 'that there exists a risk of impairing the claimant's ability to enforce a judgment or award'.[333] Again, consistent decisions in the public sphere on supervisory jurisdiction - entailing the grant of requisite relief (a preliminary injunction) in those established circumstances - demonstrate that supervisory jurisdiction is available irrespective of state immunity.[334]

Special requirements arise when applying for permanent as distinct from preliminary injunctive relief for the freezing of assets under national laws. For example, while acknowledging that 'the standard for a permanent injunction is essentially the same as for a preliminary injunction', the US Court in the *GE Transportation* case found that the claimant must show 'actual success' rather than the 'likelihood of success' on the merits to be able to obtain a permanent injunction.[335]

[3] Preservation of Contractual Rights/Status Quo

A broader objective pursued by some supervisory courts is to preserve the contractual rights of the parties under the arbitration agreement. This aim encompasses stays and other similar measures which aim at upholding the arbitration agreement per its terms.

The UK approach is conveyed by the *Channel Group Tunnel* decision.[336] The Appellants applied for an interim injunction in respect of an ICC arbitration under section 37 SCA 1981 to restrain the Respondents from taking action to vary the quality of works that had to be performed under a contract subject to the arbitration dispute. Section 37 provides the High Court with a general power to grant interim relief where it is 'just and convenient' to do so. The Court ultimately did not grant the interim injunction on the facts finding that it would largely 'pre-empt the decision of the arbitral panel' whose 'support forms the raison d'être of the injunction'. As pointed out by Lord Mustill, 'by the time that the award of the panel of arbitrators is ultimately made, with the Respondents having continued to work meanwhile it will be of very

332. In the case of France: *Soguipêche* (n 225) (considering whether the measure of security, attaching to vessels in security of the award, would be available in respect of the foreign state, thus implicitly accepting that the international legal principle of immunity *per se* does not exclude this jurisdiction).
333. *Mobil Cerro* (2008) (n 206) [35]-[37]; *GE Transportation Co Ltd v. A-Power Energy Generation Systems*, 15 Civ. 6194 (PAE) (S.D.N.Y. 2016) (US) (award issued by Hong Kong Arbitration Centre, considering a preliminary injunction according to the same criteria); *Sperry Int'l Trade v. Government of Israel*, 532 F.Supp. 901, 909 (S.D.N.Y. 1982), aff'd, 689 F.2d 301 (2d Cir. 1982) (stating the background that a preliminary injunction had been incorrectly granted because irreparable harm had not been demonstrated where potential damage was strictly monetary).
334. *Mobil Cerro* (2008) (n 206) [35]-[37]; *GE Transportation* (n 333) (US); *Sperry* (n 333).
335. *GE Transportation* (n 333) 18.
336. *Channel Tunnel* (n 242).

modest practical value, except as the basis for a claim in damages by the Respondents'.[337] Nonetheless, it is significant that the Court recognised that the power to grant an interim injunction was available in principle pursuant to section 37 SCA in respect of a foreign-seated arbitration (though, on the particular facts of that case, it was not granted). Following the approach established above, to the extent that there are representative approaches on a comparable private international law basis in the other states, this also ought to be regarded as a source for this rule and/or principle.[338] This is supported by the general aim found in Article II New York Convention, which is to uphold the contractual rights of parties under the terms of the arbitration agreement.

[F] COUNTERVAILING APPROACHES

This section considers approaches by courts which may be considered to interfere with or contradict the harmonised approach. National courts lawfully grant supervisory measures in the public sphere in respect of the arbitral proceeding. This is because this form of enforcement jurisdiction is being treated as arising as an aspect of the state's *adjudicative jurisdiction*, available irrespective of the international legal principle of state immunity, due to their widespread, consistent and representative exercises of authority in the public sphere.

However, this section will show that any countervailing approaches - which appear to suggest the prevailing approach is not consistent or widespread - can be distinguished and do not detract from this common approach.

Further, the *absence* of any countervailing practice supports the *widespread* nature of the approach thus far defended. This is because the paucity of countervailing decisions supports a finding that the approach is widespread and representative.

[1] Court at the Seat Should Grant Relief

Some case law appears to confine the possibility of supervisory jurisdiction to the seat of the arbitration rather than permitting *any* court to exercise jurisdiction.[339] In the UK decision in *U & M Mining*, a UK Court considered whether the parties were entitled to

337. *Ibid.*, 367.
338. Similarly, and further: US: *Hulley Enterprises* (2016) (n 235) (stay granted to preserve party rights to have those rights adjudicated on in the arbitration, including as here, where a state was party); *Bahrain Telecommunications* (n 257); *Mitsui* (2005) (n 192) especially [16], [18], [25] (*Mitsui* had agreed to arbitrate under the ICC arbitration rules in Switzerland. The US Court found it could not compel the arbitration because the measure was not merely to 'preserv[ing] the status quo pending arbitration'); District Court of Munich ('LG München') I, 23 June 2016, - 1 HK O 8126/16 - juris Rz. 126 [55] (measure to preserve rights of parties to arbitration - to continue participating in German football world cup in the interim before a final decision rendered as to whether revocation of licence had been lawful (in an ongoing arbitration) would have been permitted had parties not agreed to CAS Rules).
339. *See, e.g.*, *U & M* (n 180); further, Fox and Webb (n 8) 383 (this is the only circumstance which has been considered in the immunities context as being sufficient in terms of when a waiver will be removed to 'constitute' the jurisdiction - that is, when it concerns the power of the court with a *connection* to the arbitration (the 'forum' court)).

go to a Zambian Court for relief in relation to an LCIA arbitration in London. The Court expressly stated that any court which is not the seat may *only* 'exceptionally' grant interim 'if, for practical reasons, the application can only sensibly be made there and so long as the proceedings are not simply an attempt to outflank the arbitration agreement'.[340]

However, these decisions have made clear that the parties *should* apply to the court at the seat as the first port of call but not whether it or any other court should grant the relief out of a sense of obligation (international or otherwise). This reasoning - that parties should go to the court at the seat for practical reasons - acknowledges that parties would merely be exercising an *option* to go to that court but would not be bound to do so.

This point is illustrated by the decision of the Brandenburg Court of 20 June 2001.[341] The Applicant, a subcontractor of the Defendant which had carried out insulation work for it, demanded payment of the rest of its remuneration. The Defendant contested the Court's jurisdiction because the parties had agreed to arbitrate the disputes arising out of the parties' contract. In dismissing jurisdiction to decide about the claims, the Court made important remarks regarding the law relating to when the court would be available to intervene. It stated that, due to the choice of court clause in the contract in addition to the choice of arbitration, the parties would be *permitted* to go to that court (the Court at Cottbus) for any interim relief relating to the arbitration under §1033 ZPO. The language provides that this is the court to which the parties 'may' apply for interim relief.[342] This is representative of the general approach that applying to the court at the seat merely provides an option for parties rather than imposing a legal obligation.[343]

These decisions ought to therefore be viewed as dealing with a conceptually distinct question of allocation of competence between courts as a matter of private international law. They do not deal with whether any other court, with no connection to the jurisdiction, might be entitled to grant certain forms of relief.

[2] Undermined by Consent to Arbitrate

In *McCreary*, a US Court was asked to grant interim relief in respect of an ICC arbitration, stating it could not because it would frustrate the agreement to which

340. *U & M* (n 180) [63]; Similarly, finding a stay should only be granted in exceptional circumstances where the UK is not the seat: *Excalibur* (n 180).
341. Regional Court of Appeal of Brandenburg ('OLG Brandenburg'), 20 June 2001, BauR 2002, 1890 (the language of the Court stated that parties are 'permitted' to go to the Cottbus Court, using language of permissibility rather than out of a sense of obligation, in accordance with §1033 ZPO (which in any case does not require a link to German jurisdiction)).
342. OLG Brandenburg, BauR 2002, 1890 (n 341) [36] ('vor welchem Gericht Maßnahmen des einstweiligen Rechtsschutzes beantragt werden *können*' (§1033 ZPO)).
343. *See, e.g.*, *U & M* (n 180) (UK); *Hulley Enterprises* (2016) (n 235) paras 8 and 16 (in the context of proceedings for a stay of enforcement of Dutch awards, the seat being considered merely as one possible forum where relief can be applied for, not excluded others); *Société Ryanair* (n 228) (France) [8] (annulment proceedings must comply with requirements of French law *irrespective of where the award is made*).

parties have consented and thus was not available as it was a breach of Article II(3) New York Convention.[344] The reasoning of the Court in *McCreary* is also undermined by its own logic: precisely, by making supervisory relief available before any national court, this *supports* the aim underpinning Article II(3) by ensuring the arbitration agreement is upheld. Indeed, this view - that supervisory jurisdiction supports the arbitral process - is widely reflected in the prevailing approach in the arbitration literature. For example, Lew, exemplifying the approach by arbitration scholars more widely, highlights broad academic acceptance against the decision, stating that 'most would agree that [at the stage prior to establishment of a tribunal at least] national court intervention is not disruptive, and may be beneficial to the arbitration proceedings'.[345] These decisions therefore reflect a minority review and should be distinguished on the basis that they do not reflect current and prevalent approaches in arbitration.

[3] Emergency Arbitration Awards

At least one decision suggests that emergency arbitration awards are not yet recognised as available in the public sphere, absent a connection to the jurisdiction. In the Bavaria Highest Regional Court decision of 2020, the Court refused to recognise an emergency arbitration award because there was no connection to the jurisdiction - no party was domiciled there, no assets were there, and the arbitration seat was outside Germany.[346] The Court was only exercising a discretion rather than recognising its power was not available; such decisions ought not to be regarded as detracting from the otherwise harmonised approach as to the lawfulness of supervisory jurisdiction in respect of international arbitrations.[347] Thus, while in some of these decisions, the courts may have indicated that *some* connection to the territorial jurisdiction of the court is useful to justify the exercise of a discretion, this has not been decisive for the court to be able to generally grant the measure in the public sphere, as demonstrated by the otherwise consistent approach in this chapter.[348]

[4] ICSID and CAS

In respect of ICSID and the Court of Arbitration for Sport (CAS), it is widely accepted that supervisory jurisdiction is not available (apart from stays, which are recognised as available in the UK). Consequently, they represent a genuine exception, distinguishable based on the particularity of those regimes.

344. *McCreary Tire & Rubber Co v. CEAT Sp.A.*, 501 F. 2d 1032, 1038 (3d Cir. 1974).
345. Lew, 'Does National Court Involvement Undermine ...?' (n 30) 497.
346. Bavarian Supreme Court ('BayObLG'), Decision of 8 October 2020, BeckRS 2020, 28029.
347. Similarly, *U & M* (n 180) (UK) (considered above, but also as a matter of reasoning, whether the Court should find it had jurisdiction based on a territorial link was only an aspect of whether the discretion *ought* to be exercised, and not the basis upon which the Court was bound to do so).
348. *Ibid.*

Like *Soguipêche* considered above, in the *E.T.I. Telecom* decision, a UK Court refused to grant interim relief pursuant to its powers under section 44 EAA and section 25 Civil Jurisdiction and Judgments Act ('CJJA') 1982 which gives the High Court the power to grant interim relief in respect of proceedings in EU states except where it would be 'inexpedient to do so'. Article 47 provides the ICSID Tribunal with the power to grant interim relief and Article 26 that consent to ICSID shall 'unless otherwise stated, be deemed consent to arbitration to the exclusion of any other remedy'. In reliance on earlier case law where UK courts had found that the power under section 25 should only be exercised 'harmoniously with the regime and procedures of the court seized of the substantive proceedings',[349] the Court found it would be 'inexpedient' to grant the measure under section 25. Due to the parties' specific consent under ICSID, the Court effectively interpreted its supervisory jurisdiction as *excluded*.

Further, the Court clarified that section 3(2) 1966 Act, implementing the ICSID Convention as part of UK law, would not permit relief ordinarily available under sections 36, 38 and 44 EAA unless a specific Order is made by the Lord Chancellor.[350] However, section 3(2) provides that a stay under section 9 EAA is possible in respect of an ICSID arbitration.[351]

A similar approach has emerged among German courts in relation to arbitration conducted under the CAS Rules, which exclude national court supervision under r. 3.7.[352]

These court approaches relate to a specific interpretation of the ICSID or CAS Rules. They do not concern the wider question of whether the court *ought* to be able to exercise its jurisdiction in respect of *any* international arbitral proceeding irrespective of immunity. Consequently, they emerge as an exception based on the consent to those regimes, not on the lawfulness of enforcement measures in relation to international arbitration. It will be expanded upon in Chapter 6 why ICSID Tribunals ought to be subject to the same scrutiny by national courts as other arbitral tribunals, thereby supporting the general principle and its widespread application.

By way of brief introduction to the topic of excluding ICSID Tribunals from the otherwise harmonious approach, Article 26 ICSID Convention has been stated by authors to consist of a 'self-contained' regime, which means ICSID Tribunals effectively operate - at least in so far as supervisory jurisdiction is concerned - outside the public sphere of national courts.[353] This is the idea that approaches may diverge from a more general consensus as to international law on the subject, leading to particular 'sub-systems' of law which normatively diverge from international law.[354] The particular problems this causes as a theoretical and practical matter, from the perspective

349. *E.T.I. Euro Telecom* (n 226) [22], by reference to *Credit Suisse Fides Trust SA v. Cuoghi* [1998] QB 818.
350. *E.T.I. Euro Telecom* (n 226) [34].
351. *Ibid.*
352. Decision of 23 June 2016, - 1 HK O 8126/16 (n 338) [122]-[123]; Regional Court of Appeal of Munich ('OLG München'), 26/10.2000, NJW-RR 2001, 711.
353. Schreuer (n 226) 348.
354. This is a problem in international law which has been pointed out by Joost Pauwelyn, 'Bridging Fragmentation and Unity: International Law as a Universe of Inter-Connected Islands' (2004) 25 *Mich. K. Int'l* 903.

of harmonisation under international law, will be considered further in Chapter 6. Here, under examination was whether such approaches ought to be regarded as undermining the identification of state practice relating to supervisory jurisdiction in respect of which the conclusion is that consent under ICSID and CAS represent an exception to the otherwise emerging approach.

[G] CONCLUSION

The harmonised approach identified in this chapter relates to supervisory jurisdiction, a form of enforcement available irrespective of the international legal principle of state immunity. This form of jurisdiction encompasses the power of national courts to support the discrete arbitration proceeding as well as the functioning of the arbitral process.

The practical effect is that national courts and arbitral tribunals have the power to grant supervisory relief in respect of arbitral tribunals located outside the jurisdiction or when a state is party irrespective of the international legal principle of state immunity. The principle of state immunity thus ought to be regarded as a *lex specialis* in this context, i.e., not applicable to the availability or exercise of this form of enforcement. The only exception is ICSID and CAS arbitrations, where the consensus is that consent to ICSID and CAS excludes the supervisory jurisdiction of national courts, except in respect of stays. However, it will be argued in the final chapter that the general principle arising, pursuant to the harmonised approach, ought to equally apply to ICSID and CAS Tribunals as well.

Identification of the practice has at least two important practical consequences for jurisdiction in international arbitration:

(1) The first is, wider than the 'seat theory', this approach provides national courts with a principled justification for supervising arbitrations outside the territorial jurisdiction. This might help the arbitration where it is faltering, or where the form of relief (e.g., a freezing order) is only available before a national court (rather than the tribunal itself).
(2) The second is that, considering cases such as *Abaclat*, the rule and/or principle could be used to support as well as restrain the scope of supervisory measures which may be enforced by national courts.[355] This may, in turn, help ensure that the arbitral proceeding is supported in accordance with principles applicable to the arbitral process.
(3) The taking of evidence and securing attendance of witnesses are powers which are not yet universally recognised as falling within the concept of 'supervisory jurisdiction' though there is no reason in principle why these powers should not be exercisable in respect of international arbitrations, being lawful aspects of the court's enforcement powers under international law.

355. *See* Chapter 1[B].

The practice ought to be regarded as a general principle of international law, since it is widespread, consistent and representative in light of harmonising instruments and it accords with an approach to considering adjudicative jurisdiction as a manifestation of enforcement jurisdiction. Since the norms define the *lawful* scope of an international arbitral tribunal's decision-making authority, they are transposable to the international legal level. Chapter 6 cements this approach, exploring alternative methods for harmonising the principles developed in court decisions.

Methodologically, the approach goes beyond examining adjudicative jurisdiction as a mere facet of a state's prescriptive jurisdiction, analysing it as a source, based on widespread, representative and consistent state practice, when taking the UK, US, France and Germany as exemplary. Private international law may manifest itself as the public international law rule relating to supervisory jurisdiction, which has been considered in light of other court approaches and harmonising principles.

CHAPTER 4

Recognition and Review Jurisdiction

Extending the established approach – identifying national court decisions in the public sphere as a source of enforcement jurisdiction – this chapter further demonstrates the utility of such an approach to recognition and review. Crucial to enforcement of the arbitral process, and particularly any award rendered, courts are increasingly reviewing arbitral awards in comparable circumstances including where state parties are involved. This chapter identifies the extent and scope of such a principle, including identifying any differences between the extent of review of the different state courts under examination (the UK, US, France and Germany). In particular, it identifies a broadly comparable approach as to the scope of review power of national courts in respect of the substantive jurisdiction of the arbitral tribunal and considers the impact of the UK Arbitration Act 2025.

[A] DEFINING RECOGNITION AND REVIEW

When an award comes before the courts, the courts may review that award to decide whether to grant the relief that is requested.[356] That relief might be to set aside the award (with the effect of refusal of recognition) or the court may choose to recognise

356. Under Article V New York Convention, which states 'recognition and enforcement may be refused, at the request of the party against whom it is invoked, only if that parties furnishes to the competent authority where recognition and enforcement is sought, proof that ...', *inter alia*, (a) the parties were under some incapacity or the agreement was not valid under the law to which parties subjected it; (b) parties were not given proper notice of the appointment of an arbitrator, and listing other procedural grounds for challenge. There is also a ground for refusal if (as per Article V(2)): (a) the subject matter was not capable of settlement by arbitration under the law of that country (where recognition is sought); or (b) it would be contrary to the public policy of that country.

the award.[357] 'Review' is the power to review whether an award should be recognised considering certain specified grounds in law, or whether recognition should be refused on one of those grounds, and 'recognition' is the power to declare the award enforceable.

Redfern and Hunter have described the recognition and enforcement aspect of the arbitral process as a crucial factor attracting parties to arbitration: 'once this decision [i.e., the binding decision of the arbitral tribunal] has been made in the form of an award, it is an intrinsic element of every arbitration agreement that the parties will carry it out'.[358] Indeed, according to the New York Convention, states have agreed that:

> This Convention shall apply to the recognition and enforcement of arbitral awards made in the territory of a state other than the state where recognition and enforcement of such awards are sought.[359]

Expanding to national court approaches in the public sphere, may *any* national court exercise their recognition and review powers, irrespective of principles of state immunity?[360] If so, is this practice widespread and consistent between those courts? Are review powers shared across courts?

Since the *Achmea* decision, there have been limitations on the ability of courts within the EU to enforce awards based on bilateral investment treaties (BITs). While not detracting from the general principle that courts are able to recognise awards against states irrespective of immunity, these decisions impose further challenges to enforcement of ICSID and Energy Charter Treaty awards within the EU.

[B] IMPLICATIONS FOR THE IDENTIFICATION OF STATE PRACTICE

Prior to the introduction of the 2025 Arbitration Act (UK), UK courts reviewed questions of jurisdiction *de novo*. The approach followed the decision in *Dallah*. In *Dallah*, a UK Court reviewed whether the Government was a 'true party' to the agreement (containing the arbitration clause), which in that case concerned whether applying French law principles applicable to the arbitration procedure, there was a 'common intention' on the part of the parties to make the Government a party.[361] This took place as a full rehearing in the national court of the question of jurisdiction, pursuant to Article V(1)(a), which concerns whether the 'agreement is ... valid under the law to which the parties subjected it'. That power is domestically mirrored by powers available to the court under section 67 EAA which allows an English court to

357. In accordance with Article IV New York Convention, which states that to apply for recognition and enforcement, a party must apply with the duly authenticated original award; and the original agreement referred to in Article II (i.e., the arbitration agreement).
358. Blackaby et al. (n 22) para. 11.01.
359. Article I New York Convention.
360. Where there is no connection between the enforcing court's territorial jurisdiction and the arbitration dispute, or where one party is a foreign state; Chapter 1[E][1].
361. *Dallah* (n 109) [2]. Affirmed in decisions such as *GPF GP S.à.r.l. v. Republic of Poland* [2018] EWHC 409 (Comm) [64]-[65].

determine the issue of the arbitrator's jurisdiction where parties have not submitted to the arbitrator's jurisdiction.[362] In *Dallah*, this power extended to the enforcement of foreign awards because the seat of the arbitration was outside the UK. The decision in *GPF GP S.à.r.l.*[363] confirmed that this power entailed a rehearing, unfettered by the arguments which the parties put forward in the arbitration. However, since the introduction of section 11 Arbitration Act 2025, the approach has shifted again to a more limited review of the tribunal's decision, mirroring the approach by the Court in *Svenska*, to be examined further below.

[C] RECOGNITION JURISDICTION

It is clear from state practice that awards can generally be recognised as enforceable subject to only limited exceptions in the EU. The first part of this section briefly considers the general principle: that awards can be recognised and enforced, irrespective of where they are made, which is harmonised under Article I(1) NYC.

[1] Civil Law Approaches

Practice in the civil law countries examined demonstrates that arbitral awards may be recognised, irrespective of state immunity, subject to only limited exceptions. This practice arises from national court decisions in the public sphere as a source of the enforcement norm, in so far as that practice is representative, widespread and consistent.

(a) Germany

In the *Walter Bau* decision,[364] an award was rendered in the German investor's favour against Thailand under the ICC Rules in 2009. Having obtained an award pursuant to the Thailand-Germany BIT, Walter Bau applied for a declaration of enforceability (*Vollstreckbarerklärung*) against the Republic of Thailand before a German Court.

As Germany is a monist state, international law has been given automatic recognition without any need for any implementing legislation.[365] One source for court jurisdiction is the international legal principle of immunity, enacted in German law under §20(2) Courts Constitution Act (GVG) and §25 German Constitution (GG). §1061 ZPO implements Article I(1) New York Convention awards. The Court found it could

362. *Dallah* (n 109) [27].
363. *Ibid.*
364. *See*, further, Roland Kläger, 'Case Comment: Werner Schneider (Liquidator of Walter Bau AG) v Kingdom of Thailand: Sovereign Immunity in Recognition and Enforcement Proceedings under German Law' (2014) 29(1) ICSID Review 142, 144 https://doi.org/10.1093/icsidreview/sit043 (accessed 26 September 2025) (pointing to the 'significant clarification' which the BGH offered in regard to recognition and enforcement jurisdiction and state immunity); Barbara Genius, 'BGH 3. Zivilsenat, Beschluss vom 30.01.2013 - III ZB 40/12' - jurisPR-BGHZivilR 9/2013 Anm. 3.
365. Aust (n 166) 187.

exercise its jurisdiction, under §1061 ZPO, irrespective of the international legal principle of immunity. This is because it granted the declaration of enforceability pursuant to that power, with the *international* principle of state immunity from which jurisdiction derived not limiting that authority.

Part of the Court's reasoning rested on the distinction between a *Zwangsvollstreckung* (compulsory enforcement, or execution proceeding) and *Erkenntnisverfahren* (recognition proceeding, which results in the *Vollstreckbarerklärung* or declaration of enforceability).[366] The Court acknowledged that immunity does not apply to the *Erkenntnisverfahren* provided that the foreign state's capacity to act is not infringed.[367] Concerning a *Zwangsvollstreckung*, immunity would still generally apply where assets are held for sovereign purposes because state immunity would be infringed by that jurisdiction. However, an *Erkenntnisverfahren* would not infringe the foreign state's capacity to act. One source for the Court's jurisdiction was the BIT, according to which the parties consented to arbitrate.[368] However, another was the principle of review and recognition found in §1061, according to which the Court merely has the power to *declare* the award enforceable rather than to compel parties to do anything.

The decision acknowledged immunity would not be engaged by the jurisdiction. Both the decision in the public sphere as well as the reasoning of the Court (that immunity is not excluded by the jurisdiction as a matter of principle) ought to be regarded as evidence of the rule or principle.[369]

(b) *France*

Similarly, in *État du Sénégal*, the State of Senegal appealed against an order issued by the President of the Tribunal de Grande Instance of Paris for exequatur of an ICSID arbitration award ordering it to pay sums to the West African Industrial Concrete Company (Société S.O.A.B.I.), for damages suffered by it as a result of the unilateral termination of the contracts concluded between them.[370] The Court found that its jurisdiction to declare the award enforceable was an extension of the binding nature of the award under Article 54 ICSID.[371] Article 54 provides that contracting states shall 'recognize an award rendered pursuant to this Convention as binding and enforce the pecuniary obligations imposed by that award within its territories as if it were a final judgment of a court in that state'. By contrast to supervisory jurisdiction, generally

366. Walter Bau 1 (n 20) [8].
367. *Ibid.*, [10]-[11].
368. *Ibid.*, [12].
369. Similarly: Court of Appeal of Düsseldorf, Decision of 15 December 2009, I-4 Sch 10/09 (declaration of enforceability obtained in respect of an AAA award, despite no connection to the jurisdiction); BGH, Decision of 17 April 2008 – III ZB 97/06 – juris (reviewing an award rendered in Denmark; New York Convention is not the source of the jurisdiction but enshrines principles in light of which jurisdiction is exercised).
370. *État du Sénégal v. Seutin, es-qual de liquidateur de la société S.O.A.B.I*, Cour d'appel de Paris (1Ch. Suppl.), 5 December 1989.
371. This is in line with the obligation to ensure performance of pecuniary obligations under the award in its territory, as provided in Article 54 ICSID.

excluded by the ICSID,[372] Article 54 ICSID seems to import a clear obligation on national courts to declare arbitral awards enforceable. It is hard to see what else could be meant by the clear wording of Article 54.[373]

However, further widespread and consistent decisions in the public sphere show that this practice is not confined to ICSID arbitrations - nor therefore to a justification based on Article 54 ICSID alone.[374] Thus, while decisions may consider whether a power is available in light of provisions in Conventions such as ICSID, the source of the power, this book argues, is the power of the court to decide. Representative national courts render decisions in the public sphere, irrespective of state immunity, both in respect of ICSID and non-ICSID arbitrations.

[2] Common Law Approaches

Common law approaches create a similarly clear principle: arbitration awards should be recognised as enforceable provided they are not effectively set aside or otherwise rendered invalid, and state immunity does not affect the existence nor exercise of that power.

In *LR Avionics*,[375] a UK Court rendered a decision in the public sphere to recognise an award against the Republic of Nigeria.[376] State-owned premises had been leased for handling consular activities, including handling passport and visa applications. The question was whether those premises could be interpreted as being 'in use for commercial purposes' within the meaning of section 13(4) SIA, such that execution could be granted. The Court acknowledged that at least in so far as *declaring* the award enforceable was concerned - the step taken prior to execution - this had been granted, even though the award was rendered in Nigeria.[377]

One source was that a recognition proceeding is one which 'relates to the arbitration' within the meaning of section 9 SIA. Where a state has agreed in writing to submit disputes to arbitration, the state is not immune 'as respects proceedings in the courts of the United Kingdom which relate to the arbitration'.[378] The Court did not consider that Nigeria's consent to arbitrate resulted in a waiver and this was constitutive of the Court's jurisdiction. However, it did acknowledge that Nigeria had agreed to arbitrate. Considering that, the Court asked whether its enforcement proceedings are

372. Chapter 3[F][4].
373. This is also the perspective of the Schreuer ICSID Commentary (n 226) para. 1.04.
374. *See, e.g.*, CA Paris, 10 April 2018, *Société Alstom Transport SA et autre v. Société Alexander Brothers Ltd*, no RG 16/11182 (French Court of Appeal affirmed that French courts may appeal orders for the recognition and enforcement of foreign arbitration awards on the basis that such an order would breach international public policy); Cour de Cassation, 28 February 2018, *République démocratique du Congo v. Société FG Hemisphere Associates LLC*, 28 February 2018, Pourvoi No. 16-22.112 (exequatur is available in respect of a foreign state).
375. *LR Avionics* (n 107) [20]-[23]; similarly: *NML Capital Ltd* (2011) (n 109) [89]; *Dallah* (n 109); *Svenska* (2006) (n 20).
376. *LR Avionics* (n 107). Even though execution was not ultimately granted as said assets were held for consular purposes as thus excluded under section 13(4), the award was at least *declared* enforceable.
377. *LR Avionics* (n 107) [3].
378. Section 9(1) SIA.

proceedings 'which relate to the arbitration' within the meaning of section 9(1) SIA.[379] The Court found that they did constitute such proceedings. Thus, the Court exercised jurisdiction in the public sphere to grant the recognition order because it did not regard itself as prohibited from doing so by the principle of state immunity. This was partly on the basis of previous court precedent, according to which a court's power to declare an award enforceable (reflected in section 101 EAA) was found to fall within section 9 SIA.[380]

This decision is important for two reasons. First, it is representative of a general UK (and US approach under the equivalent provision, found in §1605(a)(6) FSIA) in the public sphere according to which awards may be declared enforceable by the court, irrespective of any link between the court's territorial jurisdiction and the dispute, or where a state is party.[381] The exercise of jurisdiction in the public sphere is itself evidence of the rule or principle. Second, the decision demonstrates, as a matter of reasoning, that UK and US courts generally accept that declaratory relief does not engage the principle of immunity. This is on the basis that they find that jurisdiction to decide falls within section 9 SIA or §1605(a)(6) FSIA, respectively, in the case of the US. Consequently, both for what the courts do – through exercises of jurisdiction in the public sphere – as well as the decisions for what they state (that immunity does not apply to this form of jurisdiction), UK and US practice consistently demonstrates that the power to declare an award enforceable is generally available irrespective of any immunity.

[3] EU

Considering the decisions in *Slovakia v. Achmea BV*[382] and *Micula v. Romania*,[383] the extent to which an EU Member State Court can enforce, i.e., recognise, an award rendered under a BIT has been called into question. Despite the otherwise harmonised approach demonstrated in this chapter, the decisions in *Achmea, Micula* and *Komstroy* suggest that the general principle would currently not apply to awards rendered under

379. *LR Avionics* (n 107) [21].
380. *Ibid.*; citing *Svenska* (2006) (n 20).
381. *Svenska* (2006) (n 20) (recognition of ICC award against Lithuania in UK because leave to enforce under section 101 EAA available and not excluded by principles of immunity); *Dallah* (n 109) (UK Court exercised jurisdiction to review the validity of an ICC award against the Government of Pakistan, thus deciding on this matter despite no connection to the jurisdiction); *NML Capital Ltd* (2011) (n 109) [29]; similarly (US): *Stati v. Republic of Kazakhstan*, 199 F. Supp. 3d 179 (D.D.C. 2016) (recognition of Stockholm Centre for Commerce award under Energy Charter Treaty by US Court pursuant to an implied waiver of immunity based on a similar arbitration exception, section 1605(a)(6) FSIA. The wording and effect of section 1605(a)(6) is similar to section 9 SIA mentioned above: it provides for jurisdiction of the US court where an action is brought to 'enforce an [arbitration] agreement' in the United States); *PAO Tatneft* (2018) (n 198) (similarly, consideration of whether PCA award could be recognised by US Court against Ukraine. By considering this question in the public sphere, and irrespective of immunity, this decision should be regarded as part of the rule).
382. Judgment of the Court (Grand Chamber) of 6 March 2018, Request for a Preliminary Ruling from the Bundesgerichtshof, *Slovakia v. Achmea BV* (C-284/16, ECLI:EU:C:2018:158).
383. *Micula v. Romania* [2020] UKSC 5.

intra-BITs within the EU. However, this should not detract from the approach which holds that recognition is a lawful form of enforcement jurisdiction under international law, but should merely, it will be argued, restrict the practical enforcement of certain types of awards within the EU. An exception may arise where the intra-EU BIT is enforced in a non-EU country, for example, because one of the parties' assets are in a non-EU country. In that situation, the *Achmea* decision would not bind the enforcing court as it is not within the EU.

(a) Non-ICSID Investor-State Disputes

In *Achmea*, a German Court requested the Court of Justice of the European Union (CJEU) to give a ruling on the compatibility of a BIT between the Netherlands and Slovakia with EU law. Under Article 8 of the BIT, an investor from one Member State can bring proceedings against another Member State based on the arbitration agreement contained in the BIT.

First, the preliminary ruling concerned whether Article 344 TFEU, which provides that 'Member states undertake not to submit a dispute concerning the interpretation or application of the Treaties to any method of settlement other than those provided for therein', precluded the application of an arbitration agreement in *any* BIT. Second, would Article 267 TFEU also preclude the use of an arbitration agreement in an intra-EU BIT. According to Article 267 TFEU, a 'court or tribunal' ensures the uniform application and interpretation of EU law by being able to ask the CJEU to make preliminary rulings. According to this second argument, if an 'arbitral tribunal' is not a 'court or tribunal' within the meaning of Article 267 TFEU, it would not be able to bind to interpret EU law consistently and in a uniform way and thus might escape the scrutiny which an EU court or tribunal would ordinarily give to the proper application of EU law.

Taking both questions together, the CJEU found that by application of both Articles 267 and 344 TFEU, arbitration agreements in BITs are precluded under EU law for being inconsistent with EU law. This was for two reasons:

(1) First, Article 267 TFEU ensures the 'uniform application' of EU law in accordance with the autonomy of the EU legal order, and the preliminary ruling procedure is a 'cornerstone' of that procedure. The fact that an arbitral tribunal is not a 'court or tribunal'[384] within the meaning of Article 267 TFEU and cannot make such a ruling inhibits that principle, and thus, the arbitration agreement in BITs is also contrary to Article 267 TFEU.
(2) Second, in light of the first point, under Article 344 TFEU, an international agreement 'cannot affect the allocation of powers fixed by Treaties, or ... the autonomy of the EU legal system'.[385] If arbitral tribunals, agreed upon by the Member States rather than the EU, are able to rule on questions that would

384. *Slovakia v. Achmea BV* (n 382) [49].
385. *Ibid.*, [32].

otherwise exclusively fall within the jurisdiction of EU court, then the agreement to arbitrate within the relevant BIT (here Article 8) would have an adverse effect on the autonomy of EU law.[386] Thus, Article 344 TFEU would also preclude an arbitration agreement within a BIT between Member States.

This principle that arbitration agreements concluded in BITs are prohibited by EU law was extended to awards rendered under the Energy Charter Treaty (ECT) by the CJEU in the *Moldova v. Komstroy* decision, with a preliminary reference being made by the Paris Court of Appeal in relation to the scope of 'investment' under the ECT.[387] The parties were a Ukrainian investor and Moldova, with the seat of arbitration in Paris. The CJEU, finding it had jurisdiction to interpret the ECT, found that since arbitral tribunals could not refer questions of EU law to the CJEU and domestic courts, then the autonomy of EU law would be threatened as much by the inability of the CJEU to recognise and review arbitral awards rendered under the ECT as under intra-EU BITs. It therefore appears that the recognition and review principle herein demonstrated would also not apply to awards rendered under the ECT where enforcement is sought in an EU country, in addition to its demonstrated inapplicability to intra-EU BITs after *Achmea*.

As a result of the *Achmea* and *Komstroy* decisions, it appears clear that since arbitral tribunals constituted pursuant to intra-EU BITs and under the ECT are prohibited under EU law, then these awards are not enforceable in EU courts. To date, French courts have followed this approach and annulled a number of intra-BIT awards on the basis that the arbitral tribunal did not have jurisdiction due to the applicability of *Achmea* to the awards.[388] However, it remains to be seen whether French and German courts will universally refuse to recognise awards rendered under intra-EU BITs and the ECT, though it does appear that from these decisions, they would be bound under EU law to do so.

Though this practice within the EU restricts enforcement of certain types of awards within the EU, it does not speak to the representativeness of practice in this work. The question of whether recognising an award is compatible with EU law is separate and distinct from the question of whether recognition is a lawful form of enforcement jurisdiction, more generally under international law, irrespective of immunity.

386. *Ibid.*, [57]-[59].
387. Judgment of the Court (Grand Chamber) of 2 September 2021, *République de Moldavie v. Komstroy LLC* (2 September 2021).
388. For example, annulment of two intra-BIT awards rendered against Poland: Paris Court of Appeal (Chamber 5-16), 19 April 2022, No. 20-13085 (Strabag and Raiffeisen Centrobank); Paris Court of Appeal (Chamber 5-16), 19 April 2022, No. 20-14581 (CEC Praha and Slot Group).

(b) Micula v. Romania: *National Courts' Backlash*

The picture in relation to ICSID awards is somewhat different considering the decision in *Micula v. Romania*.[389] The decision suggests that parties and national courts may be able to find ways of ensuring that despite the dicta in *Achmea*, investor-state awards are enforceable. Micula and others commenced ICSID proceedings against Romania under the Sweden-Romania BIT. An award was rendered against Romania and registered in the UK. The UK High Court granted an application by Romania to stay enforcement of the award pending resolution of proceedings in the CJEU. The question before the CJEU concerned whether implementation of the award by Romania would amount to illegal state aid.

Finding that the stay could be lifted to the effect that Micula and others could enforce the ICSID award in the UK, the Supreme Court held that the UK's obligations to enforce ICSID awards were duties which the UK had assumed to third state prior to its accession to the EU and accordingly were unaffected by the EU law duty of sincere cooperation (except in so far as review jurisdiction is concerned, which shall be considered further below).[390] The type of 'stay' under consideration was not of court proceedings but rather a stay of the enforcement of the award pending determination of an annulment decision before the General Court of the European Union (GCEU). The decision to lift the stay and enable enforcement was based on Article 351 TFEU, which provides that 'the rights and obligations arising from agreement concluded before 1 January 1958 ... shall not be affected by the provisions of the Treaties'.[391] The basis for enforcing the award was the Arbitration (International Investment Disputes) Act 1966, which gives effect to the principle that awards are to be recognised as final judgments of the court. Under the relevant provision in the ICSID Convention, Article 54(1):

> [86]: English courts are obliged ... to give effect to the Award in favour of the Claimants ... Leaving the Treaties out of the analysis, if the Award were a final judgment of an English court it would be enforced without question ... .

Article 351 TFEU means that obligation cannot be affected by anything in the Treaties.

That extended in *Infrastructure Services Luxembourg S.A.R.L* to a dispute being decided by an ICSID Tribunal under the Energy Charter Treaty, meaning that Spain could not set aside the jurisdictional Order on the basis of state immunity.[392] That was not only because of the disapplication of EU law based on consent to ICSID but also because the 1966 Act implements the ICSID Convention, whereby an award is to be recognised and enforced as a final judgment once the tribunal has determined its jurisdiction. The UK must give effect to those obligations, which it has laid down in

389. *Micula* (n 383).
390. That duty is found in Article 4(3) Treaty on European Union and the Treaty on the Functioning of the European Union 2012/C 326/01 (TEU).
391. *Micula* (n 383) [86].
392. *Infrastructure Services v. Kingdom of Spain* (n 257).

national law, which would be 'routinely undermined' if Spain, or any other state, could put forward the lengthy arguments it did.[393]

Consequently, it appears that the enforcement of ICSID awards remains supported within the UK courts, even prior to any uncoupling of the UK from EU legal provisions post-Brexit. Similar arguments could be put forward within the EU context as to the enforceability of such awards, except that it may be that EU law is regarded as having primacy over other conflicting international legal obligations, such as accession to the ICSID Convention (although the question is yet to be decided by an EU court). Until any such argument takes place, it is better to assume that in light of *Achmea*, arbitration agreements within intra-EU BITs and under the Energy Charter Treaty remain unenforceable before EU courts, which would also preclude their recognition.

[4] Conclusions Relating to Recognition

As a result of the foregoing, there is a general power to recognise arbitration awards against states irrespective of the principle of state immunity. However, exceptions arise based on EU law following the decision in *Achmea* where those awards are rendered under intra-EU BITs or the Energy Charter Treaty and enforcement is sought in an EU country. It remains to be seen whether the principle would also extend to ICSID awards within the EU, especially considering *Micula*, where UK courts have indicated they would enforce ICSID awards notwithstanding *Achmea*.

These decisions do not detract from the general principle that recognition jurisdiction ought to be a *lawful* form of enforcement in respect of states as a general principle of international law irrespective of state immunity. Even if the practical reality in light of *Achmea* is that those awards are unenforceable at the present time, the reason is not because recognition is excluded or limited by the principle of state immunity, which, as explained, is the main limitation under international law on the scope of enforcement jurisdiction.

[D] REVIEW JURISDICTION

There are procedural grounds for reviewing an arbitration award, including that the arbitral tribunal dealt with the matter referred to it by the parties under the arbitration agreement (Article V(1)(c) NYC); that the arbitral tribunal was not properly constituted in accordance with the parties' agreement (Article V(1)(d) NYC); and that the award has not yet become binding upon parties or has been set aside by a competent authority (Article V(1)(e) NYC). This part instead focuses on the powers of review of the tribunal's jurisdiction under the applicable law pursuant to Article V(1)(a) and where a party claims the award is not binding under the law where it was made (Article V(1)(e)), which might be regarded as more substantive areas, and the extent of harmonisation in those areas. Although there may be broader approaches in the UK and US as regards review of the award itself (such as under section 69 EAA), these shall

393. *Ibid.*, [161].

be excluded for the purposes of comparison under this section, which focuses rather on review of the substantive jurisdiction of the arbitral tribunal.

[1] Harmonised Approach to Review of Substantive Jurisdiction

The decision in *Svenska* is illustrative of one approach of the common law courts. The dispute concerned the exploitation of oil reserves by Svenska, a Swedish company, in the Republic of Lithuania. An ICC award was rendered in favour of Svenska in Denmark. Lithuania then challenged recognition of an ICC award on the basis that it was not a party to the arbitration agreement according to principles of the applicable law (Lithuanian law).[394] The Court recognised that the underlying transaction in the arbitration may have concerned an exercise of sovereign authority because it related to the exploitation of oil reserves within the territory of the state.[395] However, the question of whether the tribunal had jurisdiction arose as a separate question from the question of state immunity. In this regard, the Court stated:

> although we agree with the arbitrators' conclusion, we do not agree with their reasons for reaching it. However, that does not matter. If they had jurisdiction to decide whether the Government had submitted to arbitration, as we are satisfied they did, the award is binding for what it decides, right or wrong. The arbitrators, of course, did not have to decide whether the Government had agreed in writing to refer the dispute to arbitration within the meaning of Sect. 9 of the State Immunity Act, but they did have to decide whether, and if so how, the Government was bound by an agreement to arbitrate. They held that it was a party to the Agreement and in our view the Government cannot go behind that decision.[396]

According to this approach, the UK courts have accepted that once an award becomes binding, the question of state immunity would become a question for the national court to decide. At the same time, the Court seemed to state that the boundaries of this power related to reviewing whether the arbitral tribunal *could* have decided its jurisdiction the way it did (within the scope of the applicable law), and not the question of whether this decision is 'right or wrong', which included whether the tribunal's 'reasons' were right or wrong. Thus, the Court in *Svenska* appeared to subscribe to a more limited standard of review, which excluded a review of the arbitrators' justification or reasons for its exercise of jurisdiction.

The concept of a 'review' rather than a 'rehearing', which was supported by a handful of UK courts prior to *Dallah*, was said to rest on the question of whether the arbitrators reached the correct result, and not whether they were entitled to reach the decision they did.[397] *Svenska* appears to confuse the matter further: the endorsement of a review of the arbitral tribunal's 'conclusion' rather than 'reasons' seems to support

394. *Svenska* (2006) (n 20).
395. *Ibid.*, [133].
396. *Ibid.*, [116].
397. Robert Merkin and Louis Flannery, *Merkin and Flannery on the Arbitration Act 1996* (6th edn, Routledge) 685. *See, e.g.*, *Ranko Group v. Antarctic Maritime SA, The Robin* [1998] ADRLN 35, Toulson J; *Tajik Alumnium Plant v. Hydro Alumnimum AS* [2006] EWHC 1135 (Comm) [28] (while more UK courts supported the *Dallah* 'rehearing' approach even prior to *Dallah*).

an even more restrictive form of review: review rather than a rehearing is permitted, and only as regards the conclusions reached by the tribunal.

However, after *Dallah*, it was clear that UK courts were entitled to go further than the approach in *Svenska* and conduct a *de novo* rehearing: this would clearly entitle the court to conduct a rehearing of all matters of fact and law related to the substantive jurisdiction of the tribunal, that being the question of whether the tribunal was entitled to reach the decision it did.

As set out below, this appears to have changed again following the introduction of the Arbitration Act 2025. With the introduction of section 11 Arbitration Act 2025, the approach is now to not conduct a 'rehearing' but rather a review of the tribunal's decision, peddling back to an approach which is nearer to that opined by the Court in *Svenska* (though perhaps is better described in its own terms based on the wording of the Act), or at least those courts prior to *Dallah* which appeared to endorse a more limited review of whether the tribunal reached the correct decision.

(a) Review of Substantive Jurisdiction

From a UK perspective, prior to the introduction of the Arbitration Act 2025, the question of whether, and if so, to what extent a court may review a tribunal's substantive jurisdiction was determined by the decision of *Dallah.*[398] A UK Court reviewed whether an ICC award should not be enforced because it was not valid under the law to which parties submitted their substantive dispute; the Court utilised section 103(2)(b) EAA which is stated to reflect Article V(1)(a) New York Convention, as part of its reasoning.[399] This provides that recognition can be refused whether a party was 'under some incapacity' under the law applicable to it. According to the Court in *Dallah*, 'the starting point in this case must be an *independent investigation* by the court of the question whether the person challenging the enforcement of the award can prove that he was not a party to the arbitration agreement under which the award was made'.[400]

In *Dallah*, which concerned the review of an ICC award, the Court considered whether the arbitral tribunal had jurisdiction under applicable principles of French law and thus whether the arbitration agreement was valid under French law. Rejecting Dallah's argument that there should be a notion of 'deference' to the tribunal's decision, the Court made some important findings in relation to the broad scope of its review powers:

(1) There is no basis for departing from the plain language of Article V(1)(a) as incorporated by section 103(2)(b) (permitting the court to review whether the arbitration agreement was valid under the law to which parties subjected it).
(2) Article V safeguards fundamental rights, including the right of a party which has not agreed to arbitration to object to the jurisdiction of the tribunal.

398. *Dallah* (n 109).
399. *Ibid.*, [1].
400. *Ibid.*, [115].

(3) There is not anything to support Dallah's theory that the New York Convention accords primacy to the courts of the arbitral seat 'in the sense that the supervisory court should be the only court entitled to carry out a re-hearing of the issue of the existence of a valid arbitration agreement and that the exclusivity of the supervisory court in this regard ensures uniformity of application of the Convention'.[401]

The Court in *Dallah* consequently concluded that 'the English court is entitled (and indeed bound) to revisit the question of the tribunal's decision on jurisdiction if the party resisting enforcement seeks to prove that there was no arbitration agreement binding upon it under the law of the country where the award was made'.[402] This wording seemed to thus encompass the review ground for validity of the arbitration agreement (Article V(1)(a)) as well as whether the award has become binding pursuant to Article V(1)(e).

However, following the introduction of section 11 Arbitration Act 2025, a rehearing of new evidence and new grounds is expressly prohibited, and any challenge to jurisdiction will be by way of a review (rather than a rehearing). The provision states as follows, which is inserted in section 67 EAA after subsection 3A:

> (3B) Rules of court about the procedure to be followed on an application under this section may, in particular, include provision within subsection (3C) in relation to a case where the application –
> (a) relates to an objection as to the arbitral tribunal's substantive jurisdiction on which the tribunal has already ruled, and
> (b) is made by a party that took part in the arbitral proceedings.
> (3C) Provision is within this subsection if it provides that subject to the court ruling otherwise in the interests of justice –
> (a) a ground for the objection that was not raised before the arbitral tribunal must not be raised before the court unless the applicant shows that, at the time the applicant took part in the proceedings, the applicant did not know and could not with reasonable diligence have discovered the ground;
> (b) evidence that was not put before the tribunal must not be considered by the court unless the applicant shows that, at the time the applicant took part in the proceedings, the applicant could not with reasonable diligence have put the evidence before the tribunal;
> (c) evidence that was heard by the tribunal must not be re-heard by the court.

According to the new section 67(3B) 1996 Act, generally a jurisdictional challenge should be made on a ground upon which the tribunal has already ruled and the applicant has participated in the proceedings and new procedural rules to be adopted by courts should include such a provision. New questions of jurisdiction which were not considered by the tribunal cannot be considered and new evidence can similarly not be introduced. The exception, as set out in the new section 67(3C), will be where

401. *Ibid.*, [101]-[103].
402. *Ibid.* This included, for example, questions of interpretation which were not invoked during arbitral proceedings; *see, e.g., GPF GP S.à.r.l* (n 361) [125] (questions concerning interpretation of the Treaty were considered for the first time, leading to the conclusion that the determination that the Tribunal lacked jurisdiction was erroneous).

any new grounds of objection must be heard because it is in the interests of justice or if those could not have been put before a tribunal if the applicant had exercised reasonable diligence. Even in that situation, evidence will not be reheard.

Consequently, the approach has peddled back on *Dallah*. If one reads the language in *Svenska* – that the court will not review the award as to whether it was 'right or wrong' as refusing a wider question of a *merits*-based review – it would appear that the new approach under section 67 is more in-keeping with that approach. However, the language used in *Svenska* is also slightly misleading. This is because the wording of the Court, that whether the tribunal's decision was 'right or wrong' 'does not matter' could suggest that the Court is prohibited from reviewing the tribunal's reasons for reaching its decision on jurisdiction. However, if the court were, upon its review under section 67, to find that the tribunal did decide its jurisdiction correctly or incorrectly under the law applicable to the question of jurisdiction, this would necessarily include considering the tribunal's reasoning. In this regard, the words of the Court in *Svenska* are somewhat unhelpful in that they do not clarify the scope of review power of the court, suggesting that the Court's review power may be excluded entirely as the award is 'binding', which is clearly not the case under section 67. Instead, and as suggested, *Svenska* is best understood as limiting a merits-based review, but not limiting the power of courts to review the tribunal's jurisdiction decision as to whether it is wrong in law, which should include an assessment of whether its reasoning materially affected the question of law.

It will now be open to UK courts to define the level of deference which they give to arbitrators' decisions on jurisdiction, presumably within the procedural rules which they will adopt in accordance with section 67(3B) 1996 Act, as introduced by section 11 Arbitration Act 2025 or according to case law. It remains to be seen whether the court adopts an approach closer to *Dallah* (albeit not a full rehearing), in that it could review factual findings of the tribunal on jurisdiction, at least to some extent, or whether the courts will fully limit their approach to one which examines only whether the decision was wrong as a question of law (including the tribunal's reasoning) and therefore stays closer to the approach in *Svenska*. On balance, it appears that it would be within the court's power under section 67 to consider the tribunal's reasoning to the extent that this materially affected its decision on jurisdiction, but the circumstances in which new factual challenges, i.e., questions which were not before the arbitral tribunal when it decided on its jurisdiction, can be raised is limited under section 67(3C).

(b) France

The French approach had previously been more restrictive than the UK approach in that it has enabled the courts to review whether the tribunal had jurisdiction considering 'all aspects of the law and facts' though it is doubtful that this extends to a *de novo* review, except where 'international public policy' is concerned.

The basis for French review jurisdiction has varied. One legal ground was confirmed by the Paris Court of Appeal in *Kout Food Group v. Kabab-Ji*[403] as being the Dalico doctrine, according to which: (i) an international arbitration agreement is normally not governed by any national law but by a French 'material rule' (règle matérielle); and (ii) the issue of whether a party is bound by an arbitration clause has to be solved by a factual enquiry; that is, the court must assess whether the parties intended (la commune volonté des parties) to arbitrate the dispute.[404] This has enabled French courts to review arbitration awards, including by making factual enquiries, including those where the seat of the arbitration is outside of the territorial jurisdiction.

The decision in the *Arab Republic,* which has already been discussed in relation to the French approach to supervisory jurisdiction, demonstrates an approach enabling review on a question of law from the French perspective. The French Cour de Cassation held that the Court of Appeal had been entitled under Articles 1502 and 1504 *'de rechercher en droit et en fait tous les elements concernant les vices en question'* (to examine in law and in fact all the elements relevant to the alleged defects).[405] The Court of Appeal had been asked to consider whether the arbitrators had exceeded their jurisdiction. As set out in Chapter 3, the reasoning of that decision illustrates the rule or principle relating to supervisory jurisdiction since it concerned whether or not an award could be set aside, and thus whether to uphold the terms of the arbitration agreement. The reasoning may also be regarded as a source of the norm on review: its effect was to set aside or refuse to set aside the award *on the basis* of review of the tribunal's substantive jurisdiction. Such review had the legal effect of either supporting recognition of the award at the declaratory stage or refusing to declare it enforceable.[406]

Some French courts have indicated that the scope of that review is limited, as it is not for them to re-examine the merits of a contractual dispute decided by the arbitrators. In *Green Network v. Alpiq,* the Court found it could only examine the legal and factual reasons according to which the ground may be made out, but not the

403. Paris Court of Appeal, 23 June 2020, No. 17/22943.
404. Court of Cassation, First Civil Chamber, 20 December 1993, No. 91-16.828.
405. *Arab Republic* (n 217) p. 470.
406. Similarly, and further (in France): CA Paris, *République bolivarienne du Venezuela v. Société Rusoro Mining Ltd,* No. Y 19-11.551 (29 January 2019) (setting aside proceedings, *by their nature,* concern are a 'control' of the arbitral decision ('*contrôle*') which concerns the question of whether the arbitral tribunal 'could' have declared itself competent, by considering all the elements of law and facts which must be appreciated to determine whether the arbitrator could act in such circumstances. Translated from the French: 'Le juge de l'annulation contrôle la décision du tribunal arbitral sur sa compétence, qu'il se soit déclaré compétent ou incompétent, en recherchant tous les éléments de droit ou de fait permettant d'apprécier la portée de la convention d'arbitrage et d'en déduire les conséquences sur le respect de la mission confiée aux arbitres'. Thus, this decision concerned review of whether the tribunal could have had jurisdiction on the basis of the agreement between Venezuela and Canada, including a review of the facts and how this was applied by the arbitral tribunal); CA Paris, 29 November 2016, *État d'Ukraine v. Société Pao Tatneft* (even though the arbitration was seated in Paris, the jurisdiction was exercised in the public sphere as it was in respect of a foreign state, and the review included whether the Tribunal had been competent on the basis of the applicable law (Article 1520(1) CPC) which included questions as to the substantive jurisdiction of the Tribunal and whether it was competent to exercise jurisdiction on the basis of Russian-Ukrainian consent).

reasons for the decision itself.[407] This jurisdiction is called 'fullness of jurisdiction' (*plenitude de jurisdiction*). This has sometimes been criticised as entailing a full review of the merits of the award. However, the French Court in *Green Network v. Alpiq* confirmed that such review does not include the reasons for the arbitral tribunal's decision but merely review of whether any factual or legal element already established in evidence during the arbitration may amount to any alleged breach.

In the area of international public policy (though such review formally takes place under Article V(2)(b) New York Convention), French courts have been clearer that *de novo* review is permitted. In *Belokon v. Kyrgyzstan,* the French Court annulled an award where it found, contrary to the tribunal's findings, that an investor had acquired the Kyrgyz bank for the purpose of money laundering and therefore could not profit from those laundered proceeds and that would violate public policy.[408] However, there is a varied practice in the area of international public policy; the decision in *Green Network v. Alpiq* concerned a question of international public policy, and *de novo* review was expressly *not* permitted. Thus, French courts have variable approaches to the question of scope of review.

In light of disputes such as the recent *The Federal Republic of Nigeria v. Process & Industrial Developments*[409] decision in the UK, it ought to be considered whether *de novo* review should happen as a matter of course where public policy is concerned. The *P&ID* decision has given rise to a whole host of problems concerning the scope of review power which a court should have in relation to allegations of fraud, especially in circumstances where the arbitral tribunal may not have uncovered the fraud.[410] In areas such as fraud, it may be that national courts, being *public* fora which have historically dealt with these issues and have the mechanisms to do so (including disclosure and securing attendance of witnesses), would be best placed to conduct a *de novo* review in these cases in any event. Consequently, the broader approach by some French courts and at least formerly by UK courts, at least with regard to enabling *de novo* review on public policy and international public policy questions, should be welcomed. It allows an additional 'check' on the arbitral tribunal at the recognition stage, which is more substantive than simply reviewing whether the tribunal *prima facie* acted in accordance with the agreement to which the parties subjected it.

(c) ***US***

Under Article V(1)(a), the standard of review has been said to be 'deferential' to the arbitral tribunal's decision. In an earlier decision by the District Court in the same

407. *See*, recently *Green Network v. Alpiq*, Judgment of the French Cour de Cassation (First Civil Chamber) 21-20.140 (18 September 2024) [9].
408. Court of Cassation, 23 March 2022, No. 17-17.981.
409. *The Federal Republic of Nigeria v. Process & Industrial Developments* [2020] EWHC 2379 (Comm).
410. My article on the *Nigeria v. P&ID* case considers this issue: Satya Mouland, *Corruption, Nigeria v. P&ID and the Laws of Evidence: How Should International Arbitration Respond?* (Practical Law 2023).

Government of Belize case,[411] the Court considered that the standard of review under Article V(1)(a) would be similarly 'deferential' as compared with reviewing a question of arbitrability under Article V(1)(c). Considering the case in *Chevron Corp v. Republic of Ecuador,*[412] the Court referred to the deferential standard which was used there under Article V(1)(c) finding that in any dispute where a Respondent argues that the award was 'beyond the arbitrator's power' such 'merits inquiry will *always* occur'.[413] However, that is always in light of a deferential standard of review. The District Court in the *Government of Belize* decision stated that there was a 'lack of authority' for the proposition that 'the court must conduct an independent, *de novo* determination of the arbitrability of a dispute to satisfy the FSIA's arbitration exception', citing the *Chevron* case as authority for that proposition. This approach affords some degree of deference to the arbitral tribunal's reasoning, which may be regarded as similar to the approach expressed in *Svenska,* since the court must accept, to some extent, the 'binding' nature of the award but still may review the reasons of the tribunal in certain situations.[414] Indeed, US courts have recognised that such limited review is consistent with 'the basic purposes of arbitration: to resolve disputes speedily and to avoid the expense and delay of extended court proceedings'.[415]

However, this approach appears to be slightly more nuanced and dependent on the degree of reasoning of the tribunal. The exact meaning of 'deferential review' has been given some consideration; in the *Chevron Corp v. Republic of Ecuador,*[416] a US District Court stated that though there is no precise standard, it seems to be unnecessary to establish the exact level of deference though where the 'tribunal's decision appears to be well reasoned and comprehensive' and 'in no way erroneous', this would justify upholding its decision on jurisdiction.[417] Thus, as per *Chevron,* where a tribunal's decision is 'highly reasoned', then the court's review of the decision should be 'highly deferential', being a standard where, as in that case, the 'reasoned decision' is satisfied. However, that standard was again applied in the arbitrability context under Article V(1)(c) and not to the scope of an Article V(1)(e) review.

A decision outside the public sphere context suggests that such a 'deferential' approach to the arbitrator's jurisdiction would likely be the approach under Article V(1)(a). In *Commodities & Minerals Enterprise Ltd v. CYG Ferrominera Orinoco,* the Court of Appeals stated that a proceeding to confirm an arbitral award is a 'summary proceeding' as a result of which review of awards is 'very limited ... in order to avoid undermining the twin goals of arbitration, namely, settling disputes efficiently and

411. *Belize Social Development Limited v. Government of Belize,* 5 F.Supp.3d 25 (United States District Court, District of Columbia 2013).
412. *Chevron Corp v. Republic of Ecuador* 949 F. Supp. 2d 57 (United States District Court, District of Columbia, 2013).
413. *Ibid.,* at 68.
414. *Svenska* (2006) (n 20) [116].
415. *Chevron Corp* (2013) (n 412) at 68, citing *Fed. Commerce & Nav. Co. v. Kanematsu-Gosho, Ltd.,* 457 F.2d 387, 389 (2d Cir. 1972); *Rich v. Spartis,* 516 F.3d 75, 81 (2d Cir. 2008).
416. *Chevron Corp* (2013) (n 412).
417. *Ibid.,* [12].

avoiding long and expensive litigation'.[418] However, again, when reviewing Ferrominera's arguments under Venezuelan law as to whether there was a valid arbitration agreement, the Court found that no arguments had been made, and thus, the defence failed.

In relation to public policy and international public policy, the US courts accept that *de novo* review of the tribunal's jurisdiction would generally be prohibited.[419] In the *Gold Reserve* decision, for example, the Court acknowledged as a preliminary matter that 'given the FAA's favorable stance toward the enforcement of arbitration awards – both domestic and foreign – Venezuela does not, and cannot, seek de novo review of the merits of the arbitral tribunal's decision'.[420]

(d) Germany

There has been more limited practice in German courts relating to review of the merits as regards review of a tribunal's substantive jurisdiction. This may, at least in part, be due to the more restrictive approach under Article V New York Convention and Article 34 UNCITRAL Model Law, which have both been adopted in the German ZPO for defining the scope of the court's jurisdiction (including its power of review).[421] Despite this approach based on the express principles in the German ZPO, German case law in the public sphere recognises that some review of the *legality* of the tribunals under the applicable law is permissible. Thus, though the power of courts to review awards on a question of law is not recognised expressly in the ZPO,[422] the principle may be developing if decisions in the public sphere are considered the source of any potential *public international law* norm as set out further below.

A good example is the later 2016 decision in the *Walter Bau* dispute (the above considered decision being concerned with the earlier 2013 decision). Having obtained its declaration of enforceability against Thailand in respect of an ICC award, Walter Bau sought to enforce against assets. Thailand sought to challenge the declaration of enforceability on the basis that the subject matter in dispute did not fall within the scope of 'investment' within the meaning of Article 8 of the applicable Thailand-Germany BIT. This was on the ground, *inter alia*, that the subject matter concerned a sovereign matter which was therefore excluded by principles of immunity.[423] Illustrating its capacity to review whether the arbitral tribunal *could* have decided to exercise jurisdiction on the basis of Article 8 of the Thailand-Germany BIT (though formally reviewing the earlier German court's decision in this regard), the Court examined

418. *Commodities & Minerals Enterprise Ltd v. CYG Ferrominera Orinoco* 49 F.4th 902 (United States Court of Appeals, Second Circuit, 2022). Similarly: *Generali Espana de Seguros y Reaseguros, S.A. v. Speedier Shipping, Inc*, 2022 WL 1568829 (United States District Court, E.D. New York, 2022).
419. *See, e.g., Gold Reserve* (n 20).
420. *Gold Reserve* (n 20) pp. 1-2.
421. Section 1061 ZPO adopting the New York Convention verbatim and thus restricting grounds of review to those listed in Article V New York Convention.
422. Which provides for mere procedural grounds of review as per §1059 ZPO.
423. BGH, Decision of 6 October 2016 – I ZB 13/15 – juris ('Walter Bau 2').

whether the German Court had been correct to decide that the declaration of enforceability could be granted. The subject matter in dispute was whether the imposition of road tolls by a foreign state would fall within the scope of 'authorised investment' under Article 8 of the BIT. This was determined in accordance with the applicable public international law rules relating to treaties as well as under Thai Law, though it did not entail a *de novo* review of the merits of the dispute.[424] The Court found that the relevant provisions under the Thailand Investment Act had been satisfied.[425] According to the Court, this finding had been necessary for the proceeding for a declaration of enforceability (*Erkenntnisverfahren*) to be 'admissible'.[426] This was because the investment had to fall within the scope of Article 8 of the BIT for the tribunal to have the capacity for jurisdiction.

Thus, by reviewing this question, the Court acknowledged that some substantive review on whether the law was properly applied is necessary. This analysis necessarily involved reviewing the law and the facts relevant to the question of the arbitral tribunal's jurisdiction and thus review – to some degree – on a question of law. This is because the Court found it had the jurisdiction to decide whether the arbitral tribunal decided the question of its jurisdiction correctly. Thus, much like the comparison under English law of a 'rehearing' versus 'review' approach,[427] this approach appears to be closer to a more limited review, being the question of whether the tribunal reached the right conclusion on the questions considered by it (as in *Svenska*,[428] and courts prior to *Dallah*).[429] As to how review on a 'question of law' is compatible with underlying principles of arbitration will be developed further in subsection [3] of this part.

German courts have nevertheless importantly made clear that a *de novo* review of the awards (on the merits) is not possible, given the courts are mandated under section 1061 ZPO to recognise 'a potentially faulty decision of the arbitral tribunal, even if it violates mandatory domestic law'.[430] The reason is that section 1061 ZPO prohibits a 'révision au fond'. The only exception is where the award is contrary to public policy, which will be examined further below.[431]

[2] Exclusion of ICSID

Similar to the practice in relation to supervisory jurisdiction, the scope of review under the ICSID Convention is more limited: the review power of national courts is limited to reviewing the 'authenticity' of the award.[432] This has been illustrated in relation to the

424. *Ibid.*, [25]-[31].
425. *Ibid.*, [22].
426. *Ibid.*, [13].
427. Merkin and Flannery (n 397) 685.
428. *Svenska* (2006) (n 20).
429. *Dallah* (n 109).
430. High Court of Thüringen, 4 Sch 03/06 (n 299).
431. *Ibid.* (analysis of Ground IV).
432. *See, e.g.*, *Mobil Cerro Negro Ltd v. Bolivarian Republic of Venezuela*, No. 15-707 (US Court of Appeal, Second Circuit, 2017) 9. Further: *État du Sénégal* (n 370) (France) (no review on the

État du Sénégal decision.[433] The impact of such an approach, in particular on the 'self-contained' nature of the ICSID Regime, shall be examined in Chapter 6.

[3] Harmonised Approach to Review of Substantive Jurisdiction

One of the major criticisms of review on a question of law has been that it would amount to a retrial on the merits of the dispute, enabling the court to effectively replace the arbitral tribunal's decision on jurisdiction with its own.[434] For example, Moses has commented on a raft of US decisions - some of which have discussed permitting expansion of judicial review on the merits under the FAA and others have not.[435] She points out how such expanded review has been criticised on the ground that it 'further sacrifice[s] the simplicity, expediency and cost-effectiveness of arbitration' making it 'another step on the ladder of litigation'.[436] Here, we are not concerned with whether expansion would be permissible under any *national* legal instrument, nor whether it would extend to the 'merits', but merely whether it would extend to a 'question of law' - that is, review of whether the tribunal *could* have acted on the basis of the applicable law. Even though the criticism is made as regards to review of the *award*, the same criticism can be made as regards to review of the substantive jurisdiction of the tribunal, where this would essentially amount to another 'step in the ladder of the litigation'.

The principle can be illustrated by the approach which was adopted by the Court in *Svenska*. There, the Court reviewed whether the award was enforceable by examining whether the arbitral tribunal had jurisdiction under applicable principles of Lithuanian law based on the conclusions reached by the tribunal. The Court stated: 'the award is binding for what it decides, right or wrong'.[437] Thereafter, the Court explained what it meant here by 'binding': the arbitrators decided whether they had jurisdiction on the basis of the arbitration agreement but did not have to decide any question of jurisdiction within the meaning of section 9 SIA (i.e., pursuant to principles of state immunity, applicable only by national courts).[438] Much like the approach of the other examined jurisdictions, the Court in *Svenska* reviewed whether the arbitral tribunal had jurisdiction to a more limited degree. Consequently, such a review power - excluding review on the merits in principle - enables a check on the tribunal's authority. However, such a review power would not unduly encroach on the tribunal's

merits due to restriction under Article 54 ICSID which it is stated only allows the Contracting State to control the 'authenticity of the award'); *Soguipêche* (n 225) (no review of Tribunal's capacity to render interim relief permitted in accordance with Article 26 ICSID also exhibits possible trapping in relation to supervisory relief).

433. At Chapter 4[C][1](b) above.
434. *See, e.g.*, Margaret Moses, 'Party Agreements to Expand Judicial Review of Arbitral Awards' (2003) 20 *Journal of International Arbitration* 315, 316-317 https://doi.org/10.54648/joia2003025 (accessed 26 September 2025).
435. *Ibid.*, 316-317.
436. Moses, 'Party Agreements' (n 434) 318.
437. *Svenska* (2006) (n 20) [116].
438. *Ibid.*

authority to decide because the review is only to a *prima facie* standard, i.e., similar to whether the decision on jurisdiction was 'obviously wrong'.[439]

A second justification for harmonisation between courts as to their review powers is that they would ensure that the arbitral tribunal's jurisdiction accords with the international rule of law. To reiterate, this concept concerns not merely whether the tribunal could act based on the relevant jurisdictional provision in its constituent instrument but also whether decision-making authority may be *effectively implemented* (here, at the international legal level). In the *Abaclat* award described in the introduction to this study, the ICSID Tribunal found that it had jurisdiction over a 'sovereign debt'.[440] This interpretation was incorrect because only disputes pertaining to 'investments' are covered by the ICSID Convention. However, the wider question considered by Judge Abi-Saab in his dissenting judgment was whether the tribunal had jurisdiction as a more general matter of international law. In finding it did not, he stated that this was because the government bonds did not have 'any anchorage' to the host state.[441] Thus, in cases where tribunals cannot determine their jurisdiction based on the applicable jurisdictional provision in their constituent instrument or where their determination was arguably wrong, jurisdiction should be reviewable in accordance with general principles of international law as developed by national courts. In cases like *Abaclat,* where it is not clear whether the subject matter (there, a sovereign debt) would fall within the scope of the tribunal's jurisdiction ('investment' in Article 25 ICSID), the tribunal should be able to resort to general principles of international law to identify whether an exercise of jurisdiction is justified (in accordance with state immunity).

Thus, by reviewing the decisions of arbitral tribunals on jurisdiction, national court may review on questions of law and as such are contributing developing internationally as to whether arbitral tribunals have authority to act under the applicable law. Since the introduction of the Arbitration Act 2025, it appears that the UK approach is falling more in line with other court approaches, thereby supporting a more restrictive form of review of the tribunal's substantive jurisdiction rather than permitting a rehearing. This would appear to appease those arbitration scholars concerned about review being a mere step in the litigation ladder, potentially saving cost and expense for parties while allowing sufficient review to ensure tribunal has been properly established in accordance with the applicable law.

[E] COUNTERVAILING PRACTICE/EXCEPTIONS

Like in Chapter 3, it is important to consider whether any countervailing practice arises as a possible exception to the norm that review and recognition are lawful forms of

439. Under the approach in Section 69 EAA and similar to the US approach of manifest disregard of law for appeals on points of law, which are a separate matter not being considered here. However, it is suggested here that this standard summarises the extent of review power generally being exercised by courts in relation to their review of a tribunal's substantive jurisdiction.

440. *Abaclat* (n 23); *see* Chapter 1[B].

441. *Abaclat* (n 23) (Dissenting Opinion, Abi-Saab) [35].

enforcement. This is because, to the extent that these approaches can be distinguished or do not detract from the otherwise growing practice, this further cements the *representativeness* and *widespread* nature of the approaches demonstrated as a source of a general principle of international law.

[1] Must Be a Link to the Territorial Jurisdiction

In the decision in *Creighton v. Qatar*, one US Court found that it could not have personal jurisdiction in circumstances where the foreign state (here Qatar) had not consented to the New York Convention.[442] While the Court found that the award was obtained in France (such that the New York Convention would apply), it considered that the lack of consent of Qatar to the New York Convention had implications on whether the Court could hear the dispute. This was pursuant to the 'Due Process' clause of the US Constitution in circumstances where there was no link to the court's territorial jurisdiction. Due process was essentially concerned here with the fact that a court could have jurisdiction if 'the foreign state is *not* entitled to immunity either under the FSIA or any applicable international agreement'.

This decision ought to be viewed as an anomaly for two reasons. First, the New York Convention has not otherwise generally been treated as the only source of the court's jurisdiction to recognise awards. In this regard, the reasoning of the courts has indicated that the New York Convention is no more than a harmonising instrument, *in light of which* a jurisdictional basis may or may not be legally justified. This is illustrated by numerous representative decisions in all the jurisdictions examined.[443]

Second, the Court only considered the question of 'personal jurisdiction' as a question of whether the state has waived an otherwise available immunity *under the US FAA*. This was the only alternative basis upon which it was considered that there was jurisdiction to hear the case against Qatar – i.e., waiver by virtue of the consent to arbitrate. Consequently, the question answered by the Court was limited to whether jurisdiction could be implied based on consent under the adoption of the FAA (through an exercise of the state's prescriptive power) rather than as an aspect of the court's jurisdiction under public international law. The Court did not deal with the wider question of whether the jurisdiction could have been available regardless of the state's consent under the New York Convention.

442. *Creighton Limited v. The Government of the State of Qatar* 181 F.3d 118 (D.C. Cir. 1999).

443. *See, e.g.*, Walter Bau 1 (n 20) (Germany) (§1061 ZPO which gives effect to Article V treated as a principle in light of which Court decided whether to exercise decision-making authority, immunity being another relevant principle); *Stati* (2016) (US) (n 381) (One source for its jurisdiction was section 201 FAA which codifies the principle of recognition and enforcement in the New York Convention. In this regard, the Court stated that the principle that awards should be recognised and enforced is one *principle* justifying its exercise of jurisdiction to confirm the award as enforceable); *Dallah* (n 109) [1] (UK) (the source of review, from the Court's perspective, was section 103(2)(b) EAA which is stated to reflect Article V(1)(a) New York Convention); CA Paris, 18 November 2010, *Government of Region of Kaliningrad v. Republic of Lithuania*, No. 09/19535 (recognition and enforcement considered 'in light of' object and purpose of treaty).

However, this work thus far has demonstrated a separate legally justifiable basis for a court's recognition and review power – an emerging harmonised practice – which is thus not dependent on a state's consent under the New York Convention. Provided the practice is representative, widespread and consistent in the public sphere, the central argument is that it ought to be regarded as a general principle of international law. In accordance with this practice, a lawful and principled basis upon which the Court in *Creighton v. Qatar could* have had jurisdiction is evident, even if not expressly authorised by the FAA or any other provision of national law. Consequently, the 'Due Process' clause ought not to be viewed as limiting an otherwise available rule or principle.

[2] ICSID

Practice relating to ICSID Tribunals limits the scope of their review power to the 'authenticity' of the award. This includes technical questions relating to whether the correct parties are mentioned in the written award and similar matters of procedure, but excludes questions concerning whether the tribunal acted in accordance with the applicable law.

For example, in the US *Mobil Cerro* decision, the US Court stated that 'Member states' courts are ... not permitted to examine an ICSID award's merits, its compliance with international law, or the ICSID Tribunal's jurisdiction to render the award. Under the Convention's terms, they may do no more than examine the judgment's *authenticity* and enforce the obligations imposed by the award.'[444] Similarly, the French Court in *État du Sénégal* acknowledged this expressly by stating that Article 54 simplifies the exequatur for contracting states, limiting the power of the judge in each contracting state to controlling the authenticity of the award.[445]

The disparate practice in relation to ICSID raises particular concerns. The first arises for the same reasons provided in relation to the international rule of law and the concern of 'self-contained' regimes.[446] If ICSID Tribunals are able to operate outside the normative framework within which their jurisdiction is constituted – here, public international law – this would enable them to escape scrutiny of their decisions (by states).[447] This has particular implications in the area of state immunity, where an overextension of jurisdiction could enable tribunals to act outside the otherwise applicable principles which would apply to states in similar circumstances. This book seeks to demonstrate that those principles apply equally to arbitral tribunals, as they are being developed based on the implicit consent of states through their courts.

444. *Mobil Cerro* (2017) (n 432) 9. Further: *État du Sénégal* (n 370) (France) (no review on a question of law due to restriction under Article 54 ICSID which it is stated only allows the contracting state to control the 'authenticity of the award'); *Soguipêche* (n 225) (no review of Tribunal's capacity to render interim relief permitted in accordance with Article 26 ICSID also exhibits possible trapping in relation to supervisory relief).
445. *État du Sénégal* (n 370).
446. A matter to be considered in further detail in Chapter 6.
447. Schreuer (n 226) 348; *see*, Chapter 1[B] in relation to *Abaclat* (n 23).

Arbitral tribunals should not be able to escape that scrutiny. The self-contained nature of the ICSID regime is being increasingly recognised by courts; however, it is merely one interpretation of the procedural history of the Convention and is said to have only been followed by 'some delegates'.[448] From an arbitration perspective, an exclusion of review power may be viewed as desirable from an efficiency point of view. As Schreuer points out, Article 54 was modelled on Article 192 of the Treaty of Rome, which provides for *automatic* recognition (of the award as a court judgment without the need for exequatur).[449] Exclusion of national court review power would seem to speed up the recognition process by not allowing for any more comprehensive review of the arbitral award. Indeed, this is how courts seem to interpret the reason for excluding ICSID from these otherwise developing enforcement norms. This provision aims to ensure efficient execution of the award by limiting court intervention.

However, the need for efficiency of process and preservation of party autonomy (to consent to ICSID) ought not to trump wider international rule of law concerns. In addition to merely ensuring *consistency* as a source of a rule or principle of international law, review on a question of law would allow a further 'check' on the arbitral tribunal at the recognition stage as a matter of substance. Since these bodies are being increasingly regulated by national courts, as demonstrated by this work, it is hard to justify the exclusion of ICSID Tribunals from this process. These tribunals could develop a strong capacity to decide questions which may be outside the scope of their authority, otherwise limited across other arbitral tribunals exercising jurisdiction in the public sphere. This might, in turn, make the ICSID process less desirable for contracting parties if they cannot be certain that awards are rendered upon proper application of the law and then cannot pursue a review process.

Consequently, the 'self-contained' nature of the ICSID regime falls down under the weight of its own logic.[450] Its 'self-contained' nature would not necessarily heed efficiency concerns within wider international legal frameworks if the award rendered is not compliant with law and there is limited recourse to ensure this, i.e., an incorrectly decided award. The issue of 'closed' regimes, as distinct from 'self-contained' regimes, and the problem they pose in international law more generally will be considered in Chapter 6.[451]

[3] Differing Approaches under National Laws

Nuanced approaches within national law arise, which do not detract from the harmonising approach of this work. States retain their individual approaches to certain

448. *See, e.g.*, *Mobil Cerro Negro Ltd. v. Bolivarian Republic of Venezuela*, 87 F. Supp. 3d 573, 596 (S.D.N.Y. 2015) (US).
449. Schreuer (n 226) 1118-1119.
450. Even though, as Schreuer points out, national court jurisdiction is not entirely excluded at the recognition and enforcement stage, 'authenticity' still only allows a facial review of the legality of the award which essentially excludes any effective review in accordance with the international law relating to review on a 'question of law' as is being developed by this chapter; Schreuer (n 226) 1120.
451. Chapter 6[B][3] and [D][2].

issues under national law, while the general principle that the form of jurisdiction is available irrespective of immunity is maintained.

In *Société Fosmax*, the French Conseil d'Etat considered that review of arbitral awards in relation to disputes over public contracts is permissible.[452] Ultimately, the *Tribunal des Conflicts* (a special French court charged with deciding whether the administrative or ordinary French courts have jurisdiction) found that since the award conflicted with a mandatory provision in French law, it could not be recognised as enforceable.[453] In other cases, the standard against which the court has reviewed whether the award should be set aside due to fraud or corruption has been different.[454] Whichever standards the courts apply under their national laws in relation to these notions, the basic point of this work remains: each court still must ask the same question, and that is, whether the award should be refused recognition and enforcement and if so, on what legal basis? The fact that 'mandatory public law' may be differently defined across different state laws is neither here nor there: states still generally agree that the award will not be enforced if it conflicts with mandatory public law.

Consequently, even though the central aim of this work is to expose a harmonised approach, according to which national courts may *generally* grant enforcement measures in respect of the arbitral process, this does not overlook the reality that certain limitations may exist within a state's national laws when awards will not in fact be enforced under national laws. One such limitation is where enforcement conflicts with a state's mandatory public law, the principles for which will be examined comparatively below.

[F] PUBLIC POLICY AND PUBLIC LAW MATTERS

[1] Public Policy and International Public Policy

Article V(2)(b) NYC allows national courts to refuse recognition and enforcement of an arbitral award on the ground that it is contrary to the public policy of the state where enforcement is sought. Acknowledging each state's 'public policy' will be different, certain commonalities emerge relating to a more general understanding of public policy according to which recognition may be refused.

452. Nataliya Barysheva and Valentine Chessa, 'Société Fosmax v. Société TCM FR et autres, Council of State of France, ECLI:FR:CEASS:2016:388806.20161109, 09 November 2016', A contribution by the ITA Board of Reporters, Kluwer Law International.
453. Similarly: *Société Ryanair* (n 228) (recognising that the LCIA award rendered against a French company would only be enforceable provided it was compliant with mandatory principles of French law).
454. *See, e.g.*, Walter Bau 2 (n 423) [15] (Germany) (any procedural fraud could only be proven where the 'alleged illegal act did not lead to a valid decision' or 'whether criminal proceedings could be commenced') whereas fraud in other contexts may need to relate to 'basic notions of morality and justice', e.g., *Anatoli Stati et al. v. Republic of Kazakhstan, United States District Court, District of Columbia,* Civil Action No. 14-1638 (US).

(a) UK

As established in *Alexander Brothers Limited v. Alstom*,[455] 'public policy' under section 103(3) EAA, which gives effect to Article V(2)(b) NYC, is to be given a 'restrictive interpretation'. It is only to be invoked in a 'clear case' because the public policy exception to enforcement is a 'safety valve'.[456] The seat of the arbitration was Switzerland, but the Claimant sought to enforce the award in the UK. The UK Court was seized to review questions of public policy under the applicable law, which was Swiss law. It was agreed that if the conduct alleged in the case were established, it would be contrary to the 2010 Bribery Act.[457] The Court clarified that where the arbitral tribunal has jurisdiction to determine a relevant issue of illegality, there is very nearly no scope for an English court to re-open the issue of illegality.[458] The Court also stated that where there are public policy challenges at courts other than the seat, 'significant weight is given to determinations of the seat'.[459] Generally, the court will not refuse enforcement unless:

(1) there is a strong *prima facie* case, which generally suggests there must be sufficient cogency and weight to be likely to have materially influenced the arbitrator's conclusion. Where perjury is alleged, evidence must be such that it would have been expected to be decisive; or
(2) the evidence was not available or reasonably obtained either at the time of the hearing of the arbitration or at such a time as would have enabled the party concerned to have adduced it in the court at the seat.[460]

The Court also confirmed in *RBRG Trading* that it may review questions of 'international' public policy and not merely domestic public policy, which would be 'based on universal principles of morality'.[461] In that case, the Court refused to set aside an award on public policy grounds since the arbitral tribunal was expressly given jurisdiction to determine the relevant issue of public policy, namely, whether there was an illegality in the underlying contract.

Courts routinely review awards based on their own public policy. In *Stati v. Kazakhstan*, the UK courts found that the two conditions for considering allegations of fraud under the New York Convention were met in an arbitration award under the Stockholm Chamber of Commerce (SCC) Rules, being: (i) the evidence pertaining to fraud was not available to the Defendant during the arbitration, and (ii) there was a

455. *Alexander Brothers Limited v. Alstom Transport S.A & Alstom Network UK Limited* [2020] EWHC 1584 (Comm).
456. *Ibid.*, [72].
457. *Alexander Brothers* (n 455) [72].
458. Citing Hamblen LJ in *RBRG Trading v. Sinocore* [2018] EWCA Civ 838 [25], at [103] of [2020] EWHC 1584 (Comm).
459. *Alexander Brothers* (n 455) [73].
460. *Ibid.*, [74].
461. *Sinocore* (n 458) [25] (3) citing *Lemenda Trading Co Ltd v. African Middle East Petroleum Co Ltd [1998] 1 Lloyd's Rep 361* (per Phillips J).

sufficient *prima facie* case of fraud.[462] The UK Court remarked that questions of public policy 'must ultimately be a matter for the English court'. Consequently, it is possible to set awards aside based on the public policy of the forum state and this power is a clear example of enforcement review power in the public sphere, being based on Article V(2)(b) New York Convention.

(b) US

According to the decision in *Belize Bank v. Government of Belize,* the US approach is that 'public policy' is to be construed narrowly and only encompasses situations where 'enforcement would violate the forum state's most basic notions of morality and justice'.[463] In the recent *Stati* decision, a US Court found that fraud must be construed narrowly and required the state to meet a heavy burden of proving the arbitral award clearly tends to undermine 'the public interest, the public confidence in the administration of the law, or security for individual rights to personal liberty or of private property'.[464] In general, 'public policy' thus encompasses any breach of the 'basic notions' of morality and justice *within* that state. This includes fraud,[465] bribery and corruption[466] and certain elements of illegality of contracts,[467] which would violate international standards. It also generally extends to a breach of mandatory provisions of law of the forum state.

In *PAO Tatneft,* a US District Court, though rejecting the public policy defence, examined this question as one falling within its jurisdiction and not excluded by state immunity in relation to a foreign state.[468]

462. *Stati v. Kazakhstan* [2017] EWHC 1348 (Comm) (UK).
463. Further: *Bayer Cropscience AG et al. v. Dow Agrosciences LLC et al.*, 815 F. 3d 1302 (Fed. Cir. 2017), p. 6; *Parsons & Whittemore Overseas Co. v. Societe Generale de L'Industrie du Papier,* 508 F.2d 969, 974 (2d Cir. 1974).
464. *Stati* (2016) (US) (n 381).
465. *See, e.g.*, *Belokon* (n 218), Case No. 15-01650, CA Paris, *S.A. Telecel Faso v. S.A. Alcatel Lucent International,* 20 January 2015 (if arbitral proceedings are tainted by fraud, the award can be annulled, being contrary to international public policy enshrined as a ground for annulling under Article 1520(5) CPC) (France); *Stati* (2017) (UK) (n 462) [11]; *Karaha Bodas v. Perusahaan Pertambangan Minyak* 364 F.3d 274 (5th Cir. 2004) (US); Walter Bau 2 (n 423) [15] (Germany) (any procedural fraud could only be proven where the 'alleged illegal act did not lead to a valid decision' or 'whether criminal proceedings could be commenced').
466. *Alexander Brothers* (n 455); *Westacre Investments Inc v. Jugoimport SDPR Holding Co Ltd* [1999] Q.B. 740 (UK).
467. CA, Paris, *European Gas Turbines SA v. Westman International,* 30 September 1993 [22]-[30] (France) (according to the general principle of law 'fraus omnia corrumpit', the use of fraud to procure the contract which the arbitral tribunal nonetheless upheld was a ground for refusing to recognise and annul the award).
468. *PAO Tatneft (Russian Federation v. Ukraine),* United States District Court, District of Columbia, No. 17-582 (CKK), 24 August 2020.

(c) France

Similar to UK and US courts, French courts also consider the public policy defence when enforcing awards against states. In a decision in respect of the State of Libya,[469] the Court examined whether an award granted in Switzerland under a Libya-Turkey BIT could be enforced or whether exequatur would violate public policy. The French concept of public policy is set out there in paragraph 79 of the decision as being concerned with 'international public policy' as per Article 1520(5) CCP, to which Article 1525 refers, which subsumes the French concept of 'public policy'. This, the Court stated, 'is limited to examining whether the implementation of the provisions adopted by the arbitral tribunal manifestly, effectively and concretely violates principles and values included in international public policy'.[470]

Though French courts will also examine whether the award violates a French domestic concept of public policy, the concept of 'international public policy' allows courts to take wider categories into account, including not only bribery and corruption but also such matters as international terrorism, drug-trafficking and paedophilia.[471] In other jurisdictions, such as Germany, the concept has taken on a narrower meaning.

In the *State of Libya* decision, the question was whether the award was unenforceable because it was irreconcilable with a judgment handed down by the Tripoli Court.[472] The Tripoli Court issued a decision prior to the arbitration finding the tribunal had no jurisdiction,[473] but the arbitral tribunal subsequently found it did have jurisdiction without taking the Tripoli Court's decision into account. The arbitral tribunal's failure to consider *res judicata* did not itself constitute a violation of international public policy; however, another *exequatur* decision of a foreign court which was irreconcilable with the French Court decision did constitute such a 'manifest, effective and concrete' violation of public policy.[474]

The French courts have decided that in order to violate the French conception of public policy, they must ensure three conditions are met: (1) the foreign judge (where relevant, as it was in the *State of Libya* case) must have had 'indirect jurisdiction';[475] (2) the conformity of the decision with international public policy in terms of substance and procedure; and (3) the absence of fraud.

469. France No. 2024-1, *State of Libya v. Etrak Insaat Taahhüt Ve Ticaret Anonim Sirketi (Turkey)*, Cour d'Appel [Court of Appeal], Paris, International Commercial Chamber, Pole 5, Chamber 16, Case No. 24/2023, 14 March 2023.
470. *Ibid.*, [81].
471. *Alexander Brothers* (n 455) [154] (UK); CA Paris, *European Gas Turbines SA v. Westman International*, 30 September 1993 [22]-[30] (France) (according to the general principle of law 'fraus omnia corrumpit', the use of fraud to procure the contract which the Arbitral Tribunal nonetheless upheld was a ground for refusing to recognise and annul the award).
472. *State of Libya v. Etrak Insaat Taahhüt Ve Ticaret Anonim Sirketi* (n 469).
473. On the basis of annulment of a Settlement Agreement between the Parties, which was subsequently relied upon in arbitration proceedings.
474. *State of Libya v. Etrak Insaat Taahhüt Ve Ticaret Anonim Sirketi* (n 469) [83].
475. With Etrak Insaat Taahhuet Ve Ticaret Anonum Sirke arguing (unsuccessfully in this case) that the Tripoli North Court did not have indirect jurisdiction.

(d) Germany

Finally, public policy considerations have regularly entered into the analysis of German courts when parties seek to challenge awards, whether rendered against a state or in relation to a foreign-seated award. Thus, in *Deutsche Telekom AG v. Republic of India*,[476] the Higher Regional Court of Berlin considered whether a Swiss award rendered under a Germany-India BIT could be recognised as enforceable or whether the facts of the case indicated a violation of procedural or substantive public policy.

'International public policy' is a narrower concept in Germany. According to the 20 December 2012 decision of the Bundesgerichtshof, international public policy had a *narrower* meaning than domestic public policy and justified refusal of recognition and enforcement when the defect affected 'the basic principles of German social and economic life'. Comparatively, a violation of domestic public policy would ordinarily be established where the arbitral award 'is clearly incompatible with the fundamental principles of Germany, including, in particular, constitutional rights'.[477]

In the *Walter Bau 2* decision concerning fraud, the Court noted that a 'less strict' standard of review would apply where international public policy breaches are being considered because, as in that case, it was in the interests of 'international commerce' to refuse such an award which breaches international public policy.[478] Therefore, a 'less strict' standard of review may be justified in relation to international public policy where there is a particular international interest which needs to be protected. However, the standard for proving that the norm has been breached will necessarily be a high bar due to the need for the norm to be one which is 'internationally' recognised.

German public policy also extends to a breach of mandatory provisions of law of the forum state which includes such acts as a failure to register a claim in the insolvency register. This was considered by a German Court as a breach because it amounted to breach of 'the principle of equal satisfaction of all insolvency creditors'.[479]

[2] Public Matter Capable of Settlement by Arbitration: Article V(1)(a)

In addition to breaches of (international) public policy, enforcement authority may be precluded where the award breaches mandatory public law norms of the forum state.[480] In *Fosmax*, Fosmax requested the annulment of an arbitral award received against Gaz de France. Being referred by the French 'Conseil d'Etat' (the Council of State, which is a governmental body acting as legal advisor for the executive branch) to the 'Tribunal des Conflicts' (the court empowered for resolving conflicts of jurisdiction between French administrative and judicial courts), the question was whether the

476. Deutsche Telekom Case No. 12 Sch 7/21 (n 257).
477. BGH, 20 December 2012 No. 9 Sch 2/09 and No. III ZB 8/12.
478. Walter Bau 2 (n 423) [12]-[13] (Germany) [13] (in that case, any means by which the arbitral award could have been obtained by 'procedural fraud' or by 'immoral intentional harm' (running against the 'decency of a reasonably and fairly thinking person').
479. Federal Court of Justice of Germany, Decision No III ZB 178/09, 30 October 2008.
480. Conseil d'Etat ('Council of State of France'), *Société Fosmax v. Société TCM FR et autres*, 9 November 2016.

Conseil d'Etat had jurisdiction to set aside the award. The Tribunal des Conflits held that it did have jurisdiction, in order to ensure the compliance of the arbitral award with mandatory norms of French public law. Consequently, mandatory principles of public law must be complied with for recognition authority to be available.[481]

[G] APPLICATION TO INTERNATIONAL ARBITRAL TRIBUNALS AND NATIONAL COURTS

One of the wider aims of this work is to identify whether international arbitral authority is governed, and if so, to what extent, by norms of public international law. This question arises in light of disputes such as *Abaclat,* where an ICSID Tribunal found it had jurisdiction in respect of a sovereign matter which would have otherwise been excluded by principles of state immunity before national courts.[482]

Review and recognition powers are being exercised in a widespread, consistent and representative way by states, through national court decisions in the public sphere. This practice is consistent with the normative approach of adjudicative jurisdiction as a manifestation of a state's enforcement jurisdiction and with harmonising principles applicable to the scope of jurisdiction. This practice ought to be regarded as a source of a general principle of international law. This would ensure that arbitral tribunals are bound by the same principles as national courts at the recognition and review stage, when deciding the question of jurisdiction. If an award cannot be recognised where it infringes the state's 'capacity to act' at the national legal level, why should a tribunal be able to find it has jurisdiction in circumstances where the state's capacity to act would be infringed? The final part of this chapter has suggested that the tribunal should not be able to escape that scrutiny and thus the same principles should apply to states as to national courts, being organs of states and subject to international law.

If the general principles described by this work were recognised at the international level, this would provide a basis for arguing that international arbitral authority is governed by the same rules or principles of public international law as states. Thus, these bodies should be subject to the same constraints imposed by international law, including state immunity. The practice is sufficiently 'general', in that it is shared by states through representative decisions by their national courts, and it is consistent with principles of international law, i.e., those principles identified in harmonising instruments. The argument about why the discerned approach ought to be treated as a general principle of international law will be considered in greater detail in Chapter 6. For our purposes here, it is sufficient to conclude that there is a 'harmonised approach' as between representative national courts as to the scope of review and recognition jurisdiction.

481. Similarly: *Société Ryanair* (n 228); *Tamil Nadu Electricity Board v. ST CMS Electric Company Private Limited* [2007] EWHC 1713 (Comm) [16]-[17] (domestic public policy as being defined by its meaning in private international law which *includes* both whether enforcement would be breach of the 'fundamental policy' of the particular country (here, India) *and* whether it would be against 'justice and morality' (thus encompassing grounds which would fall within 'international public policy').
482. For further references to *Abaclat, see* Chapter 1[B]; Chapter 3[G]; Chapter 6[D][2].

This chapter has also examined principles of public policy and public law, including matters of a mandatory public law nature and where assets are held for public purposes, which would ordinarily be a ground for setting aside the award. To the extent that those principles are applied by national courts to review and set aside awards, they should be regarded as further norms which are harmonised and therefore being developed by national courts.

The application of this review and recognition norm is particularly important in light of awards such as *Abaclat,* where tribunals have extended jurisdiction beyond the scope of authority conferred on them by their constituent instrument. It would provide a set of general principles which tribunals may fall back on where the subject matter of a dispute - as in *Abaclat* - may not strictly fall within the tribunal's jurisdiction based on a textual reading of the Convention. This would allow courts to determine whether they nevertheless have jurisdiction over a sovereign matter, or whether this ought to be excluded by principles of state immunity.

By describing a set of practice - or *lex generalis* - relating to review and recognition jurisdiction in respect of international arbitral tribunals, this chapter has proposed a consistent and coherent basis for jurisdictional norms applicable to national courts and international arbitral tribunals. It has been suggested that this harmonised approach amounts to a general principle of international law. According to this, states have a jurisdiction to exercise recognition and review power, through their courts, irrespective of immunities. The international principle of state immunity operates as a *lex specialis* or more special set of norms in this context: there is consistent and widespread practice to this effect conforming to relevant principles of international law and international arbitration.[483]

483. Especially, International Law Commission, Fragmentation Report (n 72); *See* methodology at Chapter 1[F] (defining what is 'consistent' 'widespread' and 'representative').

CHAPTER 5
Execution Jurisdiction

This chapter addresses perhaps the thorniest form of enforcement in practice – execution jurisdiction – arguing that national court practice in this area may also be regarded as a source of the international law of enforcement jurisdiction. Homing in on the object and purpose of such jurisdiction, it is possible to regard state immunity as a lex specialis to general practice in this area. This chapter is particularly useful for practitioners seeking to enforce arbitration awards, already validly rendered, but where states invoke the principle of state immunity as a bar to execution jurisdiction. The two principles identified would hold that execution jurisdiction is generally exercisable by courts in respect of states irrespective of state immunity provided (a) the assets are within the exercising court's territorial jurisdiction; and (b) the assets are held for commercial purposes.

[A] INTRODUCTION

Execution is widely still regarded in the literature as 'the last bastion' of state immunity suggesting immunity operates as the rule or principle and jurisdiction of national courts as the exception.[484] However, this chapter will demonstrate that this assumption ought to be reversed in the area of execution against commercial assets pursuant to an arbitration award. This means that immunity now operates as a *lex specialis,*[485] or exception, to a court's jurisdiction to render execution measures in respect of a state's commercial assets within its territorial jurisdiction.

Execution is a particularly important part of the arbitration process, being the step subsequent to recognition, when a party finally gets its hands on the opposing party's assets. Born has suggested that a winning party should be able to 'recognise and

484. Ostrander (n 61).
485. The concept is explained in Chapter 1[G][2].

enforce' in any jurisdiction against a state's commercial assets.[486] Similarly, Fox and Webb have recognised that even though state immunity 'continues to bar to a very large extent the enforcement of judgments given by ... courts against foreign states' that 'change is taking place ... [in respect of] the now widely recognized exception to enforcement in respect of commercial property in commercial use'.[487]

Where the state engages in *commercial* activities, the customary international law principle of *jure gestionis* applies, which allows the state to find it has jurisdiction over a foreign state in its own territory as an exception to the general rule that a state is immune where its sovereign activities are concerned.[488] There has been increasing recognition in the arbitration literature that, at least as regards commercial assets, a court should be able to exercise its execution powers to enforce against assets pursuant to the arbitral award.[489] This chapter goes further to identify the extent of harmonisation of this norm as a source of international law, including through the identification of national court practice relating to third-party debt orders (TPDOs),[490] worldwide freezing injunctions (WFOs)[491] and any other measures sought before a court seeking to ensure execution against assets pursuant to the award including discovery or disclosure, and pre- and post-judgment attachment.

Considered only from the perspective of waiver of immunity, the orthodox state immunity literature considers state immunity as the 'rule', while court jurisdiction to render execution measures is treated as exceptional.[492] However, only some national courts have allowed for execution of foreign state assets based on a 'waiver' of state immunity implied by consent to arbitrate, with no consistency of approach from this perspective.[493] This chapter identifies representative court practice which reverses the narrative to treat *jurisdiction* as the rule and state immunity as the exception, regardless in principle of whether the state has waived immunity or not.[494]

486. Born (n 178) 3691 (enforcement should generally be carried out under the New York Convention where commercial transactions are concerned); Julien Fouret and Pierre Daureu, 'Yukos Universal Limited (Isle of Man) v The Russian Federation: Enforcement of the Yukos Awards: A Second Noga Saga or a New Sedelmayer Fight?' in Meg Kinnear and Campbell McLachlan (eds), *ICSID Review: Foreign Investment Law Journal* (2015) 336, 337; *Trendtex* (n 90) [534]-[535] (enforcement against commercial assets as a principle of customary international law).
487. Fox and Webb (n 8) 479.
488. *Ibid.*, 34.
489. Born (n 178) 3691 (in principle, awards must be recognised and enforced under the New York Convention subject to limited exceptions); presumably against commercial assets: Fouret and Daureu (n 486) 336, 337. Though which norms in fact govern *when* a national court may exercise this form of enforcement jurisdiction *as a source of public international law* has not been determined.
490. Available under English law according to CPR r. 72.1 where a debt is 'due or accruing due' to a judgment creditor.
491. *See, e.g., ArcelorMittal* (2019) (n 32) (UK).
492. As per the arbitration literature: Moses (n 22); Blackaby et al. (n 22).
493. Fox and Webb (n 8).
494. Based on the widespread, consistent and representative nature of the practice in light of harmonising principles and as is consistent with a 'public authority' approach to decision-making authority as a source of international law.

[B] BACKGROUND AND IMPORTANCE IN ARBITRATION PRACTICE

Much like the other areas of enforcement, the ability of parties to enforce against a foreign state has engaged issues of state immunity. However, the area of execution jurisdiction has been regarded in the literature as more troublesome, with a lack of harmonisation in relation to state immunity laws likely leading to non-enforcement against state assets.[495] A recent example is the well-known *Yukos* decision mentioned in the introduction to this work.

In a *Yukos*-related decision, Russia sought to argue that a security should not be granted to support execution against an award.[496] Russia argued that state immunity was a threshold matter of jurisdiction, and thus, pending resolution of the jurisdictional dispute before a Netherlands Court, the matter should be adjourned. Given the issue was pending before the Netherlands Court, Russia argued that the court's powers under section 103(5) EAA, according to which the court would have a discretion to grant security, were not available. Russia considered state immunity as a 'prior question' to whether (adjudicative) jurisdiction arises at all.[497] Since some of Russia's grounds had a realistic prospect of success, the Court concluded that the question of whether security should be granted tipped, on balance, against the party seeking the security.[498] In so deciding, the Court refused the security, sidestepping issues of jurisdiction and state immunity and deciding that granting extra security would otherwise give an 'unfair advantage' to those seeking enforcement in view of Russia's arguable claim.

The case demonstrates the need for harmonisation in ongoing execution proceedings, where immunity continues to be pleaded as an issue, when it ought not – in certain situations – to be considered an issue at all. Instead, this chapter will argue that where execution measures are sought in support of an arbitration award, in certain circumstances, state immunity ought not to limit the court's jurisdiction to grant those measures.

The central contention in this chapter in relation to easing the enforcement of arbitral awards is that in so far as this chapter identifies and describes a harmonised approach as a source of a *public international law norm,* this would assist in greater coordination of any national courts in granting execution measures, as well as, in turn, regulating the scope of international arbitral authority.

Although it did not concern execution, the 2025 *Yukos* decision suggests that the general approach of this work – promoting coordination of courts as regards jurisdictional matters – would be in-keeping with current approaches of national courts. There,

495. *See,* especially, Fox and Webb (n 8) Chapter 16 (with immunity generally being retained in respect of execution); Ostrander (n 61) 542 (stating the barriers created by the FSIA created 'unnecessarily restrictive barriers on execution').
496. *Hulley Enterprises* (2021) (n 66).
497. *Ibid.,* [71](i).
498. *Ibid.,* [255].

the UK court referred to the decisions of other national courts when interpreting its own state immunity laws.[499] Mrs Justice Cockerill had held that issue estoppel precluded Russia from re-arguing the question whether it agreed to submit the dispute to arbitration, that point having been decided previously by a Dutch court. The Court found that the appeal of Mrs Justice Cockerill's decision should be dismissed.[500] While accepting that it could review whether any of the exceptions in the SIA apply according to its own substantive and procedural rules, the Court also accepted that the principle of issue estoppel applied as part of that law. The Court therefore considered that the Dutch court's decision on Russia's submission to arbitration gave rise to an issue estoppel in relation to application of section 9 SIA, i.e., the decision on submission to arbitration by a foreign court. At paragraph 77 of its decision, the Court accordingly found that the decision of the Dutch court created an issue estoppel and there were no special circumstances which would provide a reason for not giving effect to the decision of the Dutch courts. This pragmatic (rather than principled) solution to the interaction between state immunity and jurisdiction seems to be the direction of travel of some courts, including greater cooperation *inter se*. This chapter will consider the wider question of whether there is a general principle that execution against commercial assets within the territory ought to be a generally available measure before national courts (*lex generalis*).

This chapter will begin by identifying the object and purpose of the rule according to consistent state practice. It will then look at some of the methodological contributions of this work, including the differing contributions of monist and dualist states under the functional comparative analysis and the contribution of pragmatic approaches of courts. Finally, the chapter will draw on practice relating to specific measures, such as pre- and post-judgment attachment and discovery, and identify decisions which have been excluded from the analysis.

[C] OBJECT AND PURPOSE

Two main principles arise in the case law in the public sphere, according to which a national court may render execution measures irrespective of the international legal principle of state immunity:

(1) where the assets are held for 'commercial' (as opposed to sovereign) purposes; and
(2) where those assets are located within the territorial jurisdiction of the court exercising jurisdiction.

499. *Hulley Enterprises Ltd & Ors v. The Russian Federation* [2025] EWCA Civ 108.
500. *Ibid.*, [85].

[1] Executing Against Commercial Assets of the State

(a) Germany

The first widespread and consistent shared principle is where assets are held for a 'commercial purpose'. The foundation for this norm is stated in the German *Walter Bau* 1 decision:

> German jurisdiction does not extend to foreign states in so far as they enjoy immunities. Consequently, the limits of immunity are different in respect of recognition and compulsory enforcement (i.e., execution) proceedings depending on their effects ... with regard to recognition proceedings, immunity is available according to general public international law in so far as the sovereign activities of the foreign state are affected by the legal dispute whereas immunity in execution proceedings is determined according to the capacity in which the foreign state possesses the asset.[501]

According to this approach, an otherwise available immunity may be removed depending on 'the capacity in which the state possesses the asset'. That capacity relates to whether the asset is held for commercial purposes, in respect of which there is consistent and widespread practice.

In the High Court of Munich decision of 2011, the Appellant applied to enforce a Swiss award by way of a provisional measure for security (§1063(3) ZPO). The Court found that the execution measure could not be granted because, *inter alia*, the asset against which execution was sought was not held solely for 'private purposes'.[502] §1063(3) ZPO provides that the presiding judge of the Division of Civil Matters (Zivilsenat) may direct, without having previously heard the opponent, that the petitioner may pursue compulsory enforcement pursuant to an arbitration award. Thus, at the same time as applying for a declaration of enforceability, the Appellant may apply for a security measure on the ground that though the Respondent was not located in the jurisdiction of the Court, its assets were situated there.

This was merely one of the grounds upon which the Court found the *otherwise available* jurisdiction could not be justified - the other being the question of whether the assets were located in the jurisdiction for a sufficient length of time.[503] This approach treats the manner in which the assets are held - when for commercial purposes - as a basis to render an otherwise available execution measure. This is a consistent aspect of the reasoning of German courts in the public sphere or the basis

501. Walter Bau 1 (n 20). Translation by the author ('Die deutsche Gerichtsbarkeit erstreckt sich nicht auf ausländische Staaten, soweit sie Immunität genießen. Dabei verlaufen die Grenzen der Immunität im Erkenntnisverfahren und im Vollstreckungsverfahren anders ... . Im Erkenntnisverfahren besteht nach allgemeinem Völkerrecht Immunität, soweit die hoheitliche Betätigung des ausländischen Staats durch den Rechtsstreit betroffen ist, im Zwangsvollstreckungsverfahren bestimmt sich die Immunität danach, ob der ausländische Staat das Vollstreckungsobjekt als Hoheitsträger besitzt') (vgl. Geimer, IZPR, 6. Aufl., Rn. 562).
502. OLG Munich, Decision of 4 July 2011 - 34 Sch 20/11, juris.
503. *Ibid*. This aspect will be analysed in the next section.

upon which their international jurisdiction is, in fact, exercised, i.e., when the measure is granted irrespective of immunity.[504]

The source of the court's execution jurisdiction has its foundation in the international legal principle of state immunity, which is given effect directly in Germany's national laws. In Germany, the source of a court's jurisdiction includes international law, to the extent that international law is applicable to this form of jurisdiction: *see* §20(2) Courts Constitution Act (GVG) and §25 German Constitution (GG). Consequently, the German courts have directly determined the international legal rule because international law has been given direct effect within national law. This means that those decisions, being decisions on questions of international law, become part of international law to the extent that they interpret the rule or principle consistently with other representative states. German courts have consistently found that execution may be granted within the jurisdiction against commercial assets based on the principle that such jurisdiction is not excluded by the international legal principle of state immunity.

(b) France

Similarly, in the well-known French decision of *Creighton v. Qatar,* the dispute concerned a contract between Creighton Limited and Qatar for the construction of a hospital in Qatar, which provided for the final settlement of the dispute by an ICC arbitration. Three awards were issued totalling USD 8 million. Creighton sought execution against assets held in France and the US.

The French Supreme Court found that Qatar undertook to 'carry out the awards directly' and thereby waived immunity from execution. Despite one source of the Court's reasoning being Qatar's consent to the ICC Rules and acceptance that there was thereby a waiver of immunity, the decision ultimately determined that sums held by the Ministry of Municipal Affairs and Agriculture of the Government of Qatar could be seized. This decision was based on an interpretation of the public international law rule of state immunity, whereby the Court stated that the decision was made:

504. *See,* further: The *State of Iraq v. GJV*, Oberlandesgericht [Court of Appeal], Frankfurt 1 October 1998, IPRax (1999, No. 4) pp. 247-251 (an ICC award was obtained against the State of Iraq in Paris; JGV, a German and Italian joint venture company, brought an action pursuant to the award in the Court of First Instance of Frankfurt seeking to attach assets held by the Central Bank of Iraq (CBI). The First Instance Court granted attachment. The State of Iraq appealed, arguing CBI was a separate legal entity are thus immune under Iraqi law. The Court affirmed the Lower Court's decision, finding that since the assets were not used in relation to the sovereign activities of Iraq, they were not immune from execution); *Sedelmayer* (n 531) (attachment granted in respect of commercial bank accounts held on behalf of the Russian Federation, presumed not excluded by immunity); Decision 21 W 15/03 (only because the asset under the award was held for a 'sovereign' purpose the original execution order was reversed); similarly, Hilmar Raeschke-Kessler, 'BGH: VII ZB 08/05 and VII ZB 09/05, Federal Court of Justice of Germany, VII ZB 08/05 and VII ZB 09/05, 4 October 2005', A contribution by the ITA Board of Reporters, Kluwer Law International (Russia enjoyed immunity *because* the assets were held for sovereign purposes and not because the jurisdiction (i.e., the Pfändungs- und Überweisungsbeschluss) was not available).

in light of international law principles governing state immunity, together with Article 24 ICC Rules on Arbitration.[505]

Much like the German approach, the question of whether execution could be granted in respect of an ICC award obtained by Creighton against Qatar was treated as a question of the Cour de Cassation's jurisdiction in light of public international law principles including state immunity.[506] Whether the court can grant the execution measure in question thus goes directly to the scope of its authority *to decide under public international law*: by considering the measure could be granted in light of the public international law rule, the court interprets that rule.[507]

The Court found that its jurisdiction would be available in respect of Qatari assets in France held for commercial purposes pursuant to the arbitration award.[508] This approach accepts that if assets are held for commercial purposes, the principle of state immunity does not apply to exclude a court's enforcement authority in respect of them. This is representative of further approaches between German and French courts, according to which they have consistently granted enforcement measures in the public sphere, provided the assets are held for commercial purposes.[509]

In light of the new *Sapin II* law,[510] it is questionable whether the new requirement for an express waiver of immunity[511] from execution applies also in relation to commercial assets held within the state's territory, where the assets still belong to a sovereign state. The decision in *Commisimpex* confirmed that the requirement of an express waiver, which was 'express', without any further requirement that it was

505. *Creighton* (France) (n 20) ASA Bulletin, p. 608 ('vu les principes du droit international régissant les immunités des Etats étrangers, ensemble l'article 24 du Règlement d'arbitrage de la Chambre de commerce internationale').
506. *Creighton* (France) (n 20). This case has been previously treated as standing for the proposition that the capacity of the French court to execute extended from the parties' express consent under the ICC arbitration rules; *see*, especially Fox and Webb (n 8) 387, 389. However, the Court also found that its jurisdiction would be available in respect of Qatari assets in France held for commercial purposes pursuant to the arbitration award (and thus irrespective of the rule or principle of state immunity).
507. In accordance with Article 33 CPC, Article L.411-2 §2 Code of Judicial Organization (Cour de Cassation) and para. 14 of the Preamble of the Constitution of the IVth Republic.
508. This aspect – that the assets must be located within the territorial jurisdiction of the court – will be considered a further harmonised aspect of the jurisdiction below.
509. Similarly: Cour de Cassation, 23 May 1984, *Eurodif et al v. Islamic Republic of Iran et al*, 1984 La Semaine Juridique, 20205 (France) (provided assets held for 'private purposes', they are executable); OLG Munich, Decision of 4 July 2011 (n 502) (Swiss award could be enforced by way of security measure per §1063(3) ZPO provided assets within the jurisdiction held for 'commercial purposes') (Germany); District Court of Paris ('Tribunal de grande instance de Paris') (ord. juge de l'exécution), 11 December 2002, *Banque centrale de Syrie et République arabe de Syrie v. Société Papillon Group Corp*; Cour d'Appel, 19 May 2015, *Société Chematur AB v. République de Bulgarie*, Rev. Arb. 2015, Issue 3, pp. 952-955 (execution against the Republic Bulgaria's provisional mortgages on real estate could be included, having already been the subject matter of an award in respect of which exequatur had been granted).
510. *Law on Transparency, Anti-Corruption and Modernization of Economic Life* (known as the Loi Sapin 2) No. 2016-1691.
511. An express waiver of immunity is required in respect of assets held for diplomatic purposes: *Société Commissions import export (Commisimpex) v. République du Congo, Court of Cassation of France*, First Civil Law Chamber, Arrêt No. 481 FS-P + B + R, pourvoi No. P 13-17.751, 13 May 2015.

'specific', applied in relation to diplomatic assets (and other assets held for sovereign purposes).[512] However, the same approach – requiring an express waiver – appears to have not been maintained by the courts in relation to commercial assets according to the following decisions.

The 2019 decision in *Al-Kharafi*[513] confirms that French courts continue to apply the approach in *Creighton,* notwithstanding the potential requirement of an express waiver set out above in *Commisimpex.* In *Al-Kharafi,* it was found that even though consent to arbitrate did not constitute an express waiver as required by the *Sapin II* law, an execution measure in respect of assets could still be granted where: (1) the assets were those of the entity in question (i.e., the party to the arbitration), being a state, and (2) those assets are *not* used or intended to be used for non-commercial purposes. Finding that the decision to attach state assets and seize securities should not be lifted, the decision took the *Sapin II* law into account, thereby indicating that an express waiver of immunity is not additionally required where state assets are held for commercial purposes.[514] In *SASU Financière,* it was similarly acknowledged that there was a final and binding arbitration award which constituted an 'enforceable title' in accordance with Article L.111-3 (2nd requirement) and that the asset is not intended for use for non-commercial public service purposes (3rd requirement).[515] Express waiver is considered a requirement (1st requirement) but not in the judgment and thus is not considered a prerequisite which is applied strictly by the Court.[516] Even though other French courts may disagree in the future, the approach for the time being is that it is sufficient that the assets are *not* held for non-commercial public purposes for execution jurisdiction to be available, notwithstanding a lack of express waiver of immunity, provided there is a binding and enforceable arbitration award.[517] The source of the court's power is Article L.111-1-2 du Code des procédures civiles d'exécution.[518]

An exception to the rule arises of course in respect of assets held for diplomatic (i.e., state) purposes. There must be a specific and express waiver concerning assets held for diplomatic purposes.[519] This exception ought to be viewed as further justifying

512. *Commisimpex* (n 511).
513. *See, Société Mohamed Abdel Moshen Al-Kharafi (Koweit) v. Société Libyan Investment Authority* (Libya), 18/17592 (2019); Nataliya Barysheva and Valentine Chessa, 'Société Mohamed Abdel Moshen Al-Kharafi (Koweit) v. Société Libyan Investment Authority (Libya) and other, Court of Appeal of Paris, 05 September 2019', A contribution by the ITA Board of Reporters, Kluwer Law International.
514. *Ibid.* 'les biens ne sont pas spécifiquement utilisés ou destinés à être utilisés à des fins de service public non commerciales de sorte qu'ils sont saisissables.' (the assets are not specifically used or intended to be used for non-commercial public service purposes so that they are seizable). Similarly: *SASU Financière CER (FCER) et al. v. Société Siba Plast,* Court of Appeal of Paris, 26 January 2023, Revue de l'Arbitrage (Comité Français de l'Arbitrage; Comité Français de l'Arbitrage 2024, Volume 2024, Issue 1), pp. 225-234.
515. *SASU Financière* (n 514).
516. *Ibid.,* compare p. 230 and rest of decision which does not analyse why condition 1° was met.
517. *Creighton* (France) (n 20); *Al-Kharafi* (n 513); *SASU Financière* (n 514).
518. *SASU Financière* (n 514) 227, 228, 230.
519. *See, NML Capital v. Republique Argentine No.09-72.057* (Versailles Court of Appeal finding that waiver has to be express and specific in relation to diplomatic funds, and since there was no such waiver, Commisimpex could not seize funds held in diplomatic bank accounts).

the practice in relation to commercial assets: only in so far as assets are held for sovereign purposes does France impose additional requirements.

(c) Common Law Distinctions

The common law countries examined, different from the civil law countries, have adopted legislative acts on state immunity, being dualist states.[520] This means that the decisions of their courts may not be directly illustrative of the public international law norm, but only indirectly – in so far as they are consistent with each other in the public sphere and applicable harmonising instruments.

In *Crystallex International*, upon application by Crystallex, a Canadian company, execution was granted by the United States' Court of Delaware against the Bolivarian Republic of Venezuela.[521] It found in its 2018 decision that it was sufficient that the judgment creditor demonstrated 'probable cause' that Venezuela extensively controlled the company and that the shares wholly owned by the Delaware subsidiary 'were being used for commercial purpose by the company, *and thus were subject to attachment*'.[522]

This decision was recently affirmed on appeal from the District Court to the US Court of Appeals for the Third Circuit in its 2019 Opinion.[523] There, the Court affirmed the requirement of identifying commercial assets as a prerequisite for its jurisdiction as the applicable 'standard of review'.[524] The Court found that it had jurisdiction to review the District Court's denial of PDVSA's motion to dismiss. By reviewing the earlier court's decision and affirming that assets held commercially were subject to attachment, the Court of Appeal confirmed the rule. Here, since the assets were held for commercial purposes, it follows that the principle of state immunity ought not to limit or restrict jurisdiction in respect of such assets because they are not held for sovereign purposes. This example is representative of an approach according to which US and UK courts exercise jurisdiction in the public sphere in respect of assets held for commercial purposes or, more widely, where the parties have been engaged in a commercial activity.[525]

520. SIA (UK) and FSIA (US).
521. *Crystallex International Corporation v. Bolivarian Republic of Venezuela*, 333 F. Supp. 3d 380 (D Del. 2018).
522. *Ibid.*
523. *Ibid.*
524. *Crystallex International Corporation v. Bolivarian Republic of Venezuela*, 932 F.3d 126 (United States Court of Appeals, Third Circuit) 135-136.
525. US: *Ministry of Defense and Support for Armed Forces of Islamic Republic of Iran v. Cubic Defense Systems, Inc.*, 126 S.Ct. 1193 (Supreme Court of the United States) (attachment can be granted against the property of an agency of the foreign state held for commercial purposes); *PAO Tatneft v. Ukraine, c/o Mr. Pavlo Petrenko, Minister of Justice*, 21 F.4th 829 (D.C. Cir. 2021), 840 (stating that the existence of Ukraine's commercial assets within US territory would have been sufficient for the Court to not dismiss enforcement on the basis of *forum non conveniens*); contra: *Libancell S.A.L (Lebanon) v. The Republic of Lebanon*, 06 Civ. 2765 (S.D.Y.Y, 2006) (immunity was held to exclude pre-judgment attachment against Lebanon in this case. The approach taken by the Court will be distinguished in the 'alternative approaches' section); UK: *Orascom Holding SAE v. Chad* [2008] EWHC 1841 (Comm), especially [15] (the

There are some decisions in the US which runs contrary to this practice: in *Libancell S.A.L (Lebanon),*[526] immunity was held to exclude pre-judgment attachment against Lebanon since it was found that, even if the assets had been put aside for 'commercial purposes', an express waiver of immunity in respect of those assets was required for pre-judgment attachment. This decision was based on the decision of *Banco de Seguros,* citing section 1610(d)(1), which provides expressly that '[f]oreign states are immune from prejudgment attachment of their assets used for commercial activity in the United states, unless the foreign state has *explicitly waived* its immunity from attachment prior to judgment ...'.[527] This decision ought to be viewed as limited to the issue of pre-judgment attachment, in respect of which the FSIA makes special provision for the additional requirement of an express waiver. This may be because pre-judgment attachment is a more intrusive form of execution when viewed as a measure which the parties are applying for *prior* to recognition of the award. Contrasted with section 1610(a)(6) FSIA, however, and the above-mentioned practice in relation to *post-judgment* attachment, this additional requirement of an express waiver does not apply in so far as execution measures following the recognition of the arbitration award are concerned. Consequently, it does not affect the widespread, representative and consistent nature of the practice in respect of execution measures following recognition of the arbitration award, with which this chapter is principally concerned.

(d) Interim Conclusion

To repeat the basic point being demonstrated in this work, it is the consistent, widespread and representative exercise of *decision-making authority* in the public sphere, to the extent that those decisions are consistent with harmonising principles,

Court granted execution against assets held in a bank account opened in the name of a foreign state in the UK used to receive proceeds from an oil pipeline because they were 'commercial' within the meaning of section 13(4) SIA and thus not immune from the execution action. Thus, it was sufficient for execution that assets of foreign state were held for commercial purposes within the jurisdiction); *Continental Transfer Technique Ltd v. Nigeria & Ors* [2010] EWHC 780 (Comm) (these proceedings concerned whether an award which had been set aside must be automatically suspended; however, this was in light of an interim third party debt order had already been granted against Nigeria's commercial debts held in a bank in the UK; *see,* [2009] EWHC 2898 (Comm)); *Gater Assets Limited v. National Joint Stock Company Naftogaz of Ukraine* [2008] EWHC 1108 [7] (the decision itself concerned interest payable on an *ex parte* order ordering exequatur of the award. In the statement of facts, it is stated that a third-party debt order had already been granted by a UK Court in respect of an award issued in Russia for the Defendant's commercial assets).

526. *Libancell* (n 525). *See,* further *International Insurance Company v. Caja Nacional De Ahorro y Seguro,* 293 F. 3d 392 ((United States Court of Appeals, Seventh Circuit 2002), in which pre-judgment security being granted was dependant on the alleged 'state' not in fact being an 'instrumentality of the state' and thus falling within an exception to state immunity in section 1605(a)(6)(A)).

527. *Banco de Seguros* (n 199) 261.

that is illustrative of the harmonised approach in relation to enforcement jurisdiction.[528] To reiterate, this is not 'enforcement jurisdiction' in the narrowest public international law sense, namely forcing a state's compliance with laws, but rather inducing or compelling compliance of the state through the rendering of comparable enforcement measures by national courts.

Taking into account the approaches of representative courts, there has been state practice accepting that commercial assets may be attached, but only provided that a second requirement is satisfied: those assets must be located within the court's territorial jurisdiction.

For much the same reason as given in other chapters, practice in relation to the requirement of a waiver as to immunity ought not to detract from the general availability of execution jurisdiction in respect of commercial assets pursuant to an arbitration award. In those decisions where waiver is still considered enshrining the relevant principle, such as the decision in *General Dynamics United Kingdom Limited v. The State of Libya* [2025] EWCA Civ 134, it is not denied that, according to national court approaches, national courts may be constrained in needing to consider such issues. This, however, does not detract from a general approach that, provided commercial assets are located within the territorial jurisdiction of the exercising court, they ought to be regarded as available assets to attach. According to the practice demonstrated, courts have treated execution measures as available in those circumstances, irrespective of the *international* legal principle of state immunity, as a matter of state practice. The practice is emerging in the public sphere as a source for state practice because those decisions, which are consistent, widespread and representative, demonstrate that these forms of execution pursuant to an arbitration award do not infringe the international legal principle of state immunity. The question of waiver is a separate matter which might be argued before the court, but it should not mean that such assets are not attachable *in principle.*

[2] Assets Located Within the Territorial Jurisdiction

The second widely shared general principle alongside the requirement that the assets must be held for commercial purposes is that the assets must be located within the territory of the exercising court's jurisdiction.

(a) Private International Law

Whereas from the private international law perspective, the location of assets within the jurisdiction may provide the necessary link to provide a national law justification for jurisdiction, from the public international law perspective, this may be an aspect that must be present to be constitutive of public international law enforcement

528. *See, e.g., Eurodif* (n 509) (provided assets held for 'private purposes', they are executable); OLG Munich, Decision of 4 July 2011 (n 502) (Swiss award could be enforced by way of security measure per §1063(3) ZPO provided assets within the jurisdiction held for 'commercial purposes') (Germany); *Société Papillon Group Corp* (n 509); *Société Chematur* (n 509).

jurisdiction.[529] The 'link' or connection to the territorial jurisdiction of the court which is generally required to justify jurisdiction as a matter of private international law[530] may provide a source for any public international law norm to the extent that it is consistently used to justify adjudicative jurisdiction on the same legal basis as demonstrated by the following sections.

(b) *Germany*

The German approach is demonstrated by the decision in *Sedelmayer* of 4 October 2005, which concerned the enforcement of a Stockholm Chamber of Commerce (SCC) award against Russia. Execution was not ultimately granted as the assets were held for sovereign purposes, being assets which it was found Russia had earmarked for sovereign purposes, here its diplomatic mission.[531] Nonetheless, the Court found that a German court's '*Internationale Zuständigkeit*' (international competence or jurisdiction) would have been available, in principle (had the assets not been held for sovereign purposes), against assets within the territory of the court because that court is the only one which can render such a measure. As explained by the Court in *Sedelmayer*:

> the *international competence* of German courts for execution (or compulsory enforcement) proceedings requires that execution takes place against assets within the territorial jurisdiction of the court, because only against such assets can *state authority* be exercised.[532]

Thus, the foundation for the rule in Germany is in fact recognised as being based on the fact that the court is the only body with *public* authority in respect of assets within its own territory. As stated in the previous chapter, in monist countries, the very question of adjudicative competence goes to the question of the scope of the court's jurisdiction under *international* law, since international legal principles are directly integrated into the norms which are the source of the court's jurisdiction.[533] Indeed, it

529. *See, e.g.*, Dicey (n 34) 1-027, 1-030 (conflicts are typically governed by 'links' to the jurisdiction; one example relating to immovable property, is that jurisdiction is at the situs of the property).
530. This approach is explained well in the context of state immunity claims in Goh (n 79) 687 (concerning whether a domestic court should 'not avoid adjudication of matters with foreign affairs elements'; thus a question for the particular court under private international law); further, this general approach can be illustrated by principal private international law textbooks, e.g., Dicey (n 34) 1-027, 1-030.
531. BGH, Decision of 4 October 2005, VII ZB 9/05, *Franz J. Sedelmayer (Germany) v. Russian Federation, Federal Republic of Germany* [4] Not available pursuant to the rule or principle of immunity from execution which thus exempts German court jurisdiction under Article 25 of the Constitution according to the applicable public international law rules or principles. This was fees for air traffic rights in connection with the sovereign's (in this case Russia's) territory which constituted compensation for administrative acts in the field of air traffic administration, and thus claims of a public (sovereign) nature.
532. Decision VII ZB 9/05 [15].
533. As mentioned in relation to recognition and review: *see* Chapter 4[C][1]; as well as execution: Chapter 5[C][1](a) and (b).

is notable that German jurisdiction in this area is labelled '*Internationale Zuständigkeit*': this may be regarded as recognition, at least linguistically, that the German court exercises an 'international' form of competence because it reaches beyond its own territory. Further, '*Zuständigkeit*' means 'competence', which provides a better descriptive word than 'jurisdiction' for the authority of a court to decide in accordance with the scope of its authority under international law. This descriptor is in-keeping with the broader theme of this work: namely that the decision-making authority of national courts may determine principles of international law to the extent that those decisions are in accordance with their (and an arbitral tribunal's) competence under international law.

The recognised limit on that authority would be where court competence engages the foreign state's sovereignty – i.e., would be a breach of the international legal principle of state immunity, as given effect to within Germany's national laws. This was the ultimate consequence of the *Sedelmayer* decision. The Court refused to execute against Russian assets located in Germany pursuant to the SCC award.[534] It was stated in the factual history that commercial accounts would have had to have been 'earmarked for sovereign purposes' for immunity to be available. The reasoning behind this approach is that since the capacity in which the state holds or intends to hold the asset is for a sovereign purpose, then jurisdiction in respect of sovereign assets would be a breach of the international legal principle of immunity. It would amount to compelling the state to do something which comes *outside* the jurisdictional competence of the exercising court.

Consequently, civil law courts have consistently found that they cannot order execution in respect of assets held for sovereign purposes because they simply have no jurisdiction to exercise.[535] With regard to commercial assets, states act in their private capacity.[536] Consequently, in respect of commercial assets, execution powers are not generally regarded as infringing the foreign state's sovereignty. This is more broadly reflected in the decisions of the other representative courts.[537]

534. *Sedelmayer* (n 531).

535. France: jurisdiction has extended to commercial entities on the basis that they are not the sovereign state: Cour de Cassation (1re Ch. civ.), 6 February 2007, *Société nationale des pétroles du Congo (SNPC) v. Société Walker International Holdings Ltd.*, 2007 Rev. Arb. 483 (appeal of decision according to which execution not granted against commercial entity on the ground that it was not an opposable party as was not the state. Reversed on the basis that the party was the correct party against which execution could be sought as an 'offshoot' of the state); whereas not generally sufficient that assets held for sovereign or diplomatic purposes: CA Paris (1 Ch.), 2000, *Ambassade de la Fédération de Russie en France et al. v. Compagnie Noga d'importation et d'exportation*, No. 09/19983 (one of the grounds which formed part of the reasoning as to the availability of jurisdiction (had the assets not been held for diplomatic purposes) was the location of the assets within the territory of the French Court); Cour de Cassation, 13 May 2015, *Société Commissions import export (Commisimpex) v. Republique du Congo*, No. 481 (diplomatic immunity has to be expressly waived in relation to assets, otherwise exclusion of execution is assumed); Fox and Webb (n 8) 516-517 (on *Sedelmayer*).

536. Further, Fox and Webb (n 8) 395.

537. *AIG Capital* (n 13) (UK) (assets held for a sovereign purpose, such as by the central bank, are generally excluded); *Eurodif* (n 509) (expressly stating that the 'ruling out' of immunity is to be accepted where the assets are 'allocated for private or commercial purposes'); *Orascom* (n 525) especially [15] (the Court granted execution against assets held in a bank account opened in the

(c) *France*

Similarly, in the *Creighton v. Qatar* decision set out above, whether the Court could grant the execution measure against assets of the foreign state concerned court authority *to decide under public international law*.[538] In *Creighton*, the Court found that its jurisdiction would be available in respect of Qatari assets in France held for commercial purposes pursuant to the arbitration award.[539] Jurisdiction in respect of the state's commercial assets was not excluded by the international principle of immunity precisely *because* it fell within the Court's *international* adjudicative competence (i.e., that which was available in respect of a foreign state). Recognising the 'international' nature of the jurisdiction, the French Court similarly stated: 'In light of international law principles governing state immunity, together with Article 24 ICC Rules on Arbitration'.[540]

In France, a *saisie-attribution* (a measure attaching assets) is specifically available on the basis that the assets are located within the territory of the court where enforcement is sought. This is an attachment order or writ of execution, similar to third-party debt orders (TPDOs) available in the UK under CPR r. 72.2. According to French practice, the question of the court's international jurisdiction to grant such a measure arises as a question of the court's authority to decide under section 2 of the 1991 Law reforming the law relating to execution measures.[541] In *Société Central Bank of Irak*, the Republic of Iraq challenged execution measures in respect of Iraqi assets since these were held by the Central Bank of Iraq, whose legal personality was both separate from that of the Republic of Iraq and at the same time whose activities pursued sovereign purposes and thus were subject to immunity.[542] The original execution order had been granted by the '*juge d'éxecution*' of the Tribunal de Grande Instance – the court competent for ordering such measures under section 9 of the 1991 law. It found that its international jurisdiction was available in respect of a sovereign's assets because the judge ordered Société Générale to comply with the judgment against it. The decision was reversed on appeal on the basis that the assets in question were held

name of a foreign state in the UK used to receive proceeds from an oil pipeline because they were 'commercial' within the meaning of section 13(4) SIA and thus not immune from the execution action); *Ministry of Defense of the Islamic Republic of Iran v. Gould Inc. and others*, 887 f.2d 1357 (9th Cir. 1989); also, *Ministry of Defense of the Islamic Republic of Iran v. Gould Inc. and others*, CV 87-03673 (C.D. Cal 1988) (holding that in so far as 'diplomatic relations' with another country are concerned, this limits the Defendant's *access* to the courts. This did not exclude the basis for *declaring* an award enforceable in that case in accordance with the New York Convention according to which personal and subject matter jurisdiction was still available in respect of a foreign award).

538. In accordance with Article 33 CPC, Article L.411-2 §2 Code of Judicial Organization (Cour de Cassation) and para. 14 of the Preamble of the Constitution of the IVth Republic.
539. This aspect – that the assets must be located within the territorial jurisdiction of the court – will be considered a further harmonised aspect of the jurisdiction below.
540. *Creighton* (France) (n 20), ASA Bulletin, p. 608 ('vu les princies du droit international régissant les immunités des Etats étrangers, ensemble l'article 24 du Règlement d'arbitrage de la Chambre de commerce internationale').
541. Law No. 91-650 du 9 July 1991 concerning reform of enforcement procedures.
542. CA Paris (1re Ch. C), 1 September 2005, *Société Central Bank of Irak v. Société Hochtieff Aktiengesellschaft et autres*, Rev. Arb.2006, Issue 1, pp. 214-220.

by the Central Bank, which was a separate entity from Iraq, and thus, its assets could not be attributed to Iraq in this case.[543] Nonetheless, by the mere rendering of a decision to consider whether the execution measure would be available in the public sphere, this decision could be taken as evidence of a widespread approach to this effect. The Court thereby acknowledged that one basis for its jurisdiction in the public sphere would be where the assets in question were located within its territorial jurisdiction (and thus also, such basis was not excluded by the international legal principle of immunity).[544]

(d) Common Law States

The UK courts have widely granted execution measures in respect of states, or where there is no territorial connection between their jurisdiction and the arbitration, based on CPR r. 72.1, which is part of the Civil Procedure Rules relating to TPDOs.

In *Hardy Exploration*,[545] the Claimant had obtained an arbitration award against the Government of India and subsequently applied without notice for a TPDO against India pursuant to the Civil Procedure Rules Part 72.[546] From the internal perspective of private international law as part of national law, this is the relevant 'connecting factor' according to which the jurisdiction would be available. However, taking the private international law as potentially *declaratory* of any public international law norm, it may also be constitutive of the jurisdiction. This would be to the extent that any decision is: (1) in the public sphere and (2) consistent with a sufficiently widespread number of other representative approaches in application of harmonising instruments.

In *Hardy*, the Court ultimately decided that it would grant execution against assets within the jurisdiction. This formed part of its reasoning as to why the measure would be available, based on CPR r. 72.1, which states that a third party that owes a debt to the judgment creditor must be within the jurisdiction of the court where such an order is sought[547] and the debt must be due or accruing due.[548]

In the US, meanwhile, in the *PAO Tatneft* decision in the US Court of Appeal,[549] Tatneft, a Ukrainian-owned oil company, obtained a Permanent Court of Arbitration award in France against Ukraine. The Court found that the doctrine of *forum non conveniens* (that there could be another more appropriate forum) was not available in

543. *Ibid.*
544. *See, e.g.*, *Creighton* (France) (n 20) (Qatari sums held by French bank for commercial purposes were executable); *Société Chematur* (n 509) (execution against Bulgaria's real estate within the jurisdiction permissible); *Eurodif* (n 509) (provided assets held for 'private purposes', they are executable); moreover, this might extend to whether the measure is in respect of a 'commercial' rather than sovereign entity: *Société Walker International* (n 535); whereas not generally sufficient that assets held for sovereign or diplomatic purposes: *Noga* (n 535).
545. *Hardy Exploration & Production (India) Inc v. Government of India v. India Infrastructure Finance Company (UK) Limited* [2018] EWHC 1916 (Comm).
546. *Ibid.*, [4].
547. CPR r. 72.1(1).
548. CPR r. 72.2(1).
549. United States Court of Appeals, District of Columbia Circuit, *PAO Tatneft v. Ukraine, c/o Mr. Pavlo Petrenko, Minister of Justice*, 21 F.4th 829 (D.C. Cir. 2021) 834; citing the earlier District Court decision in *Tatneft v. Ukraine*, 301 F. Supp. 3d 175, 190 (D.D.C. 2018) 192-193.

relation to recognition jurisdiction (to confirm an arbitration award) because only US courts could attach foreign commercial assets found within the US.[550] Although the decision itself concerned recognition, as a matter of reasoning, the availability of the jurisdiction was in part determined by whether the assets of Russia were located there. Thus, the 'link' with the court's jurisdiction under private international law was that the commercial assets of the foreign state were located there, which, as other US courts have stated, would constitute the 'minimum contact' with the foreign state required for the court to exercise 'personal jurisdiction' over the state.[551]

An approach accepting that execution can generally be granted in respect of commercial assets within the territorial jurisdiction has been followed by UK and US courts in the public sphere, which have consistently made execution orders in the public sphere in those circumstances – with state immunity producing no limitation on that jurisdiction, whether *prima facie* or in terms of scope.[552]

[D] ASSETS HELD FOR SOVEREIGN PURPOSES: THE EXCEPTION AS EVIDENCE OF THE RULE

Further decisions may be taken into account for what they say about an *exception* to a rule. To restate the principle established in the *Sedelmayer* decision:

> the *international competence* of German courts for execution (or compulsory enforcement) proceedings requires that execution takes place against assets within the territorial jurisdiction of the court, because only against such assets can *state authority* be exercised.[553]

The foundation for the rule, at least as acknowledged expressly by German courts, requires the court to have 'public' authority in respect of assets within its own territory, i.e., that such public authority is not limited or excluded by the international legal principle of state immunity.[554] Execution in respect of commercial assets within the jurisdiction would be a justifiable exercise of public authority since it does not infringe on the foreign state's sovereignty or authority to act. By the same logic, where assets, even if located within the territory of the exercising state, are held for sovereign purposes, immunity would be available in principle[555] in respect of them. Consequently, the *lex generalis* in respect of execution against assets would not be reversed where those assets are held for sovereign purposes.

There is a consistent line of decisions in the public sphere according to which execution measures are *not* granted for this very reason: that assets are being held or

550. *Ibid.*, *PAO Tatneft v. Ukraine* (D.C. Cir. 2021) 840.
551. *See, e.g.*, United States District Court, Southern District of New York, *Figueiredo Ferraz Consultoria e Engenharia de Projeto Ltda. (Brazil) v. The Republic of Peru et al.*, 655 F. Supp. 2d 361 (S.D.N.Y. 2009) 374.
552. US: *Ministry of Defense* 126 S.Ct. 1193 (n 525); *PAO Tatneft v. Ukraine* (D.C. Cir. 2021) (n 550) 834, 840 (as regards US courts' ability to attach foreign assets within the jurisdiction in principle); UK: *Orascom* (n 525) [15]; *Continental Transfer* (n 525); *Gater Assets* (n 525).
553. Decision VII ZB 9/05 [15].
554. *See,* Walter Bau 1 (n 20); *See* Chapter 4[C][1](a) for the facts.
555. That is, as the *lex generalis.*

earmarked for sovereign purposes.[556] The exception supports the rule: assets held for sovereign purposes are immune, as distinct from those held for commercial purposes. Where the assets are held for commercial purposes, these have been found consistently to not attract immunity *because* jurisdiction would not entail a breach of the foreign state's sovereignty: the state has acted in its private capacity when designating the assets for commercial purposes.[557]

A UK example is the decision in *AIG Capital v. Kazakhstan*.[558] The Claimants applied for enforcement of an ICSID award in the UK in respect of Kazakhstan's assets, which were being held by its central bank. Under section 14(4) SIA, a central bank's assets are immune from enforcement because that property is not to be regarded as 'in use or intended use for commercial purposes'. In its reasoning, however, the Court accepted that its jurisdiction would have been available if there was a 'debt due or accruing due' to the judgment creditor.[559] The Court then considered that under section 14(4), immunity should be afforded to the central bank as regards execution in respect of its assets under section 14(4).[560] The decision indicates that execution jurisdiction would have been available as a matter of principle had the assets *not* been held for sovereign purposes - in this case because they were being held by the central bank, which is a category of excepted assets under the SIA.

Since this practice is widespread, consistent and representative as between the selected states, it may be regarded as a further source of the practice.[561]

[E] FUNCTIONAL COMPARISONS

As a result of the differences in legal systems chosen in this book, it has been necessary to adopt a functional comparative approach.[562] This section focuses on methodology to unpick how a public authority approach enables such comparison across disparate approaches to authority.

As explained by Zweigert and Kötz, comparativists may escape the particular doctrinal quirks of each national legal system to analyse how legal systems similarly

556. *See, e.g.*, *AIG Capital* (n 13) (UK) (assets held for a sovereign purpose, such as by the central bank, are generally excluded); *Eurodif* (n 509) (expressly stating that the 'ruling out' of immunity is to be accepted where the assets are 'allocated for private or commercial purposes'); *Orascom* (n 525) especially [15] (the Court granted execution against assets held in a bank account opened in the name of a foreign state in the UK used to receive proceeds from an oil pipeline because they were 'commercial' within the meaning of section 13(4) SIA and thus not immune from the execution action); *Ministry of Defense of the Islamic Republic* (9th Cir. 1989) (n 537); also, *Ministry of Defense* (C.D. Cal 1988) (n 537) (holding that in so far as 'diplomatic relations' with another country are concerned, this limits the Defendant's *access* to the courts. This did not exclude the basis for *declaring* an award enforceable in that case in accordance with the New York Convention according to which personal and subject matter jurisdiction was still available in respect of a foreign award).

557. *See*, Fox and Webb (n 8) 395.

558. *AIG Capital* (n 13).

559. *Ibid.*, [30]-[32].

560. *Ibid.*, [7].

561. *See* (n 556).

562. *See* Chapter 1[F][2].

resolve similar legal problems.[563] Functional comparative work, by its very definition, allows for the comparison of *functionally* equivalent legal concepts – that is concepts which have the same effect, as a legal matter, on the outcome for the parties or the development of the law on a particular question, even if the norm does not expressly have the same name. By application to this work, three steps are then taken to achieve functional equivalence: (1) whether the national court is dealing with a comparable legal norm; (2) if so, to what extent it does so accord with any harmonising principles of international law; (3) whether, despite different sources, the result of the court's measure or action has the same effect in accordance with the harmonising laws.

[1] Common and Civil Law States

It has been established in the previous sections that the source of the norm may be distinct from the civil and common law court perspectives, depending at least in part on *how* the court determines whether an execution measure may be granted. For example, in German and French courts, the decision itself may be evidence of the norm because public international law is directly a source of the court's jurisdiction, i.e., the principle of immunity. In the US and UK, the authorising rule or principle may be national law(s) which give effect to principles of public and private international law, with the source of immunity being national laws to the extent that they are consistent with the international legal principle. In combination with each other, the interpretation of these different sources by the court and whether the court decides to grant the measure may be evidence of the norm. Adopting the functional comparative approach, a wider set of practice may thus be compared, even though it does not necessarily derive from the same prescription adopted as part of the state's national law.

(a) Common Law Approaches

The decision considered above in *AIG Capital* is useful to illustrate the importance of reasoning from the common law functional perspective. The Court found that since the property was held by the central bank, then the immunity was retained pursuant to section 14(4). This provides that where assets are held by a central bank, the assumption is that these are excluded by the principle of immunity. However, had this not been the case, the Court accepted in principle that its jurisdiction would have been available (provided assets were held for commercial purposes within the jurisdiction). This is clear from the reasoning of the Court, which first stated that the TPDO would be available if there was a 'debt due or accruing due' to the judgment creditor[564] and then considered whether under section 14(4), any immunity should be afforded to the central bank due to the exclusion of jurisdiction for assets held on its behalf under section 14(4).[565] The reasoning is that although the assets themselves are for a

563. Konrad Zweigert and Heinz Kötz, *An Introduction to Comparative Law* (3rd edn, OUP 1998).
564. *AIG Capital* (n 13) [30]-[32].
565. *Ibid.*, [31]-[41].

commercial purpose, the *capacity* in which they are held - by the central bank - is sovereign. The *approach* of the court is that jurisdiction *would* have been available as a matter of principle had the assets not been held for sovereign purposes and/or held by the central bank.

Had the functional comparative approach not been adopted, which takes into account the *effects* of decisions, the approach of the Court may have been overlooked as a source of the norm. Considering adjudicative jurisdiction as a facet of prescriptive jurisdiction, traditional public international lawyers might have considered the decision - which ultimately resulted in the jurisdiction *not* being exercised in respect of assets held by the central bank - as a simple interpretation of section 14(4) SIA. According to this, an *otherwise available* immunity - available in principle in respect of foreign states brought before national courts, according to section 1 of the Act - is simply preserved or upheld, since the assets are sovereign in nature. Moreover, the reasoning of the Court in relation to the TPDO - which is available as a formal matter according to CPR r. 72.1[566] may be viewed as merely a private international law rule or principle which forms part of the national law which the national court is interpreting. Thus, these decisions may have been entirely overlooked as a source of a general principle of international law if a broader approach to adjudicative jurisdiction were not adopted. The broader approach encompasses both public and private international law as a source of a harmonised approach, going beyond consideration of adjudicative jurisdiction as only an interpretation of the prescriptive norm that the state has chosen to adopt, as examined in Chapter 2.

Taking into account *AIG* as an example of the norms described in this chapter, it demonstrates the general approach of UK courts to considering the capacity in which the assets are held as determinative of whether the court will exercise jurisdiction. In this case, since the fact that the asset is held by a central bank, this is generally interpreted as falling within the principle of state immunity and thus excluded from court jurisdiction.[567]

(b) Civil Law Approaches

As stated above, it is clear from the decisions in *Creighton* and *Walter Bau* that immunity is a direct source of jurisdiction being part of international law. In practice, the application of these norms is therefore implicit in the court's decision to render the execution measure or refuse to do so.

This can be illustrated by the French decision in *Société Orion*.[568] Upon seeking seizure of assets pursuant to a Moscow Chamber of Commerce award against the Russian satellite company, Société Orion obtained an order from the French Court for

566. A TDPO is 'due or accruing due' where a third party owes a debt to a judgment creditor.
567. Similarly, and further: *Libancell* (n 525) (assets held by Lebanon's central bank in the US were immune *prima facie* under the FSIA from pre-judgment attachment, and thus immunity could not be waived).
568. *Société Orion Satellite Communications Inc. v. Société Federal State Unitary Entreprise* 'Russian Satellite Company', Court of Appeal of Paris, 31 January 2013, Revue de l'Arbitrage (Comité Français de l'Arbitrage; Comité Français de l'Arbitrage 2013, Volume 2013, Issue 2) 460.

execution. The arbitration took place under the ICC Rules against the Russian satellite company, which sought to rely on state immunity from execution. Russia argued that its assets could not be seized because they were assets of the state, not commercial assets of a separate company. The basis for execution jurisdiction is established when the creditor possesses an enforceable title for establishing a liquid and payable debt, in which case it can proceed with the sale of the goods pursuant to Article L.522-1 of the Code des procédures civiles d'exécution (Code of Civil Enforcement Procedures). Consequently, the only question arising as a matter of immunity from execution would have been the capacity in which the Respondent possessed the asset, as a state or state-affiliated entity or in a commercial capacity. Finding it did not need to decide this matter, the Court found that immunity was in any event waived because the arbitration award included the wording that it 'will be final and binding on both parties and will be subject to voluntary execution by each of the parties'.[569] However, even if immunity needed to be considered in the context of how the state held the asset, this would be separate from the Court's general jurisdiction to execute based on enforceable title pursuant to Article L.522-1. Immunity would have only affected this jurisdiction to the extent that assets were held for sovereign purposes rather than commercial purposes in respect of which jurisdiction is generally available.[570]

On the one hand, while the reasoning and approach of the court may play a role in the identification of the norms examined in this study, the *decision* itself, in the public sphere, *as a discrete aspect,* may play a greater role in the civil law countries examined. In these countries, one source of jurisdiction is the international legal principle of immunity. The court's decision for what it states may also be declaratory of the *international* norm. Whether the exercises of authority are lawful is then compared with the principles underpinning immunity and arbitration, as contained in harmonising instruments and customary international law. On the other hand, dualist states adopt their own state immunity laws. This means that the international legal norm is identified once a number of decisions are first identified and compared in the public sphere and considered in light of applicable harmonising laws. Thereafter, the decisions must similarly be analysed in light of harmonising instruments as to whether they constitute lawful exercises of authority. The decisions themselves will not always identify the international legal norm unlike the approach in monist states.[571]

Thus, the functional comparative approach adopted by this work encompasses national courts with both monist and dualist approaches to law by taking a broad approach to identifying those decisions which can be encompassed by 'the public

569. Similarly: *Société Papillon Group Corp* (n 509) 100-101 (the Republic of Syria requested the reversal of precautionary seizures in satisfaction of an arbitral award against it. The Court refused to reverse it on the basis that consent under the Article 26-8 ICC Rules was sufficient for a waiver of Arab Republic of Syria's immunity from execution. The Court found it thereby accepted enforcement of an award without delay as well as committed to rules or principles of 'international commerce'); *Société Chematur* (n 509).

570. *See Creighton* (France) (n 20).

571. *See*, further on the topic of how the private international law approach reflects the common law court's internal perspective as to the interpretation of its jurisdiction in light of *national* arbitration and state immunity laws: Chapter 1[F][2]; Chapter 2[G]; Chapter 4[C][1](a).

sphere' concept, rather than relying exclusively on the interpretation of prescriptive norms.

[F] COORDINATION UNDER PRIVATE INTERNATIONAL LAW

It has been established above that private international law traditionally requires a link to the territorial jurisdiction for there to be jurisdiction from the state's internal perspective, i.e., when considering private international law as part of national law. This section considers whether those links, to the extent that national courts consistently grant forms of enforcement based on those links, could be constitutive of, or at least *contribute to,* the *public international law* approach being demonstrated.

In the 2008 *Mobil Cerro Negro* decision, the UK Commercial Court considered its authority to grant a WFO in respect of assets of the Bolivarian Republic while a proceeding was pending before an ICC Tribunal.[572] The Court decided to set aside the freezing injunction as the Claimant was unable to show there was a real risk of dissipation of assets, that the case was one of urgency or that there was an exceptional feature such as fraud. Moreover, there was no sufficient link with the jurisdiction and the Defendant had no substantial assets in England or Wales. However, the Court did find that the power to make freezing orders in relation to arbitration proceedings is available under section 44 EAA and section 37 SCA 1981, provided that the restrictions under those are satisfied. Section 44 provides for the power of a court, with no connection to the arbitration, to order interim relief and section 37 SCA 1981 gives the court the power to order interim relief where it appears to the court to be 'just and convenient' to do so. Given that the assets were held for commercial purposes, provided that this further requirement is satisfied - i.e., real risk of dissipation or a case of urgency or an exceptional feature such as fraud - jurisdiction would be available based on section 44 EAA and section 37 SCA 1981.[573]

From a traditional private international law perspective, which would view section 44 EAA and section 37 SCA 1981 as merely *authorising principles* according to which the national court is able to found jurisdiction under national law,[574] these decisions may have been overlooked as a source of any public international law norm.

572. *Mobil Cerro* (2008) (n 206).

573. Similarly, and further, in relation to freezing injunctions: *GE Transportation* (n 333) (there would be irreparable harm where the Respondent was already held in contempt of court in Hong Kong for violating court orders by diminishing assets due under a HKIAC award) (US); *ArcelorMittal* (2019) (n 32) (UK); *Cruz City* (2014) (n 293) (the Court found it 'just and convenient' under section 37 for appointment of receivers by way of equitable execution over foreign assets in pursuit of LCIA award. Thus, although linked to arbitration, the source of the Court's power was inherent authority under section 37 and in respect of foreign assets); *Tsavliris Salvage Limited v. Ministry of Trade of the Republic of Iraq* [2008] EWHC 612 Comm (freezing injunction could be granted and was not excluded by immunity on the basis of section 9 SIA. The freezing order was granted because there was a real risk of the assets in question being dissipated); *Nedagro B.V. v. Konversbank*, No. 02 Civ. 3946 (HR) (S.D.N.Y. 21 January 2003) (a freezing order was granted in respect of assets within New York, and were attached by way of a freezing injunction *ex parte,* despite the dispute being before the ICCA in Russia) (US).

574. In accordance with the traditional private international law approach set out in the introductory chapter: Chapter 1[G][4].

However, to the extent that they are consistent in the public sphere and with harmonising instruments, they ought to also be considered evidence of the rule or principle. In *Mobil Cerro,* since the assets were held for commercial purposes and were within the jurisdiction, provided the further requirements justifying the form of relief were satisfied, a freezing injunction could be granted irrespective of principles of immunity.

In *Tsavliris Salvage v. Grain Board of Iraq (GHI),* the UK High Court specifically referred to section 9 SIA as a source of its jurisdiction to grant a freezing injunction (albeit in this case, in respect of assets within the jurisdiction).[575] Tsavliris argued that GHI was not a 'state entity' nor an instrumentality of the state for the purposes of the SIA, nor was the activity in question an exercise of the body's sovereign authority and thus did not attract state immunity from suit under section 14 SIA. Applying section 9 SIA, the Court found that regardless of the answer to the question of section 14 SIA, section 9 applied to enable the Court to have jurisdiction in a matter in which the parties had submitted to the arbitration:

> [55] s.9(1) of the Act: For my part, I prefer to begin with a consideration of the arguments as to s.9(1) of the Act – a provision capable of providing a short answer to the dispute as to immunity ... .
>
> It is beyond dispute that state immunity does not apply to proceedings relating to arbitration to which the state has agreed in writing to submit disputes: Mustill & Boyd, The Law and Practice of Commercial Arbitration in England (2nd ed., 1989), at p.151; Svenska (supra) at [117]. The only question therefore is whether the GBI (I say no more about the MOT) 'agreed in writing' to submit to the arbitration.

Finding that it had agreed to arbitrate through signature of an Lloyd's Open Form contract (LOF), the Court went on to find that it could grant a freezing injunction. The practice demonstrates that freezing injunctions would be available irrespective of state immunity when assets are located within the jurisdiction. This is provided of course that the further requirements for freezing injunctions, such as a real risk of dissipation, are otherwise met.[576] Even though section 9 and similar private international law rules, providing for an 'arbitration exception' to state immunity might be one source or justification for jurisdiction, it is not *the* source.[577] Instead, the common approach being demonstrated concerns consistent and widespread decisions on execution jurisdiction in the public sphere in circumstances where assets are held for commercial purposes within the territorial jurisdiction. However, in *Tsavliris,* the Court noted that 'a submission by GBI, agreed in writing, to submit to arbitration under and in accordance with the LOF' meant that any challenge to the award on the ground of state immunity must fail 'on this ground alone'.[578] Such an approach is supported by this work because this would be consistent with the view that these types of measures,

575. *Tsavliris Salvage Limited* (n 573).
576. Similarly: *Nedagro* (n 573) (assets within New York were attached by way of a freezing injunction *ex parte,* despite the dispute being before the ICCA in Russia).
577. *Tsavliris Salvage Limited* (n 573) [59].
578. *Ibid.*

which uphold enforcement of a valid arbitration award, merely support enforcement of the arbitration award.

Similarly, in the civil law states examined, freezing injunctions - in respect of assets within the jurisdiction - have been made available in the public sphere as an aspect of the court's authority to decide. *Société Chematur* demonstrates the French approach.[579] This concerned whether a provisional measure could be granted against assets of Bulgaria to protect against the dissipation of assets. The court's authority to decide this question was founded on Article 67 of Law No. 91-650 of 9 July 1991, reforming the civil procedure rules on execution measures, now Article L-5111-1 of the Code of Civil Procedures on Execution Measures, which provides 'any person whose claim appears to be founded may apply to the authorising judge for a protective measure against property of the debtor without prior order if it is considered justified in circumstances likely to threaten recovery'. The Court found that it had competence in respect of the real estate assets of Bulgaria which were not held for sovereign purposes.[580] The shared common basis in private international law - that the measure merely seeks to ensure compliance of the parties with the measure - here, the debt due under the arbitral award - may be regarded as a source of the public international legal norm.

As set out in *Mobil Cerro* above and the cases cited on freezing injunction, though they might be thought to have a more coercive effect than some other executory measures, as demonstrated by widespread and consistent practice, they fall within the scope of the state's adjudicative jurisdiction. These have been made available irrespective of any link between the court's territorial jurisdiction and the arbitration dispute, provided further requirements are satisfied.[581] Given this, it is all the more surprising if the decision in *UK P&I* holds weight as to the permissibility of anti-suit injunctions against states, including where their commercial assets are concerned, since freezing injunctions appear to be even more intrusive forms of relief and yet are granted as a part of the state's adjudicative jurisdiction.[582]

Even though worldwide freezing injunctions - against assets outside the court's territorial jurisdiction - have tended to be granted predominantly by UK courts, the basic requirements of a real risk of dissipation are a common basis for the jurisdiction. Specific requirements which have emerged in respect of WFOs in the jurisdictions in which they are available will be examined in the 'specific measures' section below.

579. *Société Chematur* (n 509).
580. Similarly: Kammergericht [Court of Appeal] Berlin, 20 Sch 07/04, 10 August 2006 (based on the court's power to order provisional execution under §1062(2), the Berlin Court of Appeal was competent to issue execution orders even though the Defendant did not have place of habitual residence or domicile in Germany, provided assets are within the jurisdiction); OLG Düsseldorf, I-4 Sch 10/09 (n 369); Walter Bau 1 (n 20).
581. As set out above briefly, generally 'real risk of dissipation of assets' must be proven. In the US, the additional requirement of 'irreparable harm' may also need to be proven, similarly to 'real risk of dissipation' and requiring 'course of conduct in relation to assets, actual or feared' and 'that there exists a risk impairing the claimant's ability to enforce a judgment or award' (*Mobil Cerro* (2008) (n 206) [35]-[37]); *GE Transportation* (n 333) (US); *Sperry* (n 333) (stating the background that a preliminary injunction had been incorrectly granted because irreparable harm had not been demonstrated where potential damage was strictly monetary).
582. *See*, *UK P&I Club* (2023) (n 276); *see* Chapter 3, section [D][3](b).

[G] PRAGMATISM

It is also useful to look at decisions by national courts which may be 'pragmatic' in nature as a source of any enforcement jurisdiction norm. These concern those decisions made based on what the court considers it *ought* to do in a certain set of circumstances.

Functionalism traditionally supports pragmatic approaches to the law because institutions might collectively pursue or 'stand at the centre of' a collective endeavour, as Michaels puts it.[583] This of course makes sense: if not only the decisions and reasoning themselves can be taken into account but also the effects of decisions, functionalism goes beyond the constraints of doctrinal thinking and formalism. In support of this, Zweigert describes functionalism as an anti-doctrinal method.[584] Pursued for the purposes of identifying a source of international law, the functional comparative method assists in the identification of an international legal norm.

In the *Yukos* decision mentioned in the introduction and in the sovereign equality section in Chapter 2, Yukos had obtained an award which it sought to have set aside in the UK Court based on non-recognition of a Russian annulment decision. That decision was allegedly rendered based on instruction by the Russian executive, and accordingly had been 'partial and dependant', i.e., vitiated by the improper conduct or even possibly fraud of a foreign state.[585] The Court could be viewed as adopting a pragmatic approach in the earlier 2012 Yukos decision with regard to the consideration of the Dutch decision, which found the Russian annulment 'partial and dependant'. Yukos contended that since the Dutch courts had finally determined that the annulment decisions were partial and dependent, then Rosneft Oil Company, against whom the award was rendered, would be issue estopped from denying that fact. Finding that the Defendant was not so issue estopped, the UK Court opined that the courts, being the courts of a different state, must be able to determine themselves, according to their own concept of public order, whether the decisions are in fact impartial and independent.[586]

The Court referred to the more flexible concepts of *forum non conveniens* and comity when determining whether the matter could be tried by a UK Court. *Forum non conveniens* allows a court to decline jurisdiction, finding that a foreign court's authority is more appropriate in the circumstances.[587] Applying the doctrine of comity, the Court stated the doctrine 'demands any such enquires are conducted with that proper respect which is owed in the international sphere to the courts of friendly foreign nationals'.[588] Based on comity, the UK Court found that 'English courts will require cogent grounds for any allegation that a foreign court decision should not be recognized on the grounds of a failure of substantial justice'. That, the Court stated, was 'a matter of evidence and

583. Michaels (n 48) 362.
584. *See, e.g.*, Konrad Zweigert, 'Rechtsvergleichung, System und Dogmatik', in *Festschrift für Eduard Bötticher* (1969), 443, 448.
585. *Yukos Capital Sarl v. OJSC Rosneft Oil Co* [2012] EWCA Civ 855; *see* Chapter 1[G][1] (introduction to Yukos) and Chapter 2[B].
586. *Yukos* (2012) (n 585) [155].
587. *Ibid.*, [61].
588. *Ibid.*, [125].

argument, not a matter of any immunity or the doctrine of non-justiciability'.[589] The Court made similar findings based on *forum non conveniens.*

The Court ultimately concluded that the question of whether the Russian annulment decision was 'partial and dependant' is a 'matter to be tried' on the evidence.[590] Since *forum non conveniens* was a principle in light of which the Court decided to exercise a discretion, the effect of this approach might be regarded - from the Court's perspective - as not binding as a matter of law. However, since the effect of the decision was to ensure the enforcement process could continue in relation to the already rendered arbitration award, it also ought to be considered a source of the public international law norm. This is because, based in part on those flexible principles,[591] the Court reasoned that a further review of the merits of the Dutch decision was necessary before enabling issue estoppel to take hold, with such decision ultimately leading to recognition (or refusal to recognise) the award.[592]

The extent to which the doctrines of *forum non conveniens* and comity are in fact used more directly to justify a court's jurisdiction in the public sphere to grant the measure itself is more limited. In general, the principle of comity tends to be relied on less heavily by the courts as a justification for jurisdiction, with the court preferring to decide matters based on statutory interpretation or more traditional methods. For example, in the *Dallah* decision discussed in Chapter 4, one of the parties relied upon the concept of international comity as a justification for a 'pro enforcement' approach under the New York Convention. Citing that earlier decision, the Court stated in paragraph 14 that the standard of proof as to whether a party can get recognition or enforcement under the relevant provision (section 103(2)) is determined by the wording of the New York Convention itself:

> 82. I cannot agree with this submission. It seems to me that I am bound by the wording of the Act itself, which reflects faithfully that of the Convention. A party who wishes to persuade a court to refuse recognition or enforcement of a Convention award must *prove* one of the matters set out in paragraphs (a) to (f) of section 103(2). Those paragraphs are definitive of what a party can prove in order that a court *'may'* refuse recognition or enforcement of a Convention award. If party must *'prove'* a matter, that must mean, in the context of English civil proceedings, prove the existence of the relevant matters on a balance of probabilities.[593]

This is hardly a surprising approach of the Court regarding a more straightforward question of whether an award can be enforced under the New York Convention.

589. *Ibid.*, [125].
590. *See*, recently, similar acknowledgment that the UK court will re-consider the matter in *Hulley Enterprises* (2025) (n 499), although in that case, the Court was minded recognising that Russia was issue estopped on the question of state immunity because the Dutch decision *had* decided the question of whether the award was 'partial and dependant'.
591. Shany described comity as a 'flexible regulating principle' and that description shall be adopted here: Shany (n 112).
592. Finally acknowledging in the more recent Yukos decision that Russia was estopped from relitigating questions of state immunity due to an issue estoppel based on recognition of the Dutch decision that the award was 'partial and dependant': *Hulley Enterprises* (2025) (n 499).
593. *Dallah* (n 109) [12].

With regards to more nuanced matters relating to enforcement, such as whether the court can hear the dispute at all where there are foreign annulment proceedings ongoing, the court may look to concepts such as comity and *forum non conveniens*. For example, these doctrines have been relied upon to justify why evidence can be heard in relation to enforcement[594] or whether a 'stay' can be granted in respect of recognition of an award in light of the particular interests of parties, such as awaiting grant of security.[595] It is in these types of situations that looking at doctrines such as comity and *forum non conveniens* can be useful, where a practical complexity involved in the recognition process has arisen, often where there are competing interests with foreign courts or even between the parties. Thus, they can be helpful to postpone recognition or conversely to allow a recognition process to continue notwithstanding annulment proceedings in foreign courts where there is a valid arbitration award but a strong reason to challenge the annulment process.

Ultimately, however, comity and *forum non conveniens* operate as justifications for whether a court will find it has jurisdiction and go on to render a decision notwithstanding state immunity, and thus, do not tend to be sources of the practice but rather justifying principles to whether jurisdiction was available or not. Therefore, they have been of limited assistance in identifying the practice illustrated in this work.

[H] WORLDWIDE FREEZERS AND DISCOVERY AS SPECIAL MEASURES

Subject to any additional procedural requirements under national law, the international practice examined includes attachment orders on the same basis as above: that the assets are held for commercial purposes and located within the jurisdiction.

[1] Worldwide Freezing Orders (WFOs): Assets Outside the Jurisdiction

A WFO is a particular type of freezing order which can be granted against assets worldwide rather than those within the court's territorial jurisdiction. The civil law courts examined do not grant WFOs, but rather only freezing orders *in rem*, meaning the measure must specify the form of assets, whereas WFOs are *in personam* meaning they can be granted in respect of a particular company or individual. The UK is the only jurisdiction of the common law jurisdictions examined which grants these types of wide-reaching execution measures, but only as an exceptional remedy when certain prerequisites are met. Thus, these decisions can be considered a source of the general principle in so far as the UK approach is concerned, though it would not mean that WFOs are generally available globally pursuant to any such general principle to be derived from that practice.

The *ArcelorMittal* decision mentioned in the introduction to this work serves as an example of where a court granted WFO – traditionally regarded as a more intrusive

594. For example, *Yukos* (2012) (n 585).
595. *Hulley Enterprises* (2021) (n 66).

form of enforcement relief - in respect of assets pursuant to a foreign arbitration award.[596] There was no territorial connection between the court's jurisdiction and the arbitration dispute, the award being rendered under the ICC Rules in Minnesota. As recognised by the Court, the Defendant had an insufficient connection to English jurisdiction, including no substantial assets in England, to justify an ordinary exercise of its jurisdiction under the private international law rule of a 'real and substantial' connection.[597] Nonetheless, the Court found it had jurisdiction based on there being a 'solid risk of dissipation' and it being 'just and convenient' to grant the WFO.

Apart from the *ArcelorMittal* decision, the decision in *Cruz City* is of note.[598] In that decision, although the arbitration did occur in the UK, substantial assets of the company against which enforcement was sought were in India. A particular circumstance of the case was that the Claimant was also seeking to enforce the award against third parties, meaning assets held by a third party but which were in fact beneficially owned by the Defendant.[599] Even though there was no cause of action against that third party, the Court found that it could grant the freezing order to non-parties to assist in enforcement of the arbitration award.

This extended what the UK court calls 'Chabra' jurisdiction following the decision in *TSB Private Bank International SA v. Chabra,*[600] which allowed a freezing injunction to be granted against a third party (a person against whom the Claimant had no claim) but who appeared to hold assets on behalf of the Defendant. It is interesting that this judgment appeared to extend that jurisdiction expressly as 'a remedy ... effecting ... an arbitration award' pursuant to CPR r. 62.5(1)(c). This is a gateway for 'service out of the jurisdiction' for a remedy affecting an arbitration, but where the seat of the arbitration is or will be within the jurisdiction.

WFOs, by their nature, are in the public sphere notwithstanding their connection to the territorial court's jurisdiction. They ensure that assets abroad - including potentially those held by third parties - can be frozen in satisfaction of the arbitral award. However, as with any other form of execution, the prerequisites for jurisdiction should be carefully scrutinised in light of the particular facts of the case.

The Court stated that a freezing order in relation to foreign assets can be granted only in 'exceptional circumstances' and it is this which would justify an exercise of the court's discretion under section 37(1) SCA.[601] In *ArcelorMittal,* the exceptional circumstance was where the underlying cause of action was deceit or a proprietary claim for theft of assets, there being a 'strong case of serious wrongdoing comprising conduct on a large or repeated scale'. In that situation, the UK Court stated: 'I see no reason why the English court should not be willing to intervene rather than stand by and allow the conduct to continue and, to put it more colloquially, to let the wrongdoer get away with

596. *ArcelorMittal* (2019) (n 32).
597. *Ibid.,* [69]. The Court considered it irrelevant that there were English connections of other companies within the Essar group.
598. *Cruz City* (2014) (n 293).
599. *Ibid.,* [8].
600. *TSB Private Bank International SA v. Chabra* [1992] 2 All ER 245.
601. *ArcelorMittal* (2019) (n 32) [73].

it.'[602] In that case, attempted dissipation of the Defendant's asset worth in the sum of USD 1.5 billion in the face of arbitration proceedings was sufficient to warrant intervention under what the Court deemed the 'international fraud' exception.[603]

In the US, the availability of such measures has been restricted by the *Grupo Mexicano* decision,[604] which means that national statutes have to be relied upon for pre-judgment attachment in support of the arbitration award.[605] Nonetheless, state courts have still not granted Mareva injunctions but only freezing injunctions in respect of in-state assets. In that decision, Justice Scalia famously interpreted the Judiciary Act 1789. There, he found that the Act conferred jurisdiction on federal courts only over 'all suits in equity', being equivalent remedies 'administered by the English Court of Chancery at the time of separation of the two countries' (i.e., 1789). Since the English court did not grant such remedies at the time pursuant to an equitable jurisdiction, the US court could not grant them now. Pre-judgment attachment orders have been granted by New York, California and Texas under provisions in their particular state laws (as distinct from Federal Law),[606] but these decisions have been limited to assets within US territory, and specifically only within the state where the court is located.[607] While a specific waiver may be required in respect of pre-judgment attachment, commercial assets within the jurisdiction are attachable provided the further requirement of waiver is satisfied in the US.[608]

[2] Discovery/Disclosure

Discovery or disclosure are available measures irrespective of state immunity to support the process of execution against commercial assets within the jurisdiction.[609] This section is limited to discovery, which would support execution against assets, as distinct from court support in relation to discovery in the arbitration proceedings themselves. The latter has been limited in the US, for example, by the Supreme Court decision in *Automotive US, Inc.*[610] There may be other limitations on whether discovery or disclosure will in fact be granted in respect of an award where, for example, there are outstanding issues related to state immunity. This occurred in the *P&ID v. Nigeria*

602. *Ibid.*, [75].
603. *Ibid.*
604. *Grupo Mexicano de Desarrollo v. Alliance Bond Fund, Inc,* 527 US 308 (1999).
605. *See,* especially, E Edmondson and R Ziegler, 'The Complications of Attaching Assets in the US in Aid of an Arbitral Award' (2016) 10 *DRI* 71-80.
606. N.Y. C.P.L.R. §§6201 *et seq.;* Cal. Code. Civ. Proc. §§481.010 *et seq.*; Tex. Civ. Prac. & Rem. Code Ann. §§61.001 *et seq.*
607. *See, e.g., VisionChina Media Inc v. Shareholder Representative Servs*, LLC, 109 A D.3d 49, 60 (1st Dep't 2013) (vacating order of attachment as improperly granted because of lack of showing of risk that the Defendant would fail to satisfy the judgment).
608. *Libancell* (n 525).
609. *See, e.g., Ashraf-Hassan v. Embassy of France in the U.S.*, 2014 WL 1493210 (D.D.C. 17 April 2014) (US); *Nedagro* (n 573) (US) (Court permitted discovery in respect of issue irrespective of immunity regarding arbitral proceeding in Russia).
610. *F Automotive US, Inc., et al. v. Luxshare, Ltd* 596 U.S. (2022).

decision,[611] in which the US Court of Appeals stated that the outstanding issue of immunity needs to be decided before the question of jurisdictional discovery was resolved. However, that decision did not restrict the general availability of discovery in respect of states or foreign arbitrations irrespective of immunity, but simply deferred the question because of an outstanding (unrelated) issue of immunity.

Discovery in support of execution against assets is generally a lawful form of execution jurisdiction in support of assets in the US. However, the usefulness of such process has been doubted by one US Court, where the Court rightly pointed out that since witnesses and documents were located outside the US and the Court had no power to subpoena those witnesses (with the requirement being that there is a connection to US territorial jurisdiction), the witnesses 'cannot be compelled to appear at a proceeding in the United States'.[612] In that case, it was therefore found that the more appropriate court for proceedings would be in the Ukrainian courts where the assets in dispute were also located. There may be further requirements as to whether it would be appropriate, on the particular facts of the case, to grant an order for disclosure or discovery; however, regardless of any further requirements, discovery is a generally available form of execution in respect of states.

From the French perspective, the Cour de Cassation also made findings in relation to the production of documents in the *Commisimpex* decision.[613] Earlier, the Cour d'appel de Versailles refused to order the production of documents relating to the Republic of Congo's accounts, which requested proof of the non-diplomatic use of accounts by Commisimpex. Finding this incorrectly reversed the burden of proof, the Cour de Cassation found the burden of proof was on the creditor to prove the non-diplomatic use of assets. The Court accepted that production of documents would be available in principle against a state by not dismissing the decision based on state immunity or any similar principle restricting enforcement.

In the UK, the courts have gone so far as to compel defendants to disclose assets worldwide in aid of execution in a decision in the *Cruz City* dispute, related though distinct to the earlier decision mentioned in relation to freezing orders.[614] Even though there was a link to UK jurisdiction as the arbitration took place in England, compelling disclosure of their assets worldwide engaged the court's enforcement jurisdiction and was permitted under the court's broad powers. Based on section 37 SCA 1981, the Court found that it was just and convenient to grant the order of disclosure to assist in enforcing the awards. Finding it certainly had the power to do so, the Court considered it was also 'just and convenient' to grant worldwide disclosure because the Claimants had a contractual right to the sums awarded in the arbitration and had been granted

611. *Process and Industrial Developments Limited v. Federal Republic of Nigeria and Ministry of Petroleum Resources of the Federal Republic of Nigeria* No. 18-7154 (United States Court of Appeals, District of Columbia 2019) [26] ('to defer the question is to "frustrate the significance of benefit of entitlement to immunity from suit"').
612. *Monegasque de Reassurances s.a.m. Monde Re v. NAK Naftogaz of Ukraine* 158 F. Supp. 2d 377 (Southern District of New York, 2001).
613. *Commisimpex* (n 511).
614. *Cruz City 1 Mauritius Holdings v. Unitech Limited and others* [2013] EWHC 1323 (Comm).

permission to enforce the awards as judgments.[615] Since there was evidence of potential assets in India but no further information, the Court viewed the order as material for assisting the Claimant in enforcing the awards.[616]

It is hard to find many instances in which German courts have ordered disclosure in respect of assets. However, in the decision of the Administrative Court of Berlin of November 2016, the Court considered the Claimant's request for disclosure of 'environmental information' pending an ICSID arbitration, considering such a request to not be excluded by state immunity.[617] The Court considered whether the public interest in disclosure prevailed over the Respondent's interest in preserving confidentiality, finding that such a principle ultimately did not prevail over confidentiality. However, it is understood that a power of disclosure in respect of assets would also be available in principle based on section 142 ZPO, though this would be at the discretion of the court and only in relation to specific and identifiable documents.

[3] Interim Conclusion

Given the general availability of worldwide freezing orders as well as discovery or disclosure in support of execution against assets across some of the representative states, these measures ought to be regarded as supporting a general principle of execution as falling within the state's international adjudicative authority irrespective of state immunity. WFOs may only be regarded as a source of the norm from the UK perspective and would not generally be regarded as available across all states, with the US, France and Germany not granting such measures in general. Discovery and disclosure, to varying degrees, have or ought (in the case of Germany) to be allowed in the public sphere in support of execution against commercial assets.

[I] DECISIONS EXCLUDED DUE TO LACK OF INTERNATIONAL APPROACH OR EXTRATERRITORIAL OVERREACH OF EXECUTION JURISDICTION

Despite the extent of commonalities in relation to the state practice identified, some decisions of national courts ought not be taken into account as a source of any public international law rule. As will be explained, they incorrectly interpret the Foreign Sovereign Immunities Act (FSIA) as constituting a 'comprehensive statute' rather than giving effect to the international legal principle of state immunity and thus should be excluded for failing to identify the international legal norm.

---

615. *Ibid.* [31].
616. Similarly, in respect of Germany: VG Berlin – 2 K 434.15, Administrative Court of Berlin, 2 K 434.15, 3 November 2016 (the Court, though not ultimately allowing disclosure in respect of the Claimant's environment information, did not reject the availability of disclosure in principle in relation to a pending ICSID arbitral proceeding).
617. VG Berlin decision 2 K 434.15 (n 616).

Illustrative of one such excluded decision is the *Republic of Argentina* decision.[618] In a dispute relating to enforcement against Argentina of an award obtained against it, the company, NML, applied to a US Court for post-judgment extraterritorial discovery in respect of information concerning extraterritorial assets. The Court interpreted the scope of its authority narrowly, finding that the FSIA replaced an earlier 'executive-driven, factor intensive, loosely common-law-based immunity regime with a comprehensive framework for resolving any claim of sovereign immunity'.[619] On that basis, the Court granted the order, finding that it was sufficient that its jurisdiction was 'not excluded' under §§1609, 1610, which does not limit such discovery. Accordingly, the Court found that its jurisdiction was exclusively governed by the statute which Government had enacted, and since there was *no provision forbidding* or limiting discovery in aid of execution of a foreign sovereign's assets, this would be permitted.[620]

The effects of such a decision are significant with regard to the aims of this work for deducing any consistent practice relating to an *international law* norm on execution jurisdiction. The Harvard Law Review rightly criticised the US decision in the *Republic of Argentina v. NML Capital*[621] for resting on an overly 'formalistic approach' to the question of the court's jurisdiction.[622] This is because it was founded on an interpretation of the court's jurisdiction as an exception, which was not prohibited by any FSIA rule or principle, without acknowledging the international principle of state immunity to which the Act gives effect.

Whether or not this decision was correct for what it achieved, it rested on flawed reasoning, overlooking the fact that the FSIA gives effect to the *international* law principle of state immunity. It follows that by simply accepting that its jurisdiction was available because it was *not excluded* by any provision of the FSIA, the decision is not instructive on the lawful scope of the court's jurisdiction to grant the particular measure from an *international law* perspective. It simply failed to consider this question, for example, of how the issuance of an extraterritorial discovery order might fit with the principle of immunity from execution, according to which a state is generally prohibited from exercising its execution jurisdiction where this would be a breach of a foreign state's sovereignty. An extraterritorial discovery order - by its nature - might appear to contravene such a principle in so far as it seems to authorise an extension of execution authority irrespective of any link to the court's territorial jurisdiction. Thus, without justification, the decision may be interpreted as bad law from an international law perspective. It rests on a false assumption that the legislative act, treated and interpreted in a vacuum, is the source of the court's jurisdiction, whereas principles of immunity which are of an *international nature* must be taken into account as a limit to such authority to the extent they define the scope of the court's lawful authority.

618. *Republic of Argentina* (2014) (n 152).
619. *Ibid.* (Analysis, B).
620. Such an interpretation also harks back to the *Lotus* approach criticised in Chapter 2 of this work that that which is not prohibited is therefore permitted; *see*, Chapter 2[E][1].
621. *Republic of Argentina* (2014) (n 152).
622. 'Republic of Argentina v NML Capital, Ltd' (2014) 128 *Harvard Law Review* 381.

Further, the Court in the *Republic of Argentina* case failed to provide reasons as to why jurisdiction would be justified *despite* the principle of immunity. The wording and structure of the FSIA are clear in this regard: §1604 FSIA states that subject to existing international agreements to which the US is a party, a foreign state shall be immune. The exceptions in §1605 FSIA are to be regarded as exceptions and no more - they do not *justify* or *authorise* jurisdiction but merely provide grounds upon which an otherwise available immunity may be removed. Even though the *effect* of the decision may appear to be consistent with any norm which allows execution measures to be granted irrespective of immunity, the decision rested on flawed reasoning that immunity does not limit such a power and *therefore* it is available. However, as demonstrated throughout this work, the fact that immunity does not exclude the jurisdiction is only *one* source of the court's authority.[623] Jurisdiction must also otherwise be justified according to principles underpinning authority, which may, in turn, justify the removal of an immunity.

Decisions of national courts should only be considered to the extent that they are consistent with the applicable public international law norm, and the other representative courts. In the *NML* decision, the US Court can be seen to have extended its authority beyond that which was conferred on it under the legislative Act and thus should not be taken into account as a source of the norm. This wide-reaching form of discovery has further not been permitted by other representative courts.

[J] CHAPTER CONCLUSIONS

Execution jurisdiction is a key part of the enforcement process, ensuring parties get their hands on the assets due under the arbitration award. This chapter has shed light on a harmonised approach relating to execution jurisdiction. Two grounds have been identified as prerequisites for execution jurisdiction irrespective of state immunity: (1) assets against which execution is sought are held for commercial purposes; *and* (2) those assets are located within the territorial jurisdiction of the court.

Since the practice is widespread, consistent and representative between the examined states (UK, US, France and Germany), the suggestion is that it ought to be regarded as the source of a general principle of international law - a source of public international law within the meaning of Article 38(1)(c) ICJ Statute.

Execution has been particularly problematic in practice, with states seeking to rely on the principle of state immunity to exclude a court's jurisdiction and thereby evade enforcement, the pertinent example being *Yukos*.[624] Given the norm's applicability to national courts and international arbitral tribunals, recognition of these as a general principle of international law would be useful because it would encourage these bodies to be coordinated in terms of their jurisdiction to grant measures *under*

623. *See*, Chapter 1[G][2]; the commercial/sovereign assets distinction is one recently mentioned example where state immunity norms are one source, but so are rules or principles relating to enforcement in the forum court pursuant to private international law: compare Chapter 5[D] and [F].
624. *Yukos*, PCA Case No. 2005-04/AA227 (n 66).

public international law. This would be one solution to help ease execution of arbitration awards. In addition to the practical issues mentioned, such as those illustrated by the *Yukos* dispute, where states may move their assets around the world seeking to evade enforcement, doctrinal questions relating to the interaction between jurisdiction and immunity have been left unresolved in the area of execution. The identification of this common approach provides a legal foundation for the general principle of execution in respect of an award to which the principle of state immunity ought to operate as a *lex specialis*, thus creating a framework for development of the law.

The chapter has also expanded on some of the key theoretical findings relating to the approach adopted by this work. Despite differences in dualist and monist approaches, they are both encompassed by the approach, allowing effective comparative analysis. Pragmatic approaches by courts, including in relation to comity and *forum non conveniens*, may be taken into account as justifying principles, though they were not of great assistance when identifying the practice since the court's decisions generally rest on the interaction between the applicable procedural rules and state immunity in light of the New York Convention. Decisions where the national court has adopted incorrect interpretations of state immunity under the national harmonising law – for example, when considering the FSIA as a 'comprehensive statute' – should also be excluded when identifying any 'harmonising approach'.

Part III Enforcement Jurisdiction as a General Principle of International Law

Chapter 6

National Courts as a Source of a General Principle

Drawing the strands of this book together, this chapter argues for the extension of its theoretical approach – considering adjudicative jurisdiction as a manifestation of enforcement jurisdiction – to other areas of public international law. It also further cements the public authority approach as a useful tool in the sphere of international arbitration, justifying why, as a practical matter, the practice identified would be most suitably recognised as a general principle of international law.

[A] INTRODUCTION

General principles of international law are the broadest source of international law, being 'unwritten legal norms which are common to domestic laws and which are transposable at the international level'.[625] This is a generally accepted, broad definition of general principles, including by investment tribunals.[626] General principles are both *general* in nature – in the sense that they do not require their application at the national legal level to be the *same* as that at the international law legal level – but they also must be 'transposable', i.e., require proof of application in some form in the sphere of international law.

The previous chapters described a common practice according to which national courts consistently regulate the scope of an international arbitral tribunal's decision-making authority in the public sphere. It has been suggested that this practice ought to be regarded as a source of a general principle of international law, and this chapter

625. Pellet (n 44) 768.

626. *See,* especially Patrick Dumberry, 'The Emergence of the Concept of "General Principle of International Law" in Investment Arbitration Case Law' (2020) *Journal of International Dispute Settlement* 194, 198 https://doi.org/10.1093/jnlids/idz027 (accessed 26 September 2025).

shall further investigate why. Adjudicative jurisdiction as a manifestation of enforcement power provides the jurisprudential justification for the practice as a source of public international law (Chapter 2) more generally,[627] and the state practice described is illustrative of the content of the norms (Chapters 3-5).

Dumberry has found that investment tribunals now generally recognise the term 'general principle of international law'.[628] This chapter cements the importance and validity of recognition – both by national courts and international arbitral tribunals – by considering why categorisation as a general principle is appropriate, timely and practical.

The first section examines why the practice should be recognised as a general principle of international law, considering approaches to the New York Convention and to the alternative concept of 'transnationalism'. Customary international law is excluded from this analysis. As explained in Chapter 1, it would be difficult to consider the practice as a source of customary international law.[629] This is due to the difficulties in identifying whether the practice identified is underpinned by the conscious or unconscious consent of national courts and thus whether *opinio juris* could be established, which is a requirement of customary international law.[630] Instead, general principles allow wider national court practice to be taken into account, including practice which may have emerged *unconsciously* between courts – in the sense that the court does not expressly recognise that its power derives from a sense of legal obligation.

The second section deepens the analysis as to why the practice ought to be considered a general principle by considering why it does not represent a treaty phenomenon or mere 'soft coordination' of courts.[631] Shany identifies the problem of coordination of courts as being concerned with 'jurisdictional interactions between national and international courts with respect to disputes between the same parties (or, closely connected sets of parties) over essentially identical issues, potentially or actually brought, simultaneously or consecutively, before national and international courts'.[632] Such an approach encompasses 'global approaches' to national courts, including whether they communicate through 'networks' as a form of soft coordination rather than as a concrete source of international law.[633] Globalist scholars are focused on approaches beyond or outside state structures, using the normative structure of the law as the backdrop for such interactions. The focus here is on how national courts might be regulated by a framework of law – here, public international law.

Considering adjudicative jurisdiction as a manifestation of enforcement jurisdiction goes beyond traditional consent-oriented approaches which hold that enforcement

627. Being the jurisprudential legitimacy for the general principle according to Saunders' approach (n 46); *see* Chapter 1[E][1] and Introduction to Part II.
628. Dumberry (n 626) 202.
629. Chapter 1[F][2].
630. The definition of which is itself hotly contested, *see, e.g.*, Lepard (n 53).
631. This approach is taken by authors such as Slaughter, *A New World Order* (n 112) (global coordination of courts) and Shany (n 112).
632. Shany (n 112) 2.
633. Slaughter, *A New World Order* (n 112).

jurisdiction within the territory of another state is prohibited absent the state's consent.[634] The enforcement norms identified may be useful in other areas in light of the challenges which cyberspace and other emerging areas of law which cross territorial borders pose.[635] Given the increasing deterritorialization of jurisdiction, public and private international law scholars need to develop a new and broader understanding of enforcement jurisdiction to accommodate these emerging challenges. This final section explores how the approach might apply to other areas of international law in which enforcement questions might arise, as well as how their concrete application to arbitration is useful.

[B] ALTERNATIVE APPROACHES TO SOURCES

Rather than being harmonised under a treaty or as transnational law, this section examines how the practice fits neatly within the concept of a general principle of international law. In light of the challenges which treaties and transnationalism pose for harmonisation, harmonisation being one of the central aims of this work, this conceptualisation is further justified.[636] Harmonisation is the process of 'ascertaining the admitted limits of international unification but does not necessarily amount to a vision of total uniformity'.[637] The aim is to seek the greatest degree of commonality possible in light of harmonising instruments. With this background in mind, recognition of the practice as a general principle would not only fit most closely in terms of how the practice is evolving but also, considering the alternatives, it may contribute to greater harmonisation of law.

[1] New York Convention as a Harmonising Instrument

Even though the success of the New York Convention for recognition and review of awards cannot be doubted, this study extended beyond those areas to supervision of the arbitral process, as well as execution against assets pursuant to an award. Where states are party to the arbitration, the interaction between enforcement across all three areas depends on national court approaches to state immunity. As a result, it has been necessary to examine national court decisions in the public sphere as a source of any consistent norm.

Article I(1) New York Convention provides for the recognition and enforcement of arbitral awards between two contracting states, irrespective of where they are made. It is questionable whether, by extension of the principle enshrined in Article I(1), states may have agreed to extend their enforcement jurisdiction to supervision of the arbitral process, and to execution of awards, and if so, to what extent. According to such

634. This is the definition provided in all major international law textbooks, *see* Staker (n 15); Shaw (n 15); Akehurst (n 16); Allen et al. (n 101) 384.
635. *See*, especially, Stephen Allen, 'Enforcing Criminal Jurisdiction in the Clouds and International Law's Enduring Commitment to Territoriality' in Allen et al. (n 101) 382.
636. *See*, Chapter 1[F][1].
637. Menski (n 47) 39.

argument, there would already be doctrinal harmonisation of the enforcement forms discussed under the New York Convention, and so this treaty would provide the conclusive answer to the question of scope of enforcement.

In the *Karaha Bodas* decision, which concerned the annulment of a Swiss award, a US Court made important findings in relation to the possibility of attachment (i.e., execution jurisdiction). Confirmation of the award was entered against Pertamina, and Pertamina commenced proceedings for annulment of the award and to obtain an injunction in Indonesia. KBC then sought enforcement of the award in the US Court and Pertamina applied for a stay on the basis that such proceedings were commenced in breach of its annulment proceedings in Indonesia. KBC then applied to the US Court for a preliminary injunction to prohibit Pertamina from seeking to prevent that court's execution of the arbitral award. On appeal to the United States Court of Appeals (Fifth Circuit), the Court found that the New York Convention did not divest the district court of its inherent authority to issue an injunction. Recognising the importance of the principle of enforcement under the New York Convention, the treaty-enshrined obligation to enforce therefore played into the Court's reasoning as to why (or why not) the preliminary injunction should be granted:

> Under the New York Convention and Chapter 2 of the Federal Arbitration Act (the Convention's implementing legislation), federal courts maintain jurisdiction to hear cases like this. Although these treaty obligations limit the grounds upon which the court can refuse to enforce a foreign arbitral award, there is nothing in the Convention or implementing legislation that expressly limits the inherent authority of a federal court to grant injunctive relief in respect to a party over whom it has jurisdiction.[638]

The principle of enforceability underlying the New York Convention *may* be treated as a *justification* for why the particular measure ought or ought not to be granted in view of potential future attachment (though it was not here; it was considered not to restrict enforcement authority) but is not the source of that authority; instead, that authority may be wider, including the inherent powers of courts.[639] Whether or not the New York Convention is the source of the court's authority, it tends to operate as a *principle* in light of which the court decides whether to exercise jurisdiction, or not. 'Principle' is defined here as it is in the introduction to this work, being as Koskenniemi rightly states, a norm which 'brings out arguments in favour of one way or another and thus do not determine a solution finally'.[640] Consequently, as discussed throughout this work, the New York Convention does not conclusively

638. *Karaha Bodas Co v. Perusahaan Petrambangan Minyak Dan Gas Bumi Negara*, 335 F. 3d 356 (United States Court of Appeals, Fifth Circuit 2007).

639. *See, e.g.*, Supervision: *Bahrain Telecommunications* (n 257); *Channel Tunnel* (n 242) 354; in German courts, as demonstrated, the source from the national perspective is §1033 and §1041 which give effect to principles in the New York Convention; In French courts, Article 1505 CPC similarly *gives* effect to the Article II New York Convention principle.

Recognition: *Mobil Cerro* (2015) (n 448) especially [32]-[33], [68]-[84], [87], [88] (New York Convention is the principled basis upon which execution might be pursued if a recognition order is validly obtained i.e., to ensure enforceability of arbitral awards under Article I); *Stati* (2016) (US) (n 381).

640. Koskenniemi (n 58); *see* Chapter 1[F][4].

determine the extent of a state's enforcement jurisdiction in respect of the arbitral process, but is a harmonising instrument in light of which that question is decided.

The US approach to the New York Convention in this vein is clear from the decision in *CBF*.[641] This concerned whether the Claimants ought to have applied for confirmation of an ICC award rendered in France before seeking its enforcement. The Court affirmed that Chapter 2 of the FAA, which implemented the New York Convention as a matter of US law, envisaged a single-step process of 'recognition and enforcement' meaning, under US law, the confirmation of a Convention award as a US judgment.[642] A similar approach has been followed in all the other representative jurisdictions examined.[643] However, the national courts are following the *national law* which *gives effect* to provisions of the New York Convention rather than the New York Convention itself. Thus, the New York Convention is not the *source* of court jurisdiction, but rather the national legal provisions in which it is given effect.

In so far as the New York Convention has been applied in the context of provisional relief and other supportive measures, the approach has been the same, i.e., it has not been the source for these measures in any of the representative states.[644] To

641. *CBF Industria De Gusa S/A v. AMCI Holdings, Inc*, No. 15-1133 (2d Cir. 2017) (US); similarly: *Mobil Cerro* (2017) (n 432) (similarly affirming the one-step process of 'recognition and enforcement' under the New York Convention as equivalent to 'confirmation' under US law which is merely recognising the award as being enforceable in the same way as a US court judgment).
642. *CBF* (n 641) [43].
643. *See, e.g.*, UK: *Svenska* (2006) (n 20) [102]-[104], as cited in *Dallah* (n 109) [69] (recognition under the New York Convention concerns whether the final award should be recognised as 'valid and binding' and section 103(2) gives the court the right to 'not recognize the award: if, for example, there is an error of law, *see*, *Dallah* (n 109) [7]); similarly, applications under section 101 or section 103 invariably concern whether the award may be recognised as enforceable or refused such recognition: e.g., *Dowans Holding Sa and Another v. Tanzania Electric Supply Co Ltd* [2011] EWHC 1957 (Comm); France: Republic of Lithuania, N° 09/19535 (n 443) [16] (stating that the object and purpose of the New York Convention is 'promoting the circulation of international awards by providing that contracting states shall recognize them as binding and enforce them in principle unless the parties against whom they are invoked furnish proof of one of the grounds for the refusal of enforcement [exhaustively listed]' (thus interpreting this when deciding whether to exercise jurisdiction); similarly, proceedings implicating the New York Convention have always related to recognising the award as enforceable or refusing recognition under French law: *see, e.g.*, Cour d'appel (1st and 2nd Civil Chambers of Rouen), 13 November 1984, *Société Européenne d'Etudes et d'Entreprises and Others v. Socialist Federal Republic of Yugoslavia and Others*, No. 982/82 [30]; Germany: Cases No. 9 Sch 2/09, and No. III ZB 8/12 (n 477) [1]-[3]; Walter Bau 1 (n 20) [7] (exercising jurisdiction based on §1061 ZPO which gives effect to the New York Convention as part of German law).
644. *See, e.g.*, *Stemcor USA Incorporated v. Cia Siderurgica do Para COSIPAR*, 927 F.3d 906 (United States, Court of Appeals, 5th Circuit, 2019) (US) (the source for granting attachment was not the New York Convention but the Louisiana non-resident statute. The New York Convention played a role in the decision, *inter alia*, in so far as the US is a Convention State and the Court was thus obliged to consider whether ordering the measure was inconsistent with the New York Convention or not); *E.T.I. Euro Telecom* (n 226) (UK) [30] (an argument was made that subject matter jurisdiction arose under the New York Convention. However, as is made clear in the rest of the judgment, the source of the court's jurisdiction arises under the EAA and SJJA. The New York Convention is relevant no more than for the normative argument that the debt is within the jurisdiction of the court and thus another forum (New York) is the appropriate venue); the New York Convention is not even mentioned in French and German decisions on

the extent that it has applied, it has merely been stated that the principle of consent to arbitration pursuant to Article II does not prevent the ordering of supervisory measures.[645] However, as illustrated by Chapter 2, it is clear that not all supervisory measures are made pursuant to the New York Convention, but rather the source may be national arbitration laws and state immunity laws.[646] Consequently, in so far as supervision is concerned, it has been necessary to examine national court decisions themselves to determine the extent of relief available because it appears that such powers do not arise directly under the New York Convention (though the exercise of decision-making authority may be considered in light of the Convention).

Thus, the New York Convention has not provided doctrinal harmonisation for the enforcement norms examined in Chapters 3-5. At best, it has contributed to harmonisation of some of those enforcement norms – that is, it has operated as a principle in light of which national courts have decided (or not) to exercise jurisdiction, but it has not bound them in respect of the norms examined.

Moreover, in order to take into account the *full* extent of national court decisions, which may be a source for the scope of international arbitral authority,[647] it has been necessary to examine decision-making authority of national courts as the principal source. This allows adjudicative jurisdiction to be considered in light of both national legal norms, which may give effect to the public international legal norm, *as well as* harmonising laws such as the New York Convention, in so far as they are relevant to the discrete norm under examination. In some cases, such as the power to review on the merits under the applicable law, this has been developed in more detail by national courts, some of which give greater or lesser deference to the arbitral tribunal.[648] Similarly, the New York Convention does not cover execution jurisdiction at all and relates only tangentially to supervisory jurisdiction (in so far as that power does not seem to be prohibited by Article II). In these areas, it has been necessary to look beyond treaty law and to the national court decisions themselves as the source of any international law norms.

---

interim relief; these powers are found in the relevant part of their Civil Procedure Rules (§1033 ZPO and Article 1505 CPC) e.g., LG Braunschweig, 4 August 2015 (n 214) (Germany); Decision of 27 October 2011 No. 11/11104 (n 247).

645. *See, e.g., Stemcor* (n 644) (2018) (US).
646. *See, e.g., McCreary* (n 344) (US); Chapter 3 F[2].
647. Given that the principal question is the extent of *harmonisation* of enforcement aspects of adjudicative jurisdiction, which presupposes that a *wide* definition of adjudicative authority should be considered in so far as it is consistent with international law. Harmonisation is 'the process of ascertaining the admitted limits of international unification but does not necessarily amount to a vision of total uniformity' (Menski (n 47) 39); thus the 'limits' would include *any* national court decisions which *may* be illustrative of the rule or principle, from the perspective adopted.
648. *See,* Chapter 4[D][1], comparing UK and US approaches with that of Germany and France.

[2] Transnationalism

In his seminal work on the subject, Jessup defines transnational law as being 'all law which regulates actions or events that transcend national frontiers'.[649] Transnational approaches in national court decisions invite a wider approach to the scope of the court's authority beyond merely relying on the national legal rule as a source of authority.[650] Transnational law does not have its source in any particular legal system but 'represents a convergence of rules drawn from several legal systems'.[651] This section will suggest that while the transnationalism, as a concept, may support harmonisation, whether it in fact contributes to harmonisation is dependent on whether the national court in question recognises the concept. Thus, it would not lead to as much harmonisation compared to where the source is a binding general principle of international law.

Illustrative of this approach is the decision in *République Tchèque*.[652] An arbitration award had been obtained against the Czech Republic pursuant to the Croatia-Czech Republic BIT. The Court was asked to determine whether the investment in question was an 'investment' within the BIT. The Czech Republic applied to challenge the award on jurisdictional grounds in the French courts. The Court decided it could exercise review jurisdiction in respect of the foreign award, *inter alia*, because 'the international award, which is not attached to any state legal order, is a decision of *international justice* whose regularity is examined in the light of the rules applicable in the country where its recognition and execution are requested'.[653]

According to this, the French Court viewed itself as authorised by a transnational legal approach to review the substantive decision of the arbitral tribunal. Such an approach contributes in principle to the extension of review power beyond the scope of the court's territorial jurisdiction, which may also be illustrative of the rule or principle. However, the reasoning for such an approach was dependent on recognition of the transnational legal conception within the French *national* legal system.

The harmonising effect of the approach is thus limited by the extent to which the particular legal system recognises the concept. Of the states examined, it appears that only the French legal system implements a transnational law approach to recognising arbitration as a system of 'international justice' – floating in principle above national legal orders – and justifying extensions of court authority on this basis.[654] This

649. Phillip C Jessup, *Transnational Law* (Yale University Press 1956).
650. One might argue that 'transnational' law does not have a *national* element because, by its nature, it crosses borders. However, there is no agreement on what 'transnational law' includes, except the general principle that it is a convergence of rules or principles drawn from different legal systems with at least *some* cross-border element. Thus, this does not exclude that at least one of the sources of a transnational rule or principle is national law.
651. Jessup (n 649).
652. Cour d'Appel, 20 November 2012, *République Tchèque v. Diag Human SE*, Revue de l'Arbitrage (Volume 2012 Issue 4) pp. 882-883.
653. *Ibid.*
654. Similarly: Cour de Cassation, 29 June 2007, *Societe PT Putrabali Adyamulia (Indonesia) v. Rena Holding, et al.*, 05-18,053 (Bulletin 207, I, No. 250) (justifying the application of French law which does not permit annulment in the country of origin on such a basis, thereby achieving a potentially inconsistent approach with the principles established in this chapter); Cour

approach involves the recognition of a rule or principle within the French legal system rather than recognition that the norm binds the court as a matter of law.[655]

When developed by national courts, it is difficult to see how a transnational legal approach could contribute to harmonisation, or at least as much harmonisation as international law, given that the national court has a *discretion* to recognise the transnational norm as law. In contrast, national courts are bound to recognise the binding nature of public international law norms; whether they do so or not is a distinct question.

While the norms demonstrated by this book may provide a basis for normative harmonisation in public international law, the convergence of transnational legal approaches depends on the convergence of processes through recognition of transnationalism as a concept across multiple legal systems.[656] This has not been the focus of this work, which has been grounded in potential harmonisation under public international law as the normative framework, though it would be a further potential research avenue for examining the convergence of national court approaches.

[3] Trapping of National Courts Within Sovereign Conceptions of State Immunity

Though the *source* of the norm could be regarded as national law when viewed from the perspective of that particular system, it *becomes* international law to the extent that the representative courts contribute consistently to an international legal norm shared across states. However, difficulties emerge when jurisdiction is considered as solely being based on a provision adopted in national law. Decisions based on national law provisions may fail to interpret the law in a manner which would be consistent with any public international law norms applicable to the scope of authority. The following section considers how, when adopting its own national law approach to a common international legal question, the national court does not necessarily contribute to the international legal norm but might create an (unnecessarily) divergent approach.

Consideration of the source for state immunity as being exclusively and comprehensively the national implementing statute is problematic from the perspective of harmonisation for two reasons. The first has been expanded upon in Chapter 5 in

d'appel de Paris (1re Ch. C), 31 January 2008, *Société ivoirienne de raffinage v. société Teekay Shipping Norway AS et autres*, Revue de l'Arbitrage (Volume 2008 Issue 1) pp. 163-165 (though not in the public sphere, as a matter of *reasoning*, this judgment supports this approach of French courts, more generally).

655. Similarly, and further: *République de Guinée Équatoriale* (n 222) (reliance on same principle as in *République Tchèque* (n 652) – that is, the idea that an international award is not attached to any national legal order – to justify adherence to the *narrow* scope of French court review power under its own Civil Procedure Rules); Similarly: *PT Putrabali* (n 654) (award obtained in London could be recognised despite annulment decision in London Court. This was justified in the application of French law, which does not permit annulment in the country of origin on such a basis).

656. For example, as Walker points out, international law is the 'institutionalisation' of transnational governance, transnationalism generally being the result of a more *organic* process: Walker (n 50) 60. Though the approach identified here may be organic, the proposal is that it ought to be formalised/institutionalised through recognition as a general principle.

relation to the *Republic of Argentina v. NML Capital* decision, where the Court granted extraterritorial discovery in relation to assets due under an award because it was 'not prohibited' by the FSIA. To reiterate the reasoning of the Court, it found that the FSIA replaced an earlier 'executive-driven, factor intensive, loosely common-law-based immunity regime with a comprehensive framework for resolving any claim of sovereign immunity'.[657] On that basis, the Court granted the order, finding that it was sufficient that its jurisdiction was 'not excluded' under sections 1609 and 1610, which do not limit such discovery. Accordingly, the Court found that its jurisdiction was exclusively governed by the statute which Congress had enacted, and since there was no provision forbidding or limited discovery in aid of execution of a foreign sovereign's assets, this would be permitted.[658] There have been many further US decisions which have based their decisions on such reasoning.[659]

The consequence explained in Chapter 5 is that such an approach promotes poorly reasoned decisions which do not take into account the international legal principle of state immunity to which the national implementing statute gives effect. The consequences in the area of jurisdiction can be far-reaching, because, without justification, enforcement power could compel a foreign state to do something which is not otherwise lawful or permitted.

Such an approach harks back to the *Lotus* approach examined in Chapter 2, according to which the Court found that that which is not prohibited is permitted.[660] As explained by Judge Simma, this does not go to what the *lawful* scope of the court's authority is and thus does not really provide an answer which determines how these principles should apply to that question.[661] Courts which are trapped within sovereign conceptions of state immunity do not promote nor lead to any greater harmonisation of international law.

A second consequence, which has been examined in relation to national courts inability to supervise and review the awards of ICSID Tribunals,[662] concerns the inability of tribunals thereby to move with the development of international law. This is similar to the issue of self-contained regimes, which broadly speaking relates to the issue of fragmentation, where a 'real conflict' arises between norms of international

657. *Republic of Argentina* (2014) (n 152) (Analysis, B).
658. Such an interpretation is reminiscent of the *Lotus* approach criticised in Chapter 2 of this work that that which is not prohibited is therefore permitted: *see* Chapter 2[E].
659. *See, e.g., Liberian Eastern Timber Corporation (LETCO) France v. The Government of the Republic of Liberia* 2 ICSID Rev-FILJ 188 (1987). Similarly, *see, Blue Ridge Investments v. Republic of Argentina* 902 F. Supp. 2d 367 (S.D.N.Y. 2012) p. 19 and ft 23 (the Court noted that the question of whether execution jurisdiction - if it did arise - would be interpreted solely within the confines of the FSIA, under which there would still be a presumption of immunity and thus the availability of execution would arise as an exception to this); *Ipitrade International Sa v. Nigeria* 465 F. Supp. 824 (DDC 1978); 63 ILR; *NML Capital et al v. Republic of Argentina*, 12-150L (2d Cir. 2012) (permanent injunctions granted under FSIA); *Republic of Austria v. Altmann*, 541 U.S. 677 (2004).
660. Chapter 2[E][1].
661. Judge Simma (n 119) [8].
662. For consideration in different contexts: Chapter 3[F][4] (supervision); Chapter 4[D][2] (recognition and review) and 4[E][2].

law – that is, when there is no rule or principle to decide which norm should prevail.[663] Self-contained regimes are said to operate outside the scope of a more general system of international law and therefore are said to pose a threat to the 'unity' of international law.[664] The ICSID regime has been wrongly labelled as a self-contained regime when it is in fact a closed one: its self-contained nature ought not to be regarded as posing a threat to unity in international law, but instead its 'closed' nature does not mean tribunals cannot be regulated by public international law.

Illustrative of the potential problem of closed regimes is another decision in the NML saga, this time relating to whether permanent injunctions could be granted to support attachment proceedings in respect of assets owed to NML as creditors of the Republic of Argentina.[665] The Republic of Argentina had defaulted on paying its external sovereign debt. NML Capital, a holder of Argentine bonds, filed suit in the Southern District of New York to collect the bonds, which ruled in favour.[666] This was an appeal from permanent injunctions granted by the same court. The question on appeal was whether the Court had abused its discretion to grant the injunctive relief or, alternatively, whether the injunctive relief violated the FSIA. Consequently, the question of the Court's enforcement jurisdiction arose solely as a question under the FSIA rather than whether the particular measure was permissible under the applicable norms of international law. Further evidence of this approach is in the language of the Court, which provided:

> because compliance with the injunctions would not deprive Argentina of control of any of its property, they *do not operate as attachments of foreign properly prohibited by the FSIA*. Section 1609 of the FSIA establishes that 'the property in the United States of a foreign start shall be immune from attachment arrest and execution ... courts are also barred from granting 'by injunction, relief which they may not provide by attachment'.[667]

The Court found that since the injunctions 'do not deprive Argentina of control over its property', they do not operate as attachments and thus do not fall within the scope of section 1609 FSIA. The Court failed to consider the possible *effect* of such measures, which is to attach foreign state property within the jurisdiction – ordinarily excluded by international principles of state immunity. By considering the particular execution measure as 'permitted' because it is 'not prohibited',[668] the Court failed to consider whether its jurisdiction would be *lawful* under the international legal principles to which the FSIA gives effect, which would have been the proper question in these circumstances, especially where there is no clear legislative rule or principle.

663. This problem has been noted by Pauwelyn (n 354) (giving the example of WTO rules conflicting with environmental standards, for example).
664. *See*, especially, International Law Commission, Fragmentation Report (n 72) 220-226.
665. *NML Capital* (2012) (US) (n 659).
666. *EM Ltd.* (n 151).
667. *NML Capital* (2012) (US) (n 659) [257].
668. The approach considered incorrect by Judge Simma considering the *Lotus* case: Judge Simma (n 119); *See*, further: Chapter 2[E].

[4] Interim Conclusion

Recognition of the practice as a general principle of international law overcomes the difficulties posed by the alternative approaches considered. The general principle would not require formalisation in a treaty similar to the New York Convention but rather recognition and application by arbitral tribunals and national courts, which better reflects the current practice. Furthermore, such recognition would not be reliant on globalist approaches to law, which rely on soft coordination of courts or recognition of principles such as transnationalism, and which might take a longer time to take hold within individual jurisdictions. Finally, recognition of such a general principle - one which is taking place within national courts already - would help limit the circumstances in which the courts might incorrectly interpret provisions which give effect to international law.

[C] MEANS OF REGULATION

Apart from the observations already made concerning why other sources would not contribute to greater harmonisation, further pitfalls arise in relation to considering the practice as part of treaty law or as a means for 'soft coordination'. 'Soft coordination' would concern communication between courts in the form of 'informal networks' envisaged by globalist perspectives such as Anne-Marie Slaughter rather than being bound by public international law or the relevant normative framework.[669]

[1] Treaty Law

The grounds identified upon which enforcement jurisdiction may be exercised (Chapters 3-5) *could* be formalised in a treaty. Such a treaty could include a provision regarding the interaction between the application of norms to national courts and international arbitral tribunals. The treaty could include elaboration of each of the three principles of enforcement which would apply to national courts (supervisory, recognition and review and execution) and how these interact with the international legal principle of immunity. It might also contain a provision elaborating on the interaction between those powers with any applicable arbitration rules. The aim would be to restrict arbitral tribunals from adjudicating on certain matters which fall outside their decision-making authority by virtue of the international legal principle of state immunity, as well as clarifying the grounds upon which they do have authority in respect of parties seeking enforcement.

However, as demonstrated by this book, treaties, such as the New York Convention, have not been the source of court jurisdiction: the Convention merely contains principles in light of which the court decides whether or not to find it has jurisdiction. Thus, harmonisation via a treaty is unlikely to contribute to any greater harmonisation of existing national court approaches because the national courts would still view

669. Slaughter, *A New World Order* (n 112); Shany (n 112).

national law as the source of their jurisdiction and the norm in the treaty as *merely* a 'principle'.[670] This would allow scope for the court to diverge or justify the development of the law in another direction, according to any differing national law rules.

Moreover, enshrining the common approach in a treaty would require widespread consent and a lengthy process between states. Given the existence of the New York Convention in this area and the identification of existent common approaches between national courts as the primary organs which enforce, any significant benefit of a treaty may be difficult to discern. From the perspective of those states, it might be more beneficial for the enforcement norms to be recognised as a source of international law being applied directly as a source of authority - rather than as a background principle - by national courts and arbitral tribunals. The advantage of this, for ensuring greater harmonisation of the approach identified, will be set out below in section [3] of this part.

[2] Coordination of Courts

Alternatively, some authors have considered the 'soft coordination' of courts as one means of regulation under public international law. This concept was previously used by Shany, who has identified certain general principles of international law which may coordinate national and international courts.[671] He identifies comity and '*abus de droit*' as the type of 'flexible regulating rules' which might ensure greater coordination, albeit in the context of regulation between international and national courts on issues of adjudication.[672] This is distinct from how 'coordination' is used by globalist scholars. They refer to 'transnational networks' in which national courts 'communicate' with each other to facilitate *informal* modes of communication (i.e., a non-law source) rather than contribute normatively to a source of law.[673]

In theory, soft coordination would ensure the coordination of courts through flexible regulatory rules or principles which are more informal in nature. However, since these are merely informal in nature, they would not ensure greater harmonisation under the *normative* framework of international law - instead, they would operate as rules or principles in light of which national courts *may or may not* exercise jurisdiction. Consequently, they would be more discretionary and less binding in nature than recognition of the practice as a general principle of international law.

670. In the sense described by Koskenniemi (n 58) which, as distinct from a 'rule', does not oblige the Court to follow the norm because that rule or principle is final regarding a matter, but merely provides guidance according to which the Court could determine to exercise jurisdiction in a particular way or not.
671. Shany (n 112).
672. *Ibid.*, Chapter 6.
673. Especially, Slaughter, *A New World Order* (n 112) 12-15, 18, 31-35; Anne-Marie Slaughter, 'International Law in the World of Liberal states' (1995) 6 *European Journal of International Law* 503, 515-521 https://doi.org/10.1093/oxfordjournals.ejil.a035934 (accessed 26 September 2025); Anne-Marie Slaughter, 'International Law and International Relations' (2000) 285 *Recueil des cours* 9, 41 (on the disaggregated state and how national courts are not conceived as organs of states but just bodies within networks).

Such an approach might be equated to the general treatment by courts of the principle of 'comity'. Comity is a legal principle (though not a general principle of international law) which is used by national courts in the examined area to justify a deferral of their jurisdiction to another court. Its most widely accepted definition can be found in the decision of *Hilton v. Guyot*: 'recognition which one nation allows within its territory to the legislative, execution and judicial acts of another nation'.[674] This implies that comity has the effect of allowing a state to recognise the acts of a foreign state only within *its own* territory. Thus, it would not apply to the question of how national courts may extend their jurisdiction over international arbitral tribunals operating *outside* their jurisdiction. A wider use of comity has been recognised in the scholarship on the subject.[675] According to this, whatever the *legal* nature of comity (i.e., whether it is binding or of a more discretionary nature, to be discussed further below), comity plays a 'jurisdiction-regulating role' because it ensures that one court rather than another has jurisdiction.[676]

The decision in *Ecobank*[677] is representative of the treatment of comity by UK and US courts.[678] Though 'comity' is not formally recognised in civil jurisdictions, it has gained sufficient recognition at the international legal level to be applicable there, including before arbitral tribunals.[679] Ecobank, an African bank, and Mr Tanoh, its employee, had agreed to arbitrate disputes arising out of an employment agreement

674. *Hilton v. Guyot*, 159 U.S. 113, 163-64 (1895); Ryngaert (n 15) Part 5.2; Donald E Childress III, 'Comity as Conflict: Resituating International Comity as Conflict' (2010) 44 *University of California, Davis Law Review* 11 (examining comity from the private international law perspective as a doctrine which 'encourages' courts to apply foreign law in appropriate cases); Mills (n 141) Chapter 4, ft 53 (acknowledging the uncertain nature of this norm).
675. Elisa D'Alterio, 'From Judicial Comity to Legal Comity: A Judicial Solution to Global Disorder?' (2011) 9 *International Journal of Constitutional Law* 394 https://doi.org/10.1093/icon/mor036 (accessed 26 September 2025); Ryngaert (n 15) 145 (discussing 'comity' as a principle which might justify when an exercise of jurisdiction by a state would be 'reasonable', within the framework of international law); Shany (n 112) 165-166 (considering 'comity' as a principle which regulates jurisdictional relations because such a principle serves a 'pro-coordination agenda').
676. *See*, especially, D'Alterio (n 675) 394 ('judicial comity' is the expression of a court's regulating function which is aimed at 'governing the relations between different legal systems within the global legal space'); Shany (n 112) 166 (comity serving a pro-coordination agenda).
677. *Ecobank Transnational* (n 224).
678. *See*, further: Supervisory jurisdiction: *Hulley Enterprises* (2016) (n 235) especially 285 (concerning supportive jurisdiction, specifically whether a stay could be granted to dismiss an order seeking a US Court to confirm an award in view of parallel Dutch proceedings. In this context, the Court found that it would 'have to consider the interests in international comity ... as part of its analysis as to whether such agreement [the arbitration agreement which had been set aside in the Dutch proceedings] existed'); further: Satya T Mouland, 'Rethinking Adjudicative Jurisdiction in International Law' (2019) 29 *Washington Law Review* 173, 194-195; Execution jurisdiction: *Mobil Cerro* (2008) (n 206) [86], [104]-[105] (comity is associated with other 'discretions' of the court and referred to as a mere 'consideration'), [116]-[117] (comity specifically considered in the context of whether the court may exercise its 'discretion' to grant an application to aid a freezing order affecting assets abroad).
679. Ryngaert (n 15) 145; Shany (n 112) 166; on application to ICSID Tribunals (as an example of an arbitral tribunal), *see* Thomas Schultz and Niccolo Ridi, 'Comity and International Courts and Tribunals' (2017) 50(3) *Cornell International Law Journal* 577, 578 (recognising that it should have 'regard' to earlier decisions of international courts).

between them in London under the UNCITRAL Rules. Mr Tanoh commenced proceedings against the bank in Togo and Cote d'Ivoire, obtaining judgments in both. Ecobank subsequently served notice for arbitration on Mr Tanoh and obtained a worldwide injunction preventing Mr Tanoh from enforcing the foreign judgments. On appeal, the Court considered the possible role which 'comity' might play in determining its approach to granting an anti-enforcement injunction. The Court cited its 'reluctance' to grant anti-suit injunctions where they: (1) appear to interfere with the proceedings of foreign courts; (2) were inconsistent with comity that ought to exist between courts; (3) were offensive to the foreign judiciary.[680] Comity is treated as a principle which would *justify* the Court's enforcement jurisdiction *at its discretion* - though which may not apply with regard to anti-suit injunctions where there is an express arbitration clause. Consequently, comity has a discretionary role to play in justifying or refusing to justify enforcement jurisdiction but is not the source of that authority.

Since comity operates as a discretionary rather than a binding principle of law, the extent to which it may serve in harmonisation of consistent approaches is akin to that described by globalist perspectives on law.[681] According to Slaughter's approach, national courts can only be 'coordinated' according to 'soft' principles of law.[682] This view rests on the perspective that since national courts operate in 'separate spheres' - in the sense that they operate within different legal systems without an overarching framework governing them[683] - then the greatest extent to which international law can assist in their coordination is through 'communication' and other soft law principles.[684] For example, the inclusion of international comity in §403 of the Restatement (1987) as 'jurisdictional reasonableness' to encourage balancing claims in view of international norms of jurisdiction, and any other such similar inclusion of comity in international legal instruments, ought to be encouraged.

Unless comity (as one example of such a 'soft' coordination) were to take on a more binding nature as a norm which obliges national courts to act in a certain way in a particular set of circumstances, it is difficult to see how the concept would contribute to greater harmonisation of national courts. It is in the courts' discretion to decide it has jurisdiction in view of a rule or principle such as comity, or not.

680. *Ecobank Transnational* (n 224) [82].
681. *See*, especially: Slaughter, *A New World Order* (n 112); Anne Marie Slaughter, 'A Global Community of Courts' (2003) 44 *Harvard International Law Journal* 191; Patrick Glenn, *The Cosmopolitan State* (OUP 2013) 239-240 (viewing national courts as no more able than states to contribute to the development of international law, given the characterisation of public international law is viewed as dependant on the approach which the state chooses to adopt; i.e., monist or dualist).
682. Slaughter, *A New World Order* (n 112); Slaughter, 'A Global Community of Courts' (n 681).
683. Slaughter, *A New World Order* (n 112) 103-106; Similarly, Glenn (n 681) 239-240 (views courts as operating within system which state chooses to adopt - whether monist or dualist).
684. Slaughter, *A New World Order* (n 112) 103-106 (seeing national courts as part of a 'disaggregated network' which 'coexist and interact').

[3] General Principles of International Law

If the norms illustrated in Chapters 3-5 were recognised as a general principle of international law, they could be utilised by international arbitral tribunals (as well as national courts) to delineate the scope of their jurisdiction when compared to those of national courts.

Dumberry has found that a great number of investment tribunals now recognise general principles of international law. This supports the viability of this approach, given the very bodies determining jurisdiction are beginning to recognise and apply them.[685] A treaty would also not add much because whether the source is a treaty or general principle, it would still need to be accorded a binding nature to reflect its nature under public international law.

Recognising representative national court approaches as the source of the general principle would assist investment tribunals in determining the scope of their jurisdiction. International arbitral tribunals which are tasked with making findings of fact relating to sovereign matters might refuse jurisdiction based on the principle of state immunity. A failure to refuse such jurisdiction would mean that an investment tribunal could circumvent immunity, rendering a decision which may then need to be overturned by the enforcing court.[686]

The general principle would also apply to national courts in relation to the forms of enforcement discussed. Where a tribunal is unable to act or not yet constituted, supervisory court jurisdiction may be required in view of the *international legal nature* of the principle. The court could recognise a growing 'international approach' to enforcement jurisdiction in its decision in support of the general principle. As distinct from a treaty principle, which may be further defined by adoption into a state's national laws, it is more likely that the court will be required to follow the precise content of a general principle considering its content as defined by comparative court practice. Indeed, in the *Trendtex* decision, the English Court recognised that the principle of *jure gestionis* was a customary international law principle, and thus, it was obliged to exercise jurisdiction. There is no reason that a national court should not do the same in relation to a general principle by recognising its binding nature. General principles are of course binding principles of international law within the meaning of Article 38(1)(c) ICJ Statute which have the same normative force as custom.

Even if courts were not to recognise their binding nature, recognition of the *international* nature of such principles may assist in developing international law. National court decisions are a major source in the development of customary international law in so far as they apply the same international legal principles.[687]

685. Dumberry (n 626) 202.
686. Considering *Abaclat* (n 23), *See*, Chapter 1[B]; Chapter 3[G]; Chapter 4[G]; Chapter 6[D][2].
687. As in the area of state immunity; *see* Fox and Webb (n 8) 17, 102-103.

[D] INTERNATIONAL ARBITRATION AND BEYOND

This section examines the importance of the enforcement of international arbitral tribunals by public international law, in particular focusing on how the public authority thesis provides the backbone of such an approach. It then goes on to illustrate the potential application of such an approach to other areas of international law.

[1] International Arbitral Tribunals

The 'public authority' theory identified by Von Bogdandy and Venzke has been utilised by this work as a means for analysing national court decisions as a source of a general principle of international law. According to this approach, decisions may have *effects* beyond the discrete parties to the dispute and thus cannot logically derive full meaning from that *private* party's consent alone. Von Bogdandy and Venzke focus on how, in an increasingly complex international legal order in which there is a proliferation of international courts and tribunals with a wide variety of functions, a consent-based approach to analysing authority is no longer a sufficient justification for authority.[688]

It has already been suggested throughout this work that extensions of authority beyond the scope of international legal principles are occurring in arbitration, such as in the *Abaclat* decision.[689] Judge Abi-Saab rightly pointed out that the exercise of jurisdiction would be unjustified because government bonds do not have 'any anchorage' or territorial link with the host state. As a matter of treaty interpretation, Judge Abi-Saab furthermore pointed out that there is no legal basis for construing 'investment' as extending to sovereign debts. For example, one of the purposes of resolving disputes via ICSID is to 'encourage ... investment ... by providing an international procedural guarantee ... which contributes to the economic development of the host country. However, a sovereign debt is totally unrelated to a specific project or economic operation or enterprise in the borrowing state'.[690]

Apart from the fact that the award wrongly decided that 'sovereign debt' should have fallen within the scope of 'investment', this decision illustrates a wider issue concerning the proper normative framework for the regulation of international arbitral authority which is also occurring in further ICSID awards. Based on the *Abaclat* award, the tribunals in *Ambiente Ufficio*[691] and *Giovanni Alemanni*[692] have extended authority over a state's sovereign matters. For example, in *Ambiente Ufficio*, the ICSID Tribunal relied on the reasoning in *Abaclat* to justify a finding that the dispute pertaining to a failure of Argentina to pay its bondholders, arising out of its sovereign debt crisis, was

688. Von Bogdandy and Venzke (n 31) 5-16.
689. *Abaclat* (n 23); *see*, Chapter 1[B]; Chapter 3[G]; Chapter 4[G]; Chapter 6[D][2].
690. *Abaclat* (n 23) (Dissenting Opinion, Abi-Saab) [35].
691. *Ambiente Ufficio S.p.A. and others v. Argentine Republic*, ICSID Case No. ARB/08/9; *Giovanni Alemanni and Others v. Argentina*, ICSID Case No ARB/07/8.
692. *Giovanni Alemanni and Others v. Argentina*, ICSID Case No ARB/07/8.

the type of investment falling within the scope of Article 25. It similarly concluded that 'sovereign debt' falls within the confines of the wording of Article 25.[693]

The development of incorrect interpretations of treaty law within treaty regimes (here, ICSID) could have a knock-on effect, ensuring that future tribunals interpret equivalent provisions in the same way. This has happened in this area. However, regulation of these private institutions by *public* bodies in accordance with public international law would ensure greater consistency of application of these common enforcement principles. In turn, if the international legal principles here identified applied to arbitral tribunals, they would be able to fall back on general principles without needing to strictly adhere to decisions within their treaty regime (which may promote an inaccurate interpretation of international law).

[2] The Problem of Closed Regimes

In the areas of supervisory and review jurisdiction, national court powers are either excluded[694] or circumscribed.[695] This leads to the problem of 'closed regimes', which is distinct from the issue of 'self-contained' regimes often discussed. Self-contained regimes are regimes of international law which operate outside the scope of a more general system of international law and therefore are said to pose a threat to the 'unity' of international law.[696] The emergence of these 'self-contained regimes' has been wrongly deemed a threat to the 'unity' of international law. Unity, as shown by a number of scholars, is neither a *necessity* as a matter of international law nor necessarily desirable.[697] As mentioned above, it is not a necessity because the consent-based nature of international law has meant the creation of many different constellations of treaty regimes is inevitable.[698] It may not be desirable either because the differing treaty regimes may respond to different needs within the particular contexts within which they operate.[699] However, the emergence of closed regimes within otherwise open ones – in the sense that they are open to development in accordance with rules of international law – would pose a threat to the development of international law (in this case, to the enforcement norms under examination).[700] Thus, the emergence of closed regimes within an otherwise developing regime of public international law might pose a threat to the wider system to the extent that there is an

693. *Ambiente Ufficio* (n 691) [296].
694. In the case of supervision, *see* Chapter 3[F][4].
695. Circumscribed for review: Chapter 4[D][2].
696. *See*, especially, International Law Commission, Fragmentation Report (n 72) 220-226.
697. *See*, especially, this conception that certain 'specialised' regimes pose a threat to the unity of international law has been rightly criticised by several scholars, including Rao: Pemmaraju S Rao, 'Multiple International Judicial Forums: A Reflection of the Growing Strength of International Law or its Fragmentation?' (2004) 25 *Michigan Journal of International Law* 929.
698. Pauwelyn (n 354) 903.
699. *Ibid.*, 904 (emergence of differing regimes which overlap may lead to 'better law' because they allow for the realisation of specialised rights and obligations specific to the area of law).
700. Pauwelyn (n 354) (as Pauwelyn calls this 'self-contained islands' which are 'delinked' from other branches of international law. This means that if a conflict occurs, it is difficult to find a way to reconcile conflicting obligations).

irreconcilable conflict between the developing norms and no clear norm to decide which should prevail in the case that those systems conflict.[701]

One of the principal justifications for excluding ICSID Tribunals from the scope of court enforcement jurisdiction is to heed 'efficiency' concerns related to streamlining the process into one proceeding/forum.[702] Parties *choose* ICSID precisely *because* they do not want delays in their process. Article 54 ICSID Convention was modelled on Article 192 of the Treaty of Rome, which provides for automatic recognition.[703] Exclusion of national court review power would seem to speed up the recognition process by not allowing for any more comprehensive review of the arbitral award. For example, Article 54, which provides that ICSID awards must be recognised 'as binding' and therefore 'enforce[d] within [the] territories [of Contracting states] as if it were a final judgment of a court in that state' has been interpreted by a number of courts as comporting an obligation on contracting states to enforce an award, thereby limiting the jurisdiction of judges to review the award.[704]

However, closed regimes are not desirable from the perspective of harmonisation. As explained in Chapter 2, the 'international rule of law' consists not merely of the scope of authority of a judicial body to act in accordance with its constituent instrument but also of that body's authority to be effectively implemented in accordance with the law which regulates the scope of its jurisdiction.[705] As illustrated by the *Abaclat* decision,[706] international arbitral tribunals have been rendering decisions beyond the scope of authority conferred on them by their constituent instrument. Thus, under the auspices of ICSID, it ought to be particularly important that international arbitral authority is governed consistently by any rules or principles of law applicable to the scope of authority. Otherwise, ICSID Tribunals would be able to escape the normative legal framework to which other similar arbitral regimes are subject. As is being developed by this work, this ought to include public international law norms to the extent that this is applicable to questions concerning the *scope* of authority of these bodies. These ensure that the arbitral proceeding and award are consistent with the law to which the parties subjected it.

Moreover, the norms illustrated support the underlying aims of arbitration as an alternative form of dispute resolution; then efficiency concerns *within* ICSID ought not to trump international rule of law concerns *beyond* ICSID. The 'closed' nature of the ICSID regime as being a positive development for the self-governance of arbitral tribunals under the ICSID regime falls down under the weight of its own logic.[707] Its

701. This problem has been noted by Pauwelyn (n 354) (giving the example of WTO rules conflicting with environmental standards, for example).
702. McLachlan, Shore and Weiniger (n 226) para. 1.04 (the ICSID Convention's 'uniquely self-contained process avoids many of the pitfalls that may otherwise attend the pursuit of such a claim before a national court or commercial arbitration body').
703. Schreuer (n 226) 1118-1119.
704. *See, e.g., État du Sénégal* (n 370) (France); *Mobil Cerro* (2015) (n 448) (US).
705. McCorquodale (n 136).
706. *Abaclat* (n 23); Chapter 1[B].
707. Even though, as Schreuer points out, national court jurisdiction is not entirely excluded at the recognition and enforcement stage, 'authenticity' still only allows a facial review of the legality

closed nature would not necessarily heed efficiency concerns within wider international legal frameworks if the award rendered is not compliant with law and there is limited recourse to national courts as a check on legal validity.

[3] Further Areas of International Law for Regulation by Enforcement Jurisdiction

One implication for other areas of international law is that the identified enforcement norms provide useful guidance to other international courts and tribunals grappling with the scope of their authority where there is, for example, a conflict between two principles of international law pertaining to jurisdiction with no clear hierarchical preference as to which applies.

One example is the *Enrica Lexie* dispute.[708] Two Indian fishermen were shot and killed by Italian marines outside the territorial jurisdiction of both states. India brought the ship, the Enrica Lexie, into its own territory and purported it had jurisdiction to prosecute the marines in its own courts. It claimed it could do so on the so-called *Lotus* principle, according to which a state is permitted, in principle, to do all that it is not prohibited from doing. Italy challenged the jurisdiction before the International Tribunal for the Law of the Sea (ITLOS), which has jurisdiction in so far as the dispute arises out of application on the UN Convention for the Law of the Sea (UNCLOS).[709] The contested basis for jurisdiction was Article 97 UNCLOS, which specifically grants penal jurisdiction to the state whose flag the injurious ship was flying in the event 'of a collision or any other incident of navigation'. ITLOS issued a provisional measures order, ordering the Indian proceedings to be halted.[710] As pointed out by Judge Paik in his Dissenting Opinion, the issue which went to the heart of the matter was, in fact, which state, and on which basis, could lawfully exercise its enforcement jurisdiction.[711] ITLOS clearly could not decide this: it was bound to only exercise jurisdiction based on the subject matter in dispute, which concerned Italy's challenge to jurisdiction on the basis of Article 97. However, if there were a foundation in international law for when enforcement authority *ought* to be lawful, according to a common set of principles (such as those developed by this work), that could have assisted the Court in deciding on its jurisdiction to grant the enforcement measure. Put differently, if there were a norm permitting supervision, recognition and execution irrespective of immunity, this could extend to all international courts and tribunals as a potential 'gap filler' where it is otherwise unclear whether a particular court or tribunal ought to have jurisdiction to render an enforcement measure. In that decision, the Court could

of the award which essentially excludes any effective review in accordance with the international law relating to review on the merits; Schreuer (n 226) 1120.

708. *The Enrica Lexie Incident (Italy v. India)* (Provisional Measures, Order of 24 July 2015) ITLOS Case No. 24, ICGJ 499.

709. This tribunal may hear disputes falling within the substantive scope of UNCLOS as per Article 290. United Nations Convention on the Law of the Sea, 1982, 1833 U.N.T.S. 397 (adopted 10 December 1982, entered into force 16 November 1994).

710. *The Enrica Lexie* (Provisional Measures) (n 708).

711. *Ibid.* (Dec. Judge Paik), ITLOS Case No. 24, ICGJ 499, 211 [2].

therefore have both decided it had jurisdiction to make a Provisional Measures Order both based on the subject matter falling within the scope of UNCLOS and also because the *Lotus* principle ought not to have restricted the Court's jurisdiction in that regard: supervision was a *lawful* enforcement measure to be taken in that case.

In other areas of international law, the identification of any such norms might also be used to *restrain* the scope of enforcement jurisdiction of national courts in contexts where this would constitute a potentially unlawful extension of *extraterritorial* jurisdiction. By 'extraterritorial', it is meant that the jurisdiction is beyond the state's territory (i.e., absent *any* link to the court's territory) and would thus be unlawful unless justified on the basis of consent of the foreign state. In the decision in *Microsoft Warrant,* one US Court extended its criminal enforcement jurisdiction to compel a service provider located in another territorial jurisdiction (Ireland) to hand over data.[712] The case pertained to issuance of a warrant on the basis that such jurisdiction was permitted because it was not prohibited under the US Stored Communications Act (SCA). Microsoft contended that the Government was not authorised to issue warrants outside the territorial limits of the United States. On the one hand, this extension of jurisdiction seems to breach the principle of territoriality according to which a state's consent to such a measure is generally required. On the other hand, the problem of extraterritorial data storage means that it is difficult in any concrete case to say which state should have jurisdiction to enforce its criminal jurisdiction.[713] This is in part due to the fact that it often cannot be said where the data is situated due to cloud computing arrangements. Consequently, extraterritorial enforcement jurisdiction in certain cases might be interpreted as reasonable given these types of modern-day data innovations which are widespread. In that particular case, it is unlikely that the decision ought to be considered a source of any international legal principle justifying the handing over of the data. This is, for one, due to the reasoning of the Court in that decision, which found that since the warrant was not prohibited under the US Stored Communications Act (US SCA),[714] it was permitted.[715] Thus, the Court did not put forward a principled argument as to why the warrant should be granted. For example, in considering Microsoft's counterargument that the Government was not authorised to issue warrants outside the territorial limits of the United States, the Court found that Microsoft's interpretation was 'not inconsistent with the statutory language' of the US SCA but is 'undermined by the structure of the US SCA' which authorises this extraterritorial extension of US enforcement jurisdiction.[716] Since the Court did not point to a principle of consent justifying jurisdiction, this ought to be regarded as unlawful under international legal principles applicable to the scope of that authority.

712. *Matter of a Warrant to Search A Certain E-Mail Account Controlled and Maintained by Microsoft Corporation,* No. 13 Mag. 2814 (2014).
713. Allen, 'Enforcing Criminal Jurisdiction in the Clouds' (n 635).
714. Codified at 18 U.S.C. Chapter 121 §§2701-2712.
715. 18 U.S.C. §§2701 *et seq.*
716. This decision was overturned on appeal on the basis that the issuance of the warrant violated the presumption against extraterritorial application of US law: *Microsoft Corporation v. United States,* 829 F. 3d 197 (2d. Cir 2016), p. 6 (providing that the Act 'neither explicitly nor implicitly' envision the application of its warrant provisions overseas).

In international criminal law, an approach to analysing national court decisions as a source might assist in identifying any common principles according to which the national court could *lawfully* exercise jurisdiction. One starting point would be the interaction between principles of international criminal law and state immunity, which is also frequently applied by national courts in this sphere.[717] For example, increasing recognition of the international responsibility of states in the commission of international crimes may in turn lead to the weakening of immunity which is available to a state in the courts of a foreign state.[718] It is in this space that national courts might be carving out exceptions to rules which currently prohibit the extension of a state's criminal laws over a foreign state – for example, as may be growing in relation to various acts which might be regarded to breach *jus cogens* norms.[719] Consequently, fruitful studies may be pursued across representative national jurisdictions in other areas where commonalities of approach arise, for example where crimes might be prosecuted irrespective of immunities.

Thus, considering adjudicative jurisdiction as a manifestation of enforcement jurisdiction may assist in international courts and tribunals more widely, operating within different areas of international law, such as international criminal law. International criminal law could be developed with regards to enforcement and its permissibility, where national courts may be conceived as effectively enforcing international law, as may be the case in relation to *jus cogens* and its interaction with state immunity.

[E] CONCLUSION

Drawing together the strands of this book, this chapter has examined alternative approaches to considering the practice as a source of a general principle of international law. First, it has been argued that recognition of the practice as a general principle may contribute to greater harmonisation as the New York Convention operates as a harmonising instrument and transnationalism is recognised to different extents in different jurisdictions.

Second, it has been considered that international arbitral tribunals might be more likely to recognise the binding nature of a general principle of international law, and greater harmonisation of national court approaches might similarly be better facilitated by the recognition of a general principle.

717. *See, e.g.*, Dapo Akande and Sangeeta Shah, 'Immunities of State Officials, International Crimes, and Foreign Domestic Courts' (2011) 21(4) *European Journal of International Law* 815 (where the methods of judicial enforcement in these areas are also developing in the jurisdiction of national courts; though the extent to which there are any 'common approaches' as a source for regulation of international judicial bodies in the area has not been examined).
718. Fox and Webb (n 8) 89.
719. For example, in several courts, there have been civil claims for reparation in relation to atrocities resulting in deaths of a number of civilians e.g., *Prefecture of Voiotia v. Federal Republic of Germany*, [1997] *Revue Hellénique De Droit International* 595 (Greece: Court of First Instance Leivadia, 1997). The Greek Court relied on the argument that acts which violate *jus cogens* norms do not qualify as sovereign acts and Germany had impliedly waived immunity by committing such acts; further: Akande and Shah (n 717) 891.

Third, the importance of regulating international arbitral authority under the framework of international law has been expanded upon. Since arbitral tribunals may be acting in the public sphere in matters which would ordinarily be excluded before national courts by the international legal principle of immunity, these forms of decision-making authority demand legal justification or explanation. This is particularly so considering the potential for closed regimes to emerge where the *lex generalis* is not followed.

The enforcement norms identified should be recognised as a source of international law not merely because they are emerging in a consistent, widespread and representative manner in light of harmonising principles (Chapters 3-5 of this work) but also because there is normative justification in international law and international arbitration for recognising them. This would ensure that international arbitral tribunals act in conformity with public international law norms. This ought to be applicable to the scope of their authority to restrict that authority in line with the international rule of law and sovereign equality. The identification of such enforcement norms within this sphere would also provide a starting point for identification in other areas where issues relating to the legality of jurisdiction have arisen (such as international criminal law and the international law of the sea).

CHAPTER 7
Conclusions

'Jurisdiction', as a definitional matter, stems from the latin 'ius dicere', which means 'to speak the law'. This study has shown how important national court contributions to international legal norms can be if 'jurisdiction' is considered in its widest sense as 'decision-making authority'. This conclusion reiterates some of the core findings of this work including the importance of reconsideration of adjudicative jurisdiction, not merely as a facet of prescriptive jurisdiction, but as a manifestation of enforcement jurisdiction; how that theory applies to the practice of international arbitration, currently developing between four representative states (UK, US, France and Germany); the theoretical innovation which such an approach has to offer against both the background of current practice and public and private international law literature; and the contribution of that theory, as well as the practical insights which come with it, both from comparative law and legal theoretical viewpoints.

[A] INTRODUCTION

Public and private international law scholarship has not considered adjudicative jurisdiction or decision-making authority as a source of international law in any great depth. The orthodox scholarship concludes that adjudicative jurisdiction makes a negligible contribution to international law based on states' internalisation of international legal norms;[720] the question is traditionally approached as to how the courts deal with those international norms readily identifiable by the laws which the state chooses to adopt.[721] This book has sought to deal with the reverse question of how domestic courts operate in international law, which may still be developing and undefined,

720. O'Keefe (n 76); Staker (n 15); Shaw (n 15); Akehurst (n 16).
721. Tzanakopoulos (n 76).

rather than where states have expressly consented to the norm. The wider approach to consent adopted by this book, taking into account tacit forms of consent by national courts, is consistent with the notion that international law additionally comprises '*usages generally accepted as expressing principles of law* and *established in order to regulate the relations between these co-existing independent communities* or *with a view to the achievement of common aims*'.[722]

In a world where disputes cross territorial borders and conflicts of jurisdiction arise between states, the identification of public international law norms to help remedy any such conflict becomes important. Disputes may touch several states. Where such conflicts arise, which rules or principles ought to decide which state (or court) has authority?[723] If an arbitral institution wrongly applies the law related to the question of its jurisdiction, should public international law respond to limit or exclude jurisdiction, and if so, on what basis?[724] Given enforcement jurisdiction is at the centre of international law, then what is the substance of the norm in terms of what states may *lawfully* do rather than what they are 'permitted' to do under a prescriptive rule?[725] This study has tied these strands of jurisdiction, international arbitration and public international law together in order to answer these interlinked, though distinct, legal questions. It has done so through the application of methodologies cutting across comparative law, legal theory, private and public international law.

The examined issues have arisen in the context of a 'potential conflict' of norms between the international legal principle of immunity and the enforcement jurisdiction of national courts in relation to arbitration proceedings. This is the context in which the norms might be useful in practice in view of disputes such as *Stati* and *Yukos*, where there has been protracted litigation, particularly in the area of execution.[726] In this context, it would be useful to identify common jurisdictional norms to help coordinate courts irrespective of the international legal principle of immunity, immunity being the main limitation of the jurisdiction under international law. As has been developed by this work, there *are* general norms that do *not* conflict with the international legal principle of immunity.

By reconceiving adjudicative jurisdiction as a manifestation of enforcement jurisdiction, it has been demonstrated that it is possible to identify rules or principles of a public international law nature.[727] In the area examined – international arbitration – it has been argued that the common approach identified ought to be regarded as

722. *Lotus* (n 113) [44].
723. The problem in the *Enrica Lexie* (Provisional Measures) (n 708) as set out in Chapter 6 of this work: [D][3].
724. The problem of *Abaclat* (n 23), *See*, Chapter 1[B]; Chapter 3[G]; Chapter 4[G]; Chapter 6[D][2].
725. Koh (n 14) (the centrality of enforcement in international law); Akehurst (n 16); *Lotus* (n 113) [46], *see* Chapter 2 (considering the traditional norm on enforcement, that a state is permitted to do all that it is not prohibited from doing).
726. *Stati* (n 6); *Yukos* (n 2).
727. 'Enforcement jurisdiction' here being the power to *induce* rather than just 'compel' compliance; *see*, especially, Koh (n 14). Not considered merely entailing an exercise which 'compels' action, as considered in orthodox public international law texts; e.g., Akehurst (n 16) (only considering 'enforcement' as the exercise of 'executive' power which, in the way it is considered, is compulsion). Instead, it includes the authority of states to induce compliance with international legal obligations through their courts.

governing the lawful scope of international arbitral decision-making authority under international law. This concerns the extent to which an international arbitral tribunal's jurisdiction may be enforced by states through their national courts, including measures of interim relief, declarations for enforcement, as well as review, of the award and execution against assets pursuant to the award.

The practical consequence is that in the situations described by this work, national courts ought to have a general authority to grant forms of enforcement jurisdiction regardless of the international legal principle of state immunity. This is because this is what states, through their national courts, have in fact been doing, in a widespread, consistent and representative manner, and because that practice is consistent with the normative approach described in Chapter 2. The normative approach *justifies* why the practice ought to be considered a source of international law. In these situations, the international legal principle of state immunity, which generally prohibits an exercise of state authority where it would breach the foreign state's sovereignty, ought to be regarded as *not* engaged. From a practitioner's perspective, it may now be said that enforcement measures ought to be regarded as falling within the state's *adjudicative* jurisdiction. Such an approach is also consistent with the underlying principles of international law and arbitration: it supports the coordination of courts under international law, as well as enforcement of the international arbitral process.

[B] ADJUDICATIVE JURISDICTION AS A MANIFESTATION OF ENFORCEMENT JURISDICTION

This study has developed a new conceptual premise for considering national court decisions as a source of international law: adjudicative jurisdiction as a manifestation of enforcement jurisdiction. The book then identified and determined the rules, giving content to its application in the context of international arbitration (Chapters 3, 4 and 5).

Suggesting that these norms ought to be regarded as a source of a general principle of international law within the meaning of Article 38(1)(c) ICJ Statute, among the book's central methodological innovations is the application of the 'public sphere' concept to identify national court decisions and the application of 'harmonisation' for the identification of the scope of the norm.[728] The work also considered private international law as potentially declaratory of the public international law norm on enforcement jurisdiction, which was an integral aspect of identifying the norms in the area of international arbitration.

The core tenets of the approach developed were: (1) that the court must exercise its decision-making authority in the public sphere; and (2) the sources analysed may encompass not merely decisions for what they state but also the decision as a

728. From the perspective of global law, this might be called the 'abstract-normative' scheme which has been applied within the frame of a 'convergent' leaning approach: Walker (n 50) 56, 58-59 and 70-71.

manifestation of the 'acts' of national courts, encompassing the effect of a decision to grant a particular measure.

The key decisions which were taken into account as evidence of decisions in the public sphere were:

(1) Where the court exercises jurisdiction, even though there is no territorial connection between the court's jurisdiction and the arbitration dispute.
(2) Where one party to the arbitration proceeding is a foreign state.
(3) Where the exercise of court authority in the public sphere based on a private international legal rule is a manifestation of the public international law rule.

[1] The Public Sphere Concept

The starting point was the approach of Von Bogdandy and Venzke.[729] These authors analyse international court and tribunals through the lens of public authority. One of the key aspects of their approach is how decisions may have *effects* beyond the discrete parties to the dispute and thus cannot logically derive their full meaning or contribution to public international law from the parties' consent alone. Applying this to national court decision-making authority, an approach to analysing national court decisions as a source of public international law on enforcement jurisdiction was developed.

The idea of the 'public sphere' enabled a greater number of national court decisions to be taken into account as evidence of any possible general principle of international law. No longer confined to the interpretation of a prescriptive norm, the reasoning of the court as well as the exercise of authority based on the private international law rule may be considered, in so far as the exercise is a manifestation of the public international law norm.

This approach is distinct from traditional approaches, which conceive of adjudicative jurisdiction as a mere interpretation of prescriptive jurisdiction.[730] Taking a wider approach to 'adjudicative jurisdiction' as 'authority', i.e., the authority of national courts to act in the public sphere in accordance with international law, enables adjudicative jurisdiction to be reconceived as a possible manifestation of enforcement jurisdiction.

Further, it was useful to conceptualise national court decisions as 'acts' which may contribute, or exercises of decision-making authority. This conceptualisation assisted in taking into account a wider set of decisions, not only including decisions which authoritatively decide a question of law under the court's own legal system, but which also may contribute to a public international law through reasoning, or by virtue of the effect of the particular measure granted.

729. Von Bogdandy and Venzke (n 31).
730. Using *Trendtex* as the paradigm example: *see* Chapter 2, *Trendtex* (n 90), section [B].

[2] The International Legal Principle of State Immunity

State immunity was identified throughout Chapters 3-5 as the main rule or principle of public international law which might limit or restrict a state's enforcement jurisdiction, as well as an important source for the approaches demonstrated.[731] Through the comparison of decisions, the international legal principle of state immunity was identified as an exception to the court or tribunal's jurisdiction. The argument is that this principle ought to operate as an exception to an otherwise available enforcement jurisdiction and thus a *lex specialis* to a more general set of rules or principles of enforcement jurisdiction.[732]

State immunity is an important rule of international law which limits enforcement jurisdiction. Approaches to immunity which have been considered include where the norm is expressly considered an exception,[733] where it is considered an exception as a matter of reasoning[734] and where it is not considered in the decision at all and therefore was implicitly considered by the courts *not* to restrict lawful enforcement.[735]

[3] Utilisation of the Concept of 'Decision-Making Authority'

The reconceptualisation of jurisdiction as authority, as distinct from adjudicative jurisdiction as a mere facet of prescriptive power, moved away from orthodox approaches to jurisdiction.[736] It opened up a space to consider whether, and if so, to what extent, national courts might contribute to public international law norms. This understanding of jurisdiction as decision-making authority allows for public and private international lawyers to pursue a wider range of decisions. This is because decisions can be considered to define the scope of the court authority rather than merely interpret a legal norm which the state has chosen expressly to adopt.

It has been argued that a broader analysis, concerning whether an ICSID Tribunal ought to have found it had jurisdiction in accordance with applicable public international law norms, would have also assisted the Tribunal in the *Abaclat* case. This is because it would have enabled the Tribunal to not merely consider the interpretative question of whether a 'sovereign debt' is an 'investment' under the relevant provision, but also whether, pursuant to any applicable principles of international law, such an exercise of authority would be in breach of the principle of state immunity. This study has suggested that general principles of international law should equally apply to

---

731. Drawing on approaches of authors in state immunity and arbitration, where only consent-based approaches, i.e., whether immunity is waived on the basis of consent to the arbitration agreement, is considered: Fox and Webb (n 8); Reinisch (n 61); Ostrander (n 61). However, here it is identified in so far as it may operate as an *exception* to any identified rules or principles of enforcement jurisdiction, that may be emerging as between representative courts in the public sphere considering harmonising instruments.
732. As defined in the ILC Fragmentation Report (n 72).
733. For example, *Svenska* (2006) (n 20).
734. For example, *AIG Capital* (n 13).
735. For example, *Toyo Tire* (n 188).
736. Though it has been supported by much public and private international law literature and commentary: Judge Simma (n 119); Knop, Michaels and Riles (n 139); Allen et al. (n 101).

arbitral tribunals as national courts, including the international legal principle of state immunity, which would ensure their authority is exercised in accordance with international law.

[4] Support in Public and Private International Law and Theory

Chapter 2 demonstrated how the approach is supported both by legal-theoretical approaches, including Kant, Scelle and Kelsen, as well as by public and private international law theory.

The approach is supported by public international norms underpinning authority being sovereign equality and the international rule of law. Taking those norms into consideration, they confer a wider understanding of adjudicative jurisdiction is not only a facet of prescriptive jurisdiction but may be considered a source of international law. This is because the principles underpinning decision-making authority - sovereign equality and the international rule of law - may be considered justificatory principles for a common practice among courts.

From a private international law perspective, enforcement norms have been identified by taking the private international law basis for jurisdiction into account as a source of the public international law norm rather than as merely part of national law.

[C] APPLICATION TO INTERNATIONAL ARBITRATION

The purpose of Chapters 3-5 was to identify whether, in line with the normative approach of Chapter 2, there is any state practice relating to enforcement jurisdiction in international arbitration. The chapter thus gave a solid foundation to the study, proving the viability of the approach in a particular area of law. It not only demonstrated the utility of the normative approach developed in Chapter 2 but also applied this to arbitration to demonstrate implications for national court practice in enforcement proceedings. This, in turn, made discrete contributions to three areas of enforcement in arbitration.

[1] Chapter 3 and Situating State Immunity

In Chapter 3, supervisory jurisdiction was identified as the first norm for which courts share a common approach. Drawing on the arbitration literature, various forms of supervision, not usually considered together, were considered as such.[737] This included not merely interim relief and similar measures to support the arbitral process but also setting aside proceedings, enforcement of peremptory orders and emergency arbitration awards, among other measures. Except where exceptions are identified, it has been argued that national courts generally have the power supervise the international arbitral process by ensuring the compliance of states with the international

737. For example, Blackaby et al. (n 22); Poudret and Besson (n 22); Lew (n 22); Born (n 178); Moses (n 22).

arbitral process as a matter of public international law. These norms were identified by comparing decisions across the UK, the US, France and Germany. French decisions were particularly pertinent in relation to the setting aside process and its interaction with principles of state immunity.

The principles identified were widespread, consistent and representative, though the decision in the *UK P&I Club NV v. Venezuela*,[738] gives pause for thought as to the UK court's approach to anti-suit injunctions. It was concluded in relation to this decision, and in light of *Unicredit*,[739] that anti-suit injunctions ought to be regarded as generally available irrespective of state immunity. The decision in *UK P&I* ought to be confined as an exception to an interpretation of section 13(2)(a) SIA, which is not in-keeping with wider practice in relation to supervision in the public sphere, or alternatively ought to be considered an incorrect interpretation of section 13(2)(a) SIA if it were regarded as representative of the UK approach. The supervisory jurisdiction chapter concludes section 13(2)(a) ought to be interpreted in light of section 9, which would confer a broader interpretation of when anti-suit injunctions are available *in respect of international arbitrations*. The study supports this view on the basis that properly considered, anti-suit injunctions are an enforcement aspect of *adjudicative jurisdiction* in the sphere of international arbitration rather than enforcement jurisdiction *per se*.

Further, it may be that more specific approaches emerge in relation to discovery and disclosure of assets, with French courts not generally exercising supervisory jurisdiction in this area and thus this form of supervision falling outside the scope of the concept.

[2] Chapter 4 and Harmonisation of Review of Substantive Jurisdiction

Chapter 4 similarly described national court practice in arbitration, but for the purposes of analysing it as a source of a distinct power: recognition and review jurisdiction. Even though the standard of review in this area might be different across courts, it was identified that there was a common standard more akin to the approach in *Svenska* and previous UK court decisions treating the power to review jurisdiction as closer to a review rather than a rehearing.[740]

Drawing on practice across the UK, US, France and Germany, national court practice consistently allows for review of substantive jurisdiction under the applicable law, which generally gives some level of deference to the tribunal. In view of one of the main aims of this research – to identify whether, and if so, to what extent, international arbitral authority is governed by public international law – this finding was useful. It provided a further basis upon which a national court might ensure the compliance of international arbitral authority through decisions in the public sphere. This would allow the national court to review whether the arbitral tribunal acted in accordance with the law applicable to the scope of its jurisdiction and not merely whether the arbitral process was in line with the parties' agreement.

738. *UK P&I Club* (2022) (n 207) and *UK P&I Club* (2023) (n 276).
739. *Unicredit* (2024) (n 209).
740. *Dallah* (n 109); *Svenska* (2006) (n 20) [116].

Further, even though there are limitations to the practical enforcement of awards since the decision in *Achmea*, this Chapter situates the approach under EU law as one pertaining to practical enforcement rather than whether the enforcement norms are *lawful* as a matter of international law. It has been suggested that these cases only affect whether the award will in fact be recognised as enforceable in certain situations rather than the wider question of whether state immunity limits or restricts this otherwise generally available power.

[3] Chapter 5 and Practical Enforcement Against Assets

Execution jurisdiction is widely considered in the arbitration literature as the 'last bastion' of sovereign immunity. Considering jurisdiction as the rule and immunity as the exception, Chapter 5 built both on the theoretical strands of the study as well as made doctrinal findings in this regard. From the traditional perspective, based on a consent-based approach to arbitration, a waiver of immunity is regarded as required in order for execution to be available. Further, execution may be regarded as a more coercive form of enforcement: it can compel that state to comply with measures relating to its own assets in the foreign state. This chapter cut through confusion in the literature relating to the interaction between this power and state immunity to identify those rules or principles according to which the national court may exercise jurisdiction irrespective of state immunity.

In addition to its doctrinal implications, Chapter 5 identified some of the theoretical implications of the approach developed in Chapter 2. By taking a wider approach to 'jurisdiction' as the 'authority' of national courts to 'act' in the public sphere, this allowed both national court decisions in monist and dualist states to be considered. Monist courts may *directly* interpret the public international legal norm in the text of the decision itself. By contrast, the reasoning of dualist courts may become relevant when the effect of their decision is to interpret the international legal norm, even if international law is not the direct source of authority. The study enabled exercises of decision-making authority to be considered a source of international law irrespective of the state's monist or dualist approach to international law because the method of adoption of international law into national law was not the only aspect relevant to the analysis of the existence of the norm. This is because the functional comparative approach allows for an analysis which takes into account the *effects* of decisions, and not merely what they state for their interpretation of the prescriptive norm which the state has chosen to adopt.

[4] Public and Private International Law: Viewing These Fields Together

Pursuing an approach which crosses public and private international law, the study may assist scholars interested in the intersection of those areas. The identification of norms of supervisory jurisdiction builds in part on the work of Goh.[741] He identifies

741. Goh (n 79).

that from the private international law perspective, state immunity laws may be allocative of jurisdiction. Building on this approach, it is considered how decision based on state immunity laws, which may impose links to courts from a private international law perspective, can contribute to the public international law norm. This is where the private international legal norm is, in effect, declaratory of the public international norm because it is the basis for the court's decision on enforcement.

Chapter 3 built on this private international law approach when examining supervisory jurisdiction. Though a perspective which considers private international as part of public international law has been established by theoretical works,[742] it has not been utilised identifying norms doctrinally. This study thus creates building blocks for identifying how private international law contributes to public international law in a discrete area - here, enforcement jurisdiction. Whereas private international law links had previously been considered part of national law, this book demonstrates those norms may be a manifestation of the public international law rule. In the context of execution in Chapter 5, for example, one link considered is where assets are located within the territory of the exercising court. In other words, private international law links to jurisdiction may be the basis for the exercise of jurisdiction in the public sphere, and thus declaratory of the public international law norm.

[D] METHODOLOGICAL CONTRIBUTIONS

Considering Ralf Michaels' approach to comparative law, this book supports the view that the functional comparative method can be employed to identify state practice from national court decisions. Functionalism enables the effects of court decisions to be considered even where different legal systems name proceedings differently. It allows the effects of decisions to be taken into account a source of the norm, such as reasoning or where the effect of the decision is to grant a particular enforcement measure rather than merely relying on decisions as an *interpretation* of the prescriptive jurisdictional rule.

In line with Taekema and Burg's approach, the plausibility of the argument as a whole was developed by legal theory, providing a basis for the jurisprudential legitimacy of the norm.[743] Following Saunders' approach, the jurisprudential legitimacy of the norm needed to be developed first in order to identify the content of the norm.[744] Only in so far as the norm accorded with this normative foundation, i.e., adjudicative jurisdiction as a manifestation of enforcement, was it be considered a source of state practice. This confers a unique approach to identifying general principles of international law within the meaning of Article 38(1)(c), leaving such a theoretical approach and methodology open for use by future lawyers and academics who wish to identify and expand on the field of general principles of international law applied in practical contexts such as international arbitration.

742. Mills (n 141).
743. Taekema and Burg (n 77).
744. Saunders (n 46).

'Harmonisation' provided the backdrop against which functionalism could take hold as a mechanism for determining a general principle of international law.[745] The functionalist methodology was intimately entwined with broader questions of legal theory. As stated in Chapter 1, only in so far as consistent, widespread and representative practice could be identified, could the normative approach be justified and vice-versa. Consequently, the theoretical approach developed in Chapter 2 and the common approach determined in Chapters 3-5 were iterative. Since the aim was to identify a general principle of international law, and this was dependent on both a normative and descriptive approach, this required adaptation of the theory and the practice simultaneously.

[E] PRIVATE INTERNATIONAL LAW CONTRIBUTION

The traditional private international legal approach to jurisdiction would regard the norm, as enacted in national laws, as the *authorising* principle, i.e., the permissive rule upon which a court renders a decision. This is district from the broader question of whether adjudicative jurisdiction is a source of international law in its own right, with the private international law norm being a source of public international law.

The literature which states that private international law ought to be treated, rather than as a method or policy, as a discipline in its own right, is a useful backdrop.[746] Similarly, an overly 'positivistic' approach to public international law - i.e., viewing it completely separately from private international law as a distinct discipline - may also not be useful when seeking to consider the possible regulatory function which private international law may fulfil.[747]

Drawing the strands of this literature together, this book has developed a theoretical approach to considering decisions based on the private international law norm as a source of the general principle of international law. Rather than providing the 'link' for jurisdiction within national law, the private international law link can define the object and purpose of the general principle: for example, the urgent need for interim relief as a reason for the exercise of jurisdiction (supervisory jurisdiction)[748] and assets being located in the territorial jurisdiction as the 'link' which provides the rule itself (execution jurisdiction).[749] Thus, the private international law rule, as developed in the jurisprudence of the courts, can fulfil a different function depending on its relationship to the public international law rule under analysis. The identification of the function which it plays is dependent on identifying: (a) the function of the norm under public international law, and (b) whether the exercise of authority is justified by principles of public international law. Consequently, decisions for what they say must

745. On how harmonisation was applied and how it interacts with the public authority lens, *see* Chapter 1[E][1] and [F].
746. Knop, Michaels and Riles (n 139).
747. Mills (n 141).
748. *Toyo Tire* (n 188).
749. *Sedelmayer* (n 531).

be carefully scrutinised in light of applicable public international law and international arbitration norms in order to identify their function and purpose.

[F] CHAPTER 6 AND THEORETICAL IMPLICATIONS

Chapter 6 took the study back to its normative foundations, drawing on alternative approaches to adjudicative jurisdiction exhibited by national courts in the area of arbitration. Until this point, the study hinted at how the approaches identified ought to be considered a source of a general principle of international law within the meaning of Article 38(1)(c) ICJ Statute. The wider definition of general principles as 'unwritten norms' which may be 'transposable' to the international legal level, in so far as they are applicable there, made them an ideal framework into which the common approach fitted.[750] The chapter further justified why the common approach ought to be regarded as a general principle of international law, particularly in light of the difficulties which would be faced through coordination by treaty law or soft coordination. It also deepened the normative implications for arbitration and why arbitral tribunals ought to be governed by such a general principle of international law in view of issues of legitimacy which have arisen in that area. Thus, Chapter 6 tied together some of the core normative strands of the study with the doctrinal finding that this could be applied to identify general principles of international law.[751]

[G] FINAL REMARKS

Enforcement jurisdiction scholarship has traditionally been limited to the concept of 'prohibited unless permitted'.[752] As a coercive form of relief, enforcement is viewed as only available in exceptional circumstances where the state has consented to the norm explicitly, by way of convention or possibly by custom. Considering enforcement jurisdiction more widely as '*inducing* or compelling compliance' and the potential for being formed by tacit consent, a wider range of potential sources for enforcement jurisdiction can be taken into account, namely, national court decisions. It has been argued that these ought to be considered a source of public international law enforcement jurisdiction. Importantly, it is enforcement *aspects* of adjudicative jurisdiction which have been considered by this book. This should not be confused with an analysis which holds that adjudicative is a mere subspecies of enforcement jurisdiction, or of prescriptive jurisdiction. Instead, adjudicative jurisdiction has been considered a source of international law *in its own right* - a conceptually distinct form - and here, in particular, in respect of its enforcement aspects.

This book began with the concept of 'jurisdiction' as '*ius dicere*', which means 'to speak the law'. This study has shown how important national court contribution to

750. Pellet (n 44).
751. Drawing on Saunders' recent work: Saunders (n 46). The author states that the 'jurisprudential legitimacy' of the approach to general principles may underpin what a 'general principle' is in any discrete area.
752. The principle of enforcement jurisdiction identified in the *Lotus* decision: *Lotus* (n 113) [46].

international legal norms can be if 'jurisdiction' is considered 'decision-making authority' - speaking the law through exercises of decision-making power. A central innovation of this work is to consider adjudicative jurisdiction more widely than merely an interpretation of a law which the state has chosen to adopt, but rather as 'authority' or *ius dicere*. It has been argued that by adopting this wider definition, it is not only in-keeping with an ever-evolving normative jurisdictional concept in public international law[753] but also perhaps better reflects an international legal order which is multi-layered, fragmented and is yet searching for uniformity and a harmonious approach to law.

753. Allen et al. (n 101).

Index

1. Moshe Hirsch, *The Arbitration Mechanism of the International Center for the Settlement of Investment Disputes,* 1993 (ISBN 07-923-1993-1).
2. Aida B. Avanessian, *Iran-United States Claims Tribunal in Action,* 1993 (ISBN 18-533-3902-4).
3. Isaak I. Dore, *The UNCITRAL Framework for Arbitration in Contemporary Perspective,* 1993 (ISBN 18-533-3573-8).
4. Vesna Lazić, *Insolvency Proceedings and Commercial Arbitration,* 1998 (ISBN 90-411-1115-8).
5. Joachim Frick, *Arbitration in Complex International Contracts,* 2001 (ISBN 90-411-1662-1).
6. Katherine Lynch, *The Forces of Economic Globalization: Challenges to the Regime of International Commercial Arbitration,* 2003 (ISBN 90-411-1994-9).
7. Christoph Liebscher, *The Healthy Award: Challenge in International Commercial Arbitration,* 2003 (ISBN 90-411-2011-4).
8. Hamid G. Gharavi, *The International Effectiveness of the Annulment of an Arbitral Award,* 2003 (ISBN 90-411-1717-2).
9. Abdulhay Sayed, *Corruption in International Trade and Commercial Arbitration,* 2004 (ISBN 90-411-2236-2).
10. Gabrielle Kaufmann-Kohler & Thomas Schultz, *Online Dispute Resolution: Challenges for Contemporary Justice,* 2004 (ISBN 90-411-2318-0).
11. Christopher R. Drahozal & Richard W. Naimark (eds), *Towards a Science of International Arbitration: Collected Empirical Research,* 2005 (ISBN 90-411-2322-9).
12. Ali Yeşilirmak, *Provisional Measures in International Commercial Arbitration,* 2005 (ISBN 90-411-2353-9).
13. Christian Bühring-Uhle, *Arbitration and Mediation in International Business,* second revised edition, 2006 (ISBN 978-9-041-12256-8).
14. Bernard Hanotiau, *Complex Arbitrations: Multi-party, Multi-contract and Multi-issue – A Comparative Study*, Second Edition, 2020 (ISBN 978-94-035-1261-7).
15. Loukas A. Mistelis & Julian D.M. Lew (eds), *Pervasive Problems in International Arbitration,* 2006 (ISBN 978-9-041-12450-0).
16. Julian D.M. Lew & Loukas A. Mistelis (eds), *Arbitration Insights – Twenty Years of the Annual Lecture of the School of International Arbitration, Sponsored by Freshfields Bruckhaus Deringer,* 2006 (ISBN 978-9-041-12606-1).
17. Mark Kantor, *Valuation for Arbitration: Compensation Standards, Valuation Methods and Expert Evidence,* 2008 (ISBN 978-9-041-12735-8).
18. Christoph Brunner, *Force Majeure and Hardship under General Contract Principles: Exemption for Non-Performance in International Arbitration,* 2009 (ISBN 978-90-411-2792-1).

19. Loukas A. Mistelis & Stavros L. Brekoulakis (eds), *Arbitrability: International & Comparative Perspectives,* 2009 (ISBN 978-90-411-2730-3).
20. Sam Luttrell, *Bias Challenges in International Commercial Arbitration: The Need for a 'Real Danger' Test,* 2009 (ISBN 978-90-411-3191-1).
21. Monique Sasson, *Substantive Law in Investment Treaty Arbitration: The Unsettled Relationship Between International Law and Municipal Law,* Second Edition, 2017 (ISBN 978-90-411-6103-1).
22. Ileana M. Smeureanu, *Confidentiality in International Commercial Arbitration,* 2011 (ISBN 978-90-411-3226-0).
23. Won Kidane, *China-Africa Dispute Settlement: The Law, Economics and Culture of Arbitration,* 2011 (ISBN 978-90-411-3674-9).
24. Karel Daele, *Challenge and Disqualification of Arbitrators in International Arbitration,* 2012 (ISBN 978-90-411-3799-9).
25. Crina Baltag, *The Energy Charter Treaty: The Notion of Investor,* 2012 (ISBN 978-90-411-3428-8).
26. Alexandra Diehl, *The Core Standard of International Investment Protection: Fair and Equitable Treatment,* 2012 (ISBN 978-90-411-3869-9).
27. Manuel Indlekofer, *International Arbitration and the Permanent Court of Arbitration,* 2013 (ISBN 978-90-411-4766-0).
28. Günther J. Horvath & Stephan Wilske (eds), *Guerrilla Tactics in International Arbitration,* 2013 (ISBN 978-90-411-4002-9).
29. Albert Badia, *Piercing the Veil of State Enterprises in International Arbitration,* 2014 (ISBN 978-90-411-5162-9).
30. Nadja Erk, *Parallel Proceedings in International Arbitration: A Comparative European Perspective,* 2014 (ISBN 978-90-411-5264-0).
31. Simon Vorburger, *International Arbitration and Cross-Border Insolvency: Comparative Perspectives,* 2014 (ISBN 978-90-411-5419-4).
32. Ahmad Ali Ghouri, *Interaction and Conflict of Treaties in Investment Arbitration,* 2015 (ISBN 978-90-411-5417-0).
33. Reto Marghitola, *Document Production in International Arbitration,* 2015 (ISBN 978-90-411-5159-9).
34. Alfonso Gómez-Acebo, *Party-Appointed Arbitrators in International Commercial Arbitration,* 2016 (ISBN 978-90-411-6671-5).
35. Jonas von Goeler, *Third-Party Funding in International Arbitration and Its Impact on Procedure,* 2016 (ISBN 978-90-411-5015-8).
36. Dean Lewis, *The Interpretation and Uniformity of the UNCITRAL Model Law on International Commercial Arbitration: Focusing on Australia, Hong Kong and Singapore,* 2016 (ISBN 978-90-411-6700-2).
37. Stavros Brekoulakis, Julian D.M. Lew & Loukas Mistelis (eds), *The Evolution and Future of International Arbitration,* 2016 (ISBN 978-90-411-7004-0).
38. Rémy Gerbay, *The Functions of Arbitral Institutions,* 2016 (ISBN 978-90-411-6217-5).

39. Maximilian Clasmeier, *Arbitral Awards as Investments: Treaty Interpretation and the Dynamics of International Investment Law*, 2017 (ISBN 978-90-411-8357-6).
40. Tony Cole (ed.), *The Roles of Psychology in International Arbitration*, 2017 (ISBN 978-90-411-5921-2).
41. Pietro Ferrario, *The Adaptation of Long-Term Gas Sale Agreements by Arbitrators*, 2017 (ISBN 978-90-411-8232-6).
42. Jacob B. van de Velden, *Finality in Litigation: The Law and Practice of Preclusion – Res Judicata (Merger and Estoppel), Abuse of Process and Recognition of Foreign Judgments*, 2017 (ISBN 978-90-411-8342-2).
43. Dolores Bentolila, *Arbitrators as Lawmakers*, 2017 (ISBN 978-90-411-8354-5).
44. Giacomo Marchisio, *The Notion of Award in International Commercial Arbitration: A Comparative Analysis of French Law, English Law, and the UNCITRAL Model Law*, 2017 (ISBN 978-90-411-8391-0).
45. Csaba Kovács, *Attribution in International Investment Law*, 2018 (ISBN 978-90-411-9675-0).
46. Mary Mitsi, *The Decision-Making Process of Investor-State Arbitration Tribunals*, 2019 (ISBN 978-90-411-9600-2).
47. Ahmet Cemil Yıldırım, *Interpretation of Contracts in Comparative and Uniform Law*, 2019 (ISBN 978-94-035-1130-6).
48. Beata Gessel-Kalinowska vel Kalisz, *The Legal, Real and Converged Interest in Declaratory Relief*, 2019 (ISBN 978-94-035-1244-0).
49. Maximilian Pika, *Third-Party Effects of Arbitral Awards: Res Judicata Against Privies, Non-mutual Preclusion and Factual Effects*, 2019 (ISBN 978-94-035-1273-0).
50. Yulia Levashova, *The Right of States to Regulate in International Investment Law: The Search for Balance Between Public Interest and Fair and Equitable Treatment*, 2019 (ISBN 978-94-035-0931-0).
51. Flavia Marisi, *Environmental Interests in Investment Arbitration: Challenges and Directions*, 2020 (ISBN 978-94-035-1723-0).
52. Martina Magnarelli, *Privity of Contract in International Investment Arbitration: Original Sin or Useful Tool?*, 2020 (ISBN 978-94-035-2020-9).
53. Xu Qian, *Water Services Disputes in International Arbitration: Reconsidering the Nexus of Investment Protection, Environment, and Human Rights*, 2020 (ISBN 978-94-035-2203-6).
54. Nobumichi Teramura, Ex Aequo et Bono *as a Response to the 'Over-Judicialisation' of International Commercial Arbitration*, 2020 (ISBN 978-94-035-2073-5).
55. Bruno Guandalini, *Economic Analysis of the Arbitrator's Function*, 2020 (ISBN 978-94-035-2265-4).
56. Zena Prodromou, *The Public Order Exception in International Trade, Investment, Human Rights and Commercial Disputes*, 2020 (ISBN 978-94-035-2031-5).

57. Jürg Künzle, *Multiple Contracts and Coordination in International Construction Projects: A Swiss Law Analysis*, 2020 (ISBN 978-94-035-2024-7).
58. Cornel Marian, *The State's Power to Tax in the Investment Arbitration of Energy Disputes: Outer Limits and the Energy Charter Treaty*, 2020 (ISBN 978-94-035-1752-0).
59. Luke Nottage, Shahla Ali, Bruno Jetin & Nobumichi Teramura (eds.), *New Frontiers in Asia-Pacific International Arbitration and Dispute Resolution*, 2021 (ISBN 978-94-035-2855-7).
60. Eva Litina, *Theory, Law and Practice of Maritime Arbitration: The Case of International Contracts for the Carriage of Goods by Sea*, 2021 (ISBN 978-94-035-3035-2).
61. Franco Ferrari & Friedrich Rosenfeld (eds), *Autonomous Versus Domestic Concepts under the New York Convention*, 2021 (ISBN 978-94-035-3173-1).
62. Doğan Gültutan, *Moral Damages under International Investment Law: The Path Towards Convergence*, 2022 (ISBN 978-94-035-4025-2).
63. Simon Foote QC, *The Bona Fide Investor: Corporate Nationality and Treaty Shopping in Investment Treaty Law*, 2022 (ISBN 978-94-035-4185-3).
64. George A. Bermann, *Twilight Issues in International Arbitration: Latent Choice of Law Challenges*, 2023 (ISBN 978-94-035-1746-9).
65. Emmanuel Obiora Igbokwe, *Dealing with Bribery and Corruption in International Commercial Arbitration: To Probe or Not to Probe*, 2023 (ISBN 978-94-035-2066-7).
66. Peter Sester, *Contract Law in International Commercial Arbitration*, 2023 (ISBN 978-94-035-1036-1).
67. Julian Bickmann, *Fact-Finding in International Arbitration: The Emergence of a Transnational* Lex Evidentiae, 2023 (ISBN 978-94-035-1886-2).
68. Giovanna E. Gismondi, *International Environmental Law and International Human Rights Law in Investment Treaty Arbitration: The Contribution of Host States' Argumentation in Re-Shaping International Investment Law*, 2023 (ISBN 978-94-035-3047-5).
69. Fabricio Fortese, *Early Determination of Jurisdiction*, 2024 (ISBN 978-94-035-0268-7).
70. Sabrina Pearson-Wenger, *Good Faith in International Commercial Arbitration: Its Application by Arbitral Tribunals to the Parties' Contract and the Arbitration Agreement*, 2024 (ISBN 978-94-035-0738-5).
71. Charalampos Tagaroulias, *International Investment Law and the Law of the European Union: How Regionalism and Interregionalism Have Shaped the Relationship in the Post-Lisbon Era*, 2024 (ISBN 978-94-035-0708-8).
72. Dan Xie, *Transnational Due Process and Article V(1)(b) of the New York Convention: Grounding Interpretation and Application of the Due Process Defence in the Public International Law Framework for Treaty Interpretation*, 2024 (ISBN 978-94-035-2437-5).
73. Thomas Lehmann, *Investment Arbitration and International Climate Change Law: Revaluing Legitimate Expectations*, 2025 (ISBN 978-94-035-2799-4).

74. Ylli Dautaj, *Sovereign Immunity from Execution and International Arbitration: Theory and Practice*, 2025 (ISBN 978-94-035-0858-0).
75. Satya Talwar Mouland, *Enforcement Jurisdiction in International Law and Arbitration*, 2026 (ISBN 978-94-035-4158-7).

www.ingramcontent.com/pod-product-compliance
Ingram Content Group UK Ltd.
Pitfield, Milton Keynes, MK11 3LW, UK
UKHW020813290926
15470UKWH00003B/1121

9 789403 541587